The Providential Aesthetic
in Victorian Fiction

The Providential Aesthetic in Victorian Fiction

THOMAS VARGISH

University Press of Virginia
Charlottesville

THE UNIVERSITY PRESS OF VIRGINIA
Copyright © 1985 by the Rector and Visitors
of the University of Virginia

First published 1985

Library of Congress Cataloging in Publication Data

Vargish, Thomas.
  The providential aesthetic in Victorian fiction.

  Includes bibliographical references and index.
  1. English fiction—19th century—History and criti-
cism.   2. Providence and government of God in literature.
I. Title.
PR878.P734V37 1985   823'.8'09382   84–29098
ISBN 0-8139-1062-5

Printed in the United States of America

To

Elizabeth Deeds Ermarth

Contents

Preface

In this book I trace the development of a particular way of seeing the world as it found representation in English novels. Specifically, my study explores a mode of perception, the providential habit of mind, as it informed and shaped major works of Victorian fiction. Such an undertaking involves attention to cultural and religious history, in this case chiefly in order to advance the history of the novel—its changes and developments in techniques of representation. I propose to offer a body of information pertinent to our reading of nineteenth-century fiction and then to present critical examples of how that information can enlarge and sharpen our methods of interpretation and our understanding of the texts. This approach assumes that a knowledge of past values and sensibilities can make a significant contribution to our perception of form in art, particularly in literary art. A formulation such as providential aesthetic *inherently asserts the intimate (I believe inseparable) integration of ideological and historical elements with the principal constituents of narrative representation. It assumes that the rigorous exercise of our historical imagination has high critical value and can, with scholarly discipline and qualification, be applied successfully to the practice of textual interpretation.*

I have made regular use of nineteenth-century reviews and of other commentary that voices the religious and philosophical expectations of Victorian novel readers because my own interpretations depend in part on the reconstruction of a varied providential ethos. On the other hand, I have tried to avoid giving the impression that all fiction from Defoe to George

Eliot qualifies as providential. The history of the novel in England may be seen, and often was seen, as broadly secular. Many important novelists—such as Scott, Thackeray, and Trollope—were not deeply committed to the providential habit of mind or at least not to its representation in literature, and consequently they receive minimal attention here. I do not want to force the entire genre into a category of thought; rather, I am interested in the complex integration of a mode of perception that preceded the novel by millennia with its last great expression in Victorian realistic fiction.

My introductory chapter offers a general historical and methodological account of the providential aesthetic as it informs the English novel between the early eighteenth and the early twentieth centuries. Here I define my terms and suggest certain adjustments to current critical perspectives. The case for these generalizations is made in the following three chapters, each of which examines in detail the work of a single author. Charlotte Brontë's novels frame the subject by demonstrating the range of structures and techniques accessible within the providential tradition. Dickens's work completes the aesthetic by comprising the fullest extended exploration of the possibilities for the novel inherent in this habit of mind. George Eliot demonstrates the power of the narrative conventions generic to the providential aesthetic as she redirects them to the representation of an entirely human world. In these three chapters the interpretations of individual novels show the progress of the providential aesthetic through English realistic fiction. Much of the value of the enterprise, however, must come from the refinement and comprehension it gives to our reading of particular novels. The success of what follows thus depends on the realization of a double aim, the recovery of a determining theme in our literary tradition and the consequent enlargement of our appreciation of the individual texts.

I would like to thank the Guggenheim Foundation for a fellowship grant that supported my initial research and enabled me to define my subject. Dartmouth College furthered its development with a senior faculty grant for one term's leave of absence. Patricia Hawthorne typed the manuscript and considerably reduced its technical inconsistencies. Darrel Mansell and U. C. Knoepflmacher read individual chapters and made important suggestions for revision. So did Patricia Spacks, and to her I owe substantial clarifications that grew out of periodic discussions of my main theme. George Ford's advice on the entire manuscript helped me to strengthen its scholarly underpinnings. Gerald Trett of The University Press of Virginia has significantly sharpened the stylistic accuracy of the presentation. Finally, my greatest debt is to Elizabeth Deeds Ermarth for her acute criticism and generous encouragement throughout the writing of this book.

The Providential Aesthetic
in Victorian Fiction

1

INTRODUCTION
The Providential Aesthetic in Victorian Fiction

AMONG THE SEVERAL concerns that seemed of central importance to literate Victorians the action of God's will in the world was the most transcendent, and it is also the one that has lost most ground with us. Our current intellectual life as expressed in our literature and criticism, speaking generally, either does not deal with that concern or offers it the status of a historical curiosity or a minority report. The subject matter of this book thus brings with it an antecedent problem that may threaten the reception of the whole inquiry. This problem is one of interest, interest dependent on the critical status of our historical imagination. Why should it matter to us that most major English novelists before George Eliot assumed the existence of a providential order to the cosmos and found evidence for a providential intention at work in it, that their representations of human life in the world presuppose a representation of this order or intention?

Such a question is vulnerable to scholarly rebuke, to some assertion defending the intellectual validity of cultural history and the moral primacy of the historical imagination. But although such assertion and rebuke have a certain pedagogical value in some contexts—perhaps especially for the pedagogue—they will not work here because the initial problem is not one of willful ignorance or denial. Most present-day readers of Victorian novels allow for the assumption of providential intention inherent in the genre. They accept it as an obvious thematic staple of that literature. Then (with notable exceptions) they let it go either as an essentially uninteresting anachronism or as an aesthetic convention so monolithic and opaque as to be inaccessible to lively critical discourse. This tacit dismissal is evident in the organization of our university courses, in the emphases of our formal criticism, and even in our selections for reprint of critical commentary by the Victorians themselves. The problem is one of interest, of engagement, and we do not become interested in a subject because we are told we ought to be interested. We become interested in a subject when the discourse that surrounds it becomes lively.

It may be true that apprehension of an active providence in the human world has ceased to be a vital intellectual resource for most people who read Victorian novels and that as an assumption about the world it has become anachronistic in relation to life outside of books. But with that life this discussion has very little to do. My aim here is to show that in English novels, particularly in major Victorian fiction, the assumption of a providence at work in the fictional representation of reality is neither monolithic nor opaque but richly various, particularized, diverse; and that attention to it leads not to confirmation of its intellectual opacity or obviousness but to an illumination of its fundamental relation to major questions of form and structure. I will argue that the fictional representation of providence at work in the world is a major unifying thematic direction of the English novel before George Eliot—and that her work itself is largely engaged with its adaptation to secular imperatives. Attention to what I will define as a *providential aesthetic* leads immediately to issues of causality in narrative (sequence, coincidence, determinism, will), to the confines and opportunities of temporal modes (history, linearity, and their interruptions), to the relation between typological or parabolic significance and the credibility of character or event (psychological verisimilitude and particularity).

A deeper understanding of the providential tradition in its variety and complexity helps both to focus our apprehension of the genre and to refine our reading of individual novels. To read, for example, *Villette* or *Bleak House* or *The Mill on the*

Floss without awareness of this tradition—one which they build on and add to—seems to me analogous to listening to a major symphony from which great sections of the orchestration have been omitted or to standing too close to one corner of a large painting. Such failures of comprehension and perspective not only account for some of the peculiarity and special pleading of current criticism (and here I am aware that this study is vulnerable to similar correction) but, far more important, they diminish and impoverish experience of the art. The more tones we can hear, the more formal relationships we can perceive, the deeper our engagement and pleasure in the text will be—provided that the tones are clear and the relationships coherent.

The first step toward validating these claims—they cannot be *proved* without the more detailed discussion of my succeeding chapters—seems to me to be the elementary one of acknowledging the width of the gap separating a culture that possesses an essentially providential view of life and art from one that does not. In a thoroughgoing providential worldview no event can be fully apprehended without some acknowledgment of its potential spiritual or moral content. No circumstance can be assumed to exist and no event to occur simply for its own sake. All being and action are suspectible to meaning beyond themselves. The fall of any sparrow may have significance. The universe is a moral theater, a spiritual classroom. As Robert Colby puts it, "Our age shuns didacticism in art. The nineteenth century novelist believed that art was didactic precisely because life was didactic." The English novel before George Eliot imitates life in revealing a moral intention in the universe, and as it heightens and clarifies other aspects of life—the nature of society, individual development, the action of historical forces—so it heightens and clarifies the evidence for cosmic design and divine presence. Most Victorian novels admit of no clear distinction between moral ends and aesthetic means because no corresponding distinction existed in the perceived world they attempt to represent. Experience for most people had no form without moral content. In 1853 the *Westminster Review* observed that a novel "may carry its moral openly on its very title page, through all its conclusions; or it may carry within it, not one but many moral illustrations, naturally arising out of the way incidents are grouped, and the way characters express themselves." The distinction may have seemed useful, but it does not allow for a novel without a moral. Even during the 1870s and eighties, when the possibility of a literature devoid of moral didacticism became the fashionable critical topic, the intensity of the debate suggests the strength and persistence of the earlier tradition. Kenneth Graham describes the difficulty for late Victorian critics: "Their obsessive concern for the relationship of art and morality is easily guyed, but cannot be dismissed as irrelevant. For all of the limitations of their enquiry, they were confronting a problem which is still largely unanswered and which is still vital to our understanding of art; the exact nature of a literary 'idea.' "[1]

It will shortly become important to distinguish between the idea of providence in fiction and the correlative and more diffuse idea of moral content, but here I wish to notice only the distance of these allied ideas from those we usually take to be definitive of our own time. The possible ways of demonstrating this are overwhelming in volume and range, but the following passage from Camus's *The Plague* illustrates it very well:

> "My question's this," said Tarrou. "Why do you yourself show such devotion, considering you don't believe in God? I suspect your answer may help me to mine."
>
> His face still in shadow, Rieux said that he'd already answered: that if he believed in an all-powerful God he would cease curing the sick and leave that to Him. But no one in the world believed in a God of that sort; no, not even Paneloux, who believed that he believed in such a God. And this was proved by the fact that no one ever

[1]Robert Colby, *Fiction with a Purpose* (Bloomington: Indiana Univ. Press, 1968), p. 24; *Westminster Review*, NS 3 ([old vol. 59]1853), 475-76; Kenneth Graham, *English Criticism of the Novel, 1865-1890* (Oxford: Clarendon, 1965), p. 71.

threw himself on Providence completely. Anyhow, in this
respect Rieux believed himself to be on the right road—
in fighting against creation as he found it.[2]

The moves here are typical of twentieth-century dismissals of
providentialism. In the first place, Dr. Rieux does not understand the tradition. He assumes that belief in providence logically entails the abdiction of moral responsibility, whereas Jane
Eyre or even Oliver Twist could have told him that human
volition has a central though undetermined role in the divine
scheme. Next we observe an attempt at psychological undermining. Paneloux thinks he believes in providence, but Rieux
knows he really does not because he does not throw himself
"on Providence completely." This assumes what no intelligent
providentialist would allow, that Paneloux's will operates
somehow outside the providential order and that he can somehow distinguish between that order and himself, as if he could
choose not to participate in it. Finally, that seems to be what
Rieux in this passage has chosen to do, "fighting against creation as he found it," an idea that succeeds in being totally
alien to a providential worldview. What is important here,
however, is not the secular coherence of Camus's fictional
structure but Rieux's failure to understand what—in a rare
moment of self-expression—he allows himself to criticize.

Lionel Trilling observes that "perhaps the greatest distress
associated with the evanescence of faith, more painful and
disintegrating than can now be fully imagined, was the loss
of the assumption that the universe is purposive. This assumption, which as Freud says, 'stands and falls with the religious
system,' was, for those who held it, not merely a comfortable
idea but nothing less than a category of thought; its extirpation
was a psychic catastrophe."[3] My effort in the chapters that
follow is to understand this "category of thought" as it operates

[2]Albert Camus, *The Plague,* trans. Stuart Gilbert (New York: Vintage,
1972), p. 120.

[3]Lionel Trilling, *Sincerity and Authenticity* (Cambridge: Harvard Univ.
Press, 1973), p. 116.

in the English novel, especially in the novels of Charlotte Brontë, Charles Dickens, and George Eliot. I have chosen these three writers for extended discussion because in their work the providential worldview reaches its fullest and richest expression. Brontë and Dickens provide in their early novels a splendid celebration of its powers as a structuring principle and in their later work increasingly radical and brilliant defenses against what proved in the end to be its "extirpation" as a general cultural and aesthetic premise. George Eliot produced the first and greatest examples of the ways in which the aesthetic conventions and structural devices of the providential tradition can be turned to the service of what has become a generally secular art. In all cases I am concerned with historical forces and cultural change only as represented in fiction or as affecting the evolution of the novel. The multifarious and complex extraliterary forces that led to the pervasive secularism of our own age—the historical, economic, technological, demographic "causes" for the disappearance of providence—are not my central concern. Excellent studies dealing with those subjects have been written and more will certainly appear.[4] This one is about fiction and how it is shaped.

The Providential Aesthetic

I introduce the formulation *providential aesthetic* to mean those devices or conventions characteristic of literary works in which the assumption of providential design and intention at work

[4]See, for example, Alexander Welsh, "Realism as a Practical and Cosmic Joke," *Novel,* 9 (1975), 23-26 and 26-39 passim; Owen Chadwick, *The Secularization of the European Mind in the Nineteenth Century* (London: Cambridge Univ. Press, 1976); and Bernard M. G. Reardon, *From Coleridge to Gore: A Century of Religious Thought in Britain* (London: Longman, 1971), pp. 216-320. I didn't see Barry Qualls's *The Secular Pilgrim in Victorian Fiction* (New York: Cambridge Univ. Press, 1982) until after the present study was accepted for publication. Qualls selects the same three novelists for attention, especially to certain limited religious motifs in their work. Otherwise our two books are notably free from substantive and methodological similarities.

in the fictional world is a major premise or concern. I have made it a condition that this premise or concern be explicit in the texts, that the narrators or the characters make explicit and repeated reference to it. I have not made it a condition that all the works discussed support a providential worldview—none of George Eliot's novels do that, and final resolution of the question has sometimes been regarded as doubtful in *Villette* and the later Dickens. Finally, the idea of a providential aesthetic in fiction is not rigorously prescriptive: no one set of conventions and techniques applies to all the serious fiction that qualifies thematically for discussion. Each major novel discussed ultimately creates its own aesthetic, even its own providential aesthetic as it participates in the tradition.

Nevertheless, certain characteristic elements appear with great regularity. The most recurrent of these is the use of coincidence in plot. A *coincidence* in its basic meaning is merely the concurrence or juxtaposition in time and space of two or more events or circumstances. Pip and Estella happen to meet at the end of *Great Expectations,* either in a London street or on the grounds of Satis House depending on which of the two available endings we select. But coincidence in its common and most important literary use carries with it an element of surprise or astonishment that derives from the lack of apparent causal connection. We do not know what brought the events or circumstances to concurrence, and our ignorance allows us to be surprised. The degree of our astonishment depends upon our sense of probability, our awareness of what is more or less likely to occur. In the canceled conclusion to *Great Expectations* neither Pip nor Estella appears to be much surprised: "The lady and I looked sadly enough on one another." They know—everybody knows—that you eventually meet the whole world along Piccadilly. In the ending Dickens chose to publish, however, Pip does show surprise:

> "Estella! . . .
> ". . . After so many years, it is strange that we should thus meet again, Estella, here where our first meeting was! Do you often come back?"

"I have never been here since."
"Nor I."[5]

Pip knows that you are not likely to meet the whole world on the cleared grounds of an obscure estate. It is not probable. And Dickens intentionally stresses the temporal improbability. He could have had Estella wandering remorsefully about the grounds for months to be there when Pip turns up (heroines do a lot of waiting in Dickens). But this is the first and only night of her return. It is a *true* coincidence, one designed to push the reader toward a different level of causality from that which can satisfactorily explain the Piccadilly encounter, an idea of causality perfectly real and comfortable to readers educated in the providential tradition.[6]

Dickens told Collins that he made his new ending "a very pretty piece of writing . . . and I have no doubt the story will be more acceptable through the alteration."[7] He had a good ear—to put it mildly— for his audience. He could count on their application of a causality that was not naturalistic. Most twentieth-century readers, certainly most critics, have preferred the canceled conclusion partly because there the concurrence of events points toward a naturalistic causality. The published coincidence seems to some a time-serving compromise for the sake of popularity rather than aesthetic truth or validity. But if a reader possesses a providential view of the world, then the meeting on the grounds of Satis House is true, true in the sense that moral development and spiritual refinement do merit

[5]*Great Expectations,* ed. Earle Davis (New York: Holt, Rinehart, Winston, 1972), pp. 470, 468; ch. 59.

[6]Norman Goldhawk observes in a summary of William Paley's *Natural Theology* (a primary source for eighteenth- and nineteenth-century providentialism), "It may be that, owing to the ignorance of the observer, events will have the appearance of chance, whereas they may well proceed from intelligence and design. This is particularly true of our judgments about God's actions" ("William Paley: or the Eighteenth Century Revisited," in *Providence,* ed. Maurice Wiles [London: S.P.C.K., 1969], p. 55).

[7]Quoted by Edgar Johnson, *Charles Dickens: His Tragedy and Triumph* (New York: Simon and Schuster, 1952) II, 969.

and receive acknowledgment by or in the temporal course of events. Rewards do come. Pip and Estella deserve to be rewarded and acknowledged.

In the providential aesthetic, then, coincidence is not necessarily a failure in realism or (as is sometimes implied) a cheap way out of difficulties in plot and structure—though of course it can be both in a bad novel.[8] Instead, coincidence is a sign or pointer. As Barbara Hardy observes, "Coincidence is a symbol of providence." Coincidence characteristically refers the reader to causes and patterns beyond the immediate or empirical range of what we perceive as probable in physical nature, the naturalistic range. When coincidences occur, a reader may view them as invitations to widen awareness of the fictional cosmos, to see a larger pattern, to entertain the possibility of a unity not limited to the street. Of course a reader may decline the invitation by rejecting the fictional assumption of a providential intention in the novel by classifying it as unreal, sentimental, or conventionally obligatory—"an unpardonable mannerism of style" in Oscar Wilde's cheerful phrase.[9] Some readers do this, and for them the larger unity either goes unperceived or is rejected as bogus. But for readers sympathetic to the providential aesthetic—and such readers need not be themselves believers in a providential intention in the world outside of books—the invitation issued by coincidence is not

[8]See David Goldknopf's discussion of coincidence as a "tacit metaphysical statement," a choice "in preference to . . . a naturalistic pattern of motivation," by which "the authors are in effect commanding the readers, believe!" (*The Life of the Novel* [Chicago: Univ. of Chicago Press, 1972], pp. 159, 162, 163). Nevertheless, much specifically Christian criticism of the Victorian novel objected to excessive use of improbable events and characters as inauthentic and therefore inappropriate to a representation of God's moral universe. See John O. Waller, "A Composite Anglo-Catholic Concept of the Novel, 1841-1868," *Bulletin of the New York Public Library*, 70 (1966), 368, and 356-67 passim.

[9]Barbara Hardy, *The Appropriate Form: An Essay on the Novel* (London: Athlone, 1964), p. 63 (She attributes the point to Kathleen Tillotson in *Novels of the Eighteen-Forties* [Oxford: Clarendon, 1956], where I have been unable to find it); Oscar Wilde, Preface to *The Picture of Dorian Gray* (Harmondsworth: Penguin, 1962), p. 5.

an arbitrary superimposition of a dogmatic construct. Instead, it provides an aesthetic transition from ignorance to knowledge, from confusion to order. As readers and characters learn to interpret the particular coincidences correctly, as they correct their ignorance of the causality, the energy initially released by the element of surprise or astonishment transfers itself to apprehension of form or design.

In some novels, like *Villette* or *Great Expectations* or *Daniel Deronda*, the formal unities suggested are (as we shall see) thematically elaborate and profound. In others, like *Oliver Twist* and *Jane Eyre*, they seem more perfunctory or geometric. But coincidences in the providential tradition are always more than the arbitrary manipulation of events modern readers often take them to be. They signal a purposiveness beyond the natural accident. In *Hard Times* as Mrs. Sparsit drags the unwilling and unwelcome mother of Mr. Bounderby from her coach she cries, "It's a coincidence. . . . It's a Providence! come out, ma'am!"[10] Mrs. Sparsit's motives may be impure, but her association of ideas moves in a significant direction.

Closely related to the function of coincidence in the providential aesthetic is the phenomenon I will label *inconsequent actualization*. By this I mean the fulfillment or realization of a desire or fear by causal sequences which the characters do not initiate or control. In *Great Expectations* Pip and Estella both desire reconciliation. Both endings show that they have come to recognize each other's real worth. But they neither plan nor anticipate the reunion they experience in the published conclusion. That opportunity comes to them, in a providential reading of the novel, from beyond the pale of human calculation and contrivance. In *Jane Eyre*, when the protagonists reach the state of moral and spiritual development that suits them to each other, the obstacles to their equal union are removed: Jane receives her inheritance and Bertha Mason Rochester dies. Neither event is arranged by the principals.

[10]*Hard Times,* ed George Ford and Sylvère Monod (New York: Norton, 1966), p. 196; bk. III, ch. 5.

The actualization of the necessary and desired circumstances is not consequent on their planning or manipulation. If we accept Jane's reading of events, the causality implied can be nothing less than divine. Such supernaturalistic causality ultimately brings David Copperfield to Agnes Wickfield, Amy Dorrit to Arthur Clennam, Lizzie Hexam to Eugene Wrayburn. And the device works as well for punishments as for rewards. The unplanned death of Smike punishes his father Ralph Nickleby. Monks and Sikes are caught up in loops and coils of unforeseen circumstances. Steerforth drowns. Miss Havisham is purified by fire. Mrs. Reed goes down in lonely despair.

Such actualization gives characters in providential fiction a sense of plan or pattern in their lives.[11] Readers participate in this patterning provided that they accept the required premise of a causality, a providential intention functioning beyond (though often through) the naturalistic concatenations resulting from willed human action. The providential aesthetic thus intensely engages readers in the act of witnessing characters interpret events. Characters "read" the "text" of their own lives in an attempt to discover meaning and order there. Readers not only interpret the events of those lives but also must evaluate the characters' interpretations of them. Readers interpret characters interpreting, a process that constitutes much of the excitement of the providential aesthetic and perhaps of most dramatic narrative. Characters, of course, can misinterpret events, as Pip disastrously misinterprets his great expectations or as Lucy Snowe misinterprets M. Paul's intentions on the night of the carnival in *Villette*. This process of interpreting interpretations receives a good deal of attention in this study, largely because the apprehension of a providential intention

[11]Marianna Torgovnick observes that "in completing the 'circle' of a novel, endings create the illusion of life halted and poised for analysis. . . .In part we value endings because the retrospective patterning used to make sense of the texts corresponds to one process used to make sense of life: the process of looking back over events and interpreting them in light of 'how things turned out' " (*Closure in the Novel* [Princeton: Princeton Univ. Press, 1981], p. 5).

at work in the fictional world involves so directly major problems of causality and because it raises immediate questions about the status of the reality represented and the status of the characters' understanding of it. The action of interpreting interpreting quickly grows very involved, especially in analysis of novels where the device of inconsequent actualization deeply influences the structure of the work and is treated with great sophistication, as in *Villette* or *Little Dorrit* or *Daniel Deronda*.

For the moment, however, I wish to refine certain customary distinctions that tend to blur into one another in critical examination of the interpreting that goes on within Victorian novels. The first and most troublesome of these has to do with the metaphorical functions of events and circumstances presented to the reader and experienced by the characters. This is ground bearing heavy critical traffic, where it seems difficult to be clear without appearing naive. On a most basic level it is now often pointed out—sometimes with appalling intensity and elaboration—that everything in a literary work must be metaphorical because language is metaphor and literary works exist only in language. I grant this without qualification in order to move to another, perhaps secondary, level of discussion. On this level readers and critics—even some accomplished critics—show a tendency to assume that the reality represented in fiction is in some way opposed to metaphor, especially to elaborated forms of metaphor such as typology, allegory, or parable. This duality between realistic and metaphorical representation may work well (though I doubt it) for some literary forms. It does not work in Victorian providential fiction. As we have already seen, it can be said that events and circumstances in a providential novel may be metaphorical to the extent that they participate in the providential aesthetic, that they point beyond naturalistic causalities.[12] It does not

---

[12]Of course this does not mean that *all* events and circumstances in a providential novel are metaphorical in this sense or that they necessarily do participate in the providential aesthetic. G. A. Starr observes in a discussion of *Moll Flanders* that "some portions of the narrative are not spiritualized

follow, however, that they therefore cease to be realistic or that they lose their importance as naturalistic representations.

But the apparent duality has become embedded in our critical discourse. For example, Barbara Hardy, a foremost student of the genre and highly sensitive to its religious content, dealing with what she calls "dogmatic form" in the novels of Defoe and Charlotte Brontë among others, makes this formulation: "All the novelists I have taken to illustrate dogmatic form, attempt, with unfortunate results, to do what Lawrence calls applying the world to their metaphysic, but they are all happily incapable of doing this consistently. At times they apply the metaphysic to the world which breaks or enlarges the scheme and makes the novel more than a treatise or a fable." This is a typically loaded response. If they could, it implies, these novelists would force the world to conform to their "dogmatic" preconception of it, their ideology. But as novelists they are too good for that—they imitate life too accurately in spite of themselves. And life, the world, is in the critic's view patently undogmatic. A similar criticism—the moves are the same— was made of George Eliot by Henry James. George Eliot had admitted that she found Balzac's *Le Père Goriot* "a hateful book." This, says James, is a revealing remark: "It illuminates the author's general attitude with regard to the novel, which, for her, was not primarily a picture of life, capable of deriving a high value from its form, but a moralized fable, the last word of philosophy trying to teach by example."[13]

But what if, as George Eliot thought (without believing in providence), life *is* didactic? What if the artist's premise about

---

at all, either implicity or explicitly; or, at any rate, they are not fully assimilated into the spiritual framework" (*Defoe and Spiritual Autobiography* [Princeton: Princeton Univ. Press, 1965], p. 62). This kind of qualification would apply to much of what goes on in high Victorian fiction. Nevertheless, events and circumstances may not contradict—though they may threaten— the providential design.

[13]Hardy, *The Appropriate Form*, p. 82; Henry James's review of Cross's biography, *Atlantic Monthly* (May 1885), is reprinted in *George Eliot: The Critical Heritage*, ed. David Carroll (New York: Barnes & Noble, 1971), p. 497.

the world—Defoe's and Charlotte Brontë's premise—is that reality is in its nature didactic, significant, symbolic? In what sense can such writers be seen as imposing dogma on experience or as arbitrarily moralizing from purely neutral, formal (Jamesian) life? The criticism is not only historically unimaginative but metaphysically hubristic, assuming as it does that the nature of reality has somehow been proved to *be* morally neutral. In his 1855 essay on "The Relation of Novels to Life," Fitzjames Stephen applied a similar standard to the characters in Dickens's early fiction: "They all depart in different dramatic positions, each with his appropriate piece of poetical justice. Can anyone pretend that this is like life?" The answer, obviously, is no, not like life as Fitzjames Stephen sees it. But Stephen, closer than James in time and sensibility to the providential tradition in fiction, goes on to show that it is not Dickens's didacticism he objects to but its inauthenticity as revealed by the coarsely mechanical dispensation of rewards and punishments, what current critical discourse might term its lack of validity. By way of contrast he praises not some work innocent of dogmatic content but Defoe's handling of providence in *Robinson Crusoe*: "To invent facts in order to justify a theory is one thing,—to apply facts fairly represented in a particular manner is quite another thing." A good novel is not the successful justification of a theory about life. It is the successful representation of life as the author perceives it. The reality of fiction, Stephen implies, is reality as perceived by the author. Even Defoe's use of omens and presentiments must be viewed as realistic in this sense: "Believing in them as matters of fact, it is natural that he should introduce them into a picture of life."[14]

The omens and presentiments in *Robinson Crusoe* are at once naturalistic phenomena and indices of providential intention.[15] So, indeed, are the "dramatic positions" of the characters at

---

[14]Fitzjames Stephen, *Cambridge Essays* (London: John W. Parker, 1855), pp. 188, 191.

[15]As has been persuasively demonstrated by Starr in *Defoe and Spiritual Autobiography*, pp. 74–125, 194–97, and J. Paul Hunter in *The Reluctant Pilgrim* (Baltimore: Johns Hopkins Univ. Press, 1966), pp. 188–201, 207–8, and 126–88 passim.

the end of Dickens's novels, however mechanical they might seem. Such events and circumstances may appear from a present-day perspective to exercise a dual function or to occupy a double agenda, naturalistic and parabolic, mimetic and metaphorical. But the realism of the providential aesthetic admits of no such constant duality because there the reality of nature and the evidence for divine intention can at any moment prove reciprocal or integral.

This is as true of the delineation of character as it is of the representation of external circumstances. Psychological phenomena become, in serious providential fiction, a part of that reality which embodies and evinces divine intention. This does not mean that characters are allegorical in the simpler sense, like the more easily abstracted personae of a morality play. On the contrary, in Victorian providential fiction they tend to be highly individual, particularized. George Landow has recently suggested that perhaps *typological* might prove the more useful term because "whereas in typology both signifier and signified are real, in allegory the signifier can be cast off like an empty husk once its meaning has been understood." He goes on to point out that "what is perhaps unique about Victorian typology is that it comes into being during an age when men have increasingly come to accept that reality inheres in present fact and not in the realm of ideas, forms, or spirituality."[16] Another way of putting this is to say that "present fact"—empirical, concrete phenomena—participates in a world order seen as providential, and that psychological realism—complexity and depth of character—actually helps to signify this.

For example, we now understand very well the causes and effects of Pip's feeling of guilt throughout *Great Expectations*. It has clearly drawn naturalistic causes and effects. These do not prevent his feeling of guilt from also having religious significance, from leading to his spiritual maturation in a providential universe and to a profound, almost Boethian acceptance of the limitations of human time. Lucy Snowe in *Villette* has excellent psychological reasons for becoming the wary,

---

[16]George Landow, *Victorian Types, Victorian Shadows* (Boston: Rutledge and Kegan Paul, 1980), pp. 52, 54.

distrustful, secretive person she presents herself to be, but her reserve and distrust prove to be liabilities when they bring her into conflict with what she finally sees as the dark providential leadings of her circumstances. If the fictional universe is pervasively providential, verisimilitude of character, the devices that promote psychological credibility, are integral to that universe. Given the premise inherent in the providential aesthetic, the more fully developed the character, the greater its reality, the more fully it participates.[17]

This does not mean that psychological credibility is never sacrificed in the interest of the moral line—Helen Burns and Florence Dombey leap to mind—but that there is no inherent or necessary conflict between the providential worldview as it exists in high Victorian fiction and the concrete representation of highly individualized characters. The persistent post-Jamesian assumption that in order to possess credibility characters must be divorced from larger philosophical, especially religious, patterns and contexts has no place in the providential aesthetic. There is no such independence and there can be none. On the contrary, all reality—inner and outer—is assumed to be ultimately interdependent, and this interdependence gains richness and power from the uniqueness and complexity, the individuation, of its constituents.

Providence, Decorum, and Poetic Justice

As with most subjects of a certain range, it is difficult to treat this one without trying to talk about all aspects of it at once. This book could have begun with a definition and history of

---

[17]In *The Providential Order of the World*, A. B. Bruce gives an interesting analysis of the relation of the idea of self to his paradigm of providential order: "Personality is as necessary to morality as is society. We must be 'selves' before we begin to be moral." Selfhood, personality, he goes on, is therefore a providential provision (New York: Scribners, 1897; AMS reprint, 1979), pp. 136 ff.

the idea of providence, or at least with a discussion of that idea in Victorian culture. Such a beginning, however, might have proved misleading because my subject is not providence but a providential worldview as it relates to the thematic content and structure of Victorian fiction, its providential aesthetic, and I wanted to begin with some suggestion of the limitations and possibilities of that. In so doing I have used the terms *providence, providential intention,* and *providential worldview* as if present-day readers of English novels could have no difficulty with them, as if they have a clear and distinct meaning that permitted their free use in critical and scholarly discourse. Pedagogical and collegial experience, however, has taught me that this is not necessarily the case, at least not if one wants to make precise and extended application of these words to a literature otherwise sufficiently rich and complicated. What follows, therefore, is a development and explanation of the principal terms of the study. The definitions are as brief as I could make them, but I have tried to establish precision and clarity as my priorities and to avoid arcane or arbitrary vocabulary.

Historically, in Western civilization at least, the idea of providence has been coincident with ideas of moral and ethical responsibility. It is in fact a commonplace of historical generalization to say that until quite recently, perhaps until the seventeenth or eighteenth centuries for Western intellectuals and much later for most others, human beings saw themselves as living at the center of an ethical universe. We were part of a natural world that was fundamentally moral and intimately connected with human action. We made no consistent distinction between nature and society; we were part of an ordered cosmos at whose heart was an ordered ethos. What human beings did had an ethical effect on the nature of which we were the most important manifestation and which reflected to our apprehension the ethical value of our activities. In the Judeo-Christian tradition this human interaction with the natural world came to be seen as the process of the working out of the divine purpose, and the word that came to comprehend the fulfilling of God's will for humanity in time, in the working out of history, was *providence,* so that *Providence* has also been used to mean *God* as he fulfills his will in human destiny.[18]

The English word *providence* means, by derivation, foresight, and in practice refers to the thoughtful preparation for human needs. In a theistic sense it denotes "the care of God for his creatures, His general supervision over them, and the ordering of the whole course of things for their good." Christian discussions of providence often refer to St. Paul's assertion in his Epistle to the Romans "that all things work together for good to them that love God, to them who are the called according to his purpose" (8:28). Augustine took an epoch-making approach to the entire matter in part by "rejecting the concepts of both chance and fate, and holding that divine providence operates in all things, no matter how minute and obscure." This of course includes all social interaction because, in Augustine's words, "it is impossible to suppose that [God] would have excluded from the laws of his providence the kingdoms of men and their denominations and servitudes."[19] Milton's sustained attempt in *Paradise Lost* to "assert eternal Providence" (I, 25)—surely for English literature the greatest and

[18]This lightning summation of religious history and prehistory is partly transcribed and paraphrased from my essay on providentialism and dystopia in *Technological Forecasting and Social Change,* 16 (1980), 180. Among extensive background materials not cited elsewhere in this study I have found the following helpful and suggestive: Karl Löwith, *Meaning in History* (Chicago: Univ. of Chicago Press, 1958); Mircea Eliade, *The Myth of the Eternal Return* (Princeton: Princeton Univ. Press, 1971); James Martineau, *A Study of Religion* (Oxford: Clarendon, 1888); Leslie Stephen, *Essays on Freethinking and Plainspeaking* (London: Longman, 1873); and the *Oxford English Dictionary* S.V. "Providence." Hunter provides admirable definitions of "providence" and "special providence" as essential to Defoe and to eighteenth-century fiction in *The Reluctant Pilgrim,* pp. 52–60.

[19]*Encyclopedia of Religion and Ethics,* ed. James Hastings (New York: Scribners, 1919), X, 415 (This definition is elaborated by Jacob Viner in *The Role of Providence in the Social Order* [Princeton: Princeton Univ. Press, 1972], pp. 4–5); *Schoff-Herzog Encyclopedia of Religious Knowledge,* ed. Samuel Macauly Jackson (London, 1911), p. 308; Augustine, *The City of God against the Pagans,* trans. William M. Green (Cambridge: Harvard Univ. Press, 1963), II, 189.

most influential statement on the subject outside the King James Bible—adopted and dramatized this view of providence as working in and through all things; or, as God sums it up to his Son:

> Boundless the deep, because I am who fill
> Infinitude, nor vacuous the space.
> Though I uncircumscribed myself retire,
> And put not forth my goodness, which is free
> To act or not, necessity and chance
> Approach not me, and what I will is fate.
>
> (VII. 168–73)

In these philosophically compressed observations Milton has God asserting at once his presence and prescience throughout the universe and also his unlimited option to determine or to refuse to determine the outcome of events, an option that bears directly on human freedom of choice in the Garden of Eden and later in the historical world from the Fall to the Last Judgment.

Beyond *Paradise Lost* the assertion is fundamental to any understanding of a providential worldview that stresses human responsibility. The chief providential tradition in Western culture does not merely make room for human freedom: it presents itself as pertinent to human understanding primarily because human beings are free. Ultimately no doubt all things work together for them that love God, but human beings can choose whether or not to love God—as Old Testament prophets, Jesus, St. Paul, Augustine, Aquinas, Milton, and numberless others repeatedly assert. I belabor this point because this particular aspect of the providential vision is subject to ideological slippage in the twentieth century, as much discussion of the problem in criticism of *Paradise Lost* attests. But this was not, as a rule, a primary difficulty for Victorian readers, who tended to find plenty of scope for freedom and responsibility within the providential order.

In nineteenth-century England there were perhaps two major versions of the providential worldview.[20] The first, inherited from the previous century and perpetuated by the sustained attention given such works as Joseph Butler's *The Analogy of Religion, Natural and Revealed, to the Constitution and the Course of Nature* (1736) and William Paley's *Natural Theology, or Evidence of the Existence and Attributes of the Deity Collected from the Appearances of Nature* (1802), emphasized the order of the world and the evidence to be found there for a divine planner—not, as these writers insist, the absent watchmaker of the deists, but a being of order, foresight, power, and benevolence. The design of the universe suggests these moral attributes for contemplation and imitation. More important for the providential aesthetic in fiction, the very idea of design—plenitude, plan, pattern, order, symmetry, form—as evincing moral qualities, as having what might be termed ethical prestige, gives the structuring impulse tremendous force. If there is virtue in design, in formal arrangement, then believers in providence will wish to see everywhere, even in their fiction, the fullest possible design, the roundest plot—complete with foreshadowings, parallels, and analogies—compatible with the representation of that particularization or individuation of circumstances, characters, and events that qualify as reality.[21]

[20]Of course this represents a simplification, but a workable one. Other categorizations are numerous. Huw Owen, in a recent essay, finds that "the idea of Providence has four main aspects. It indicates firstly that God foresees future events, secondly that he controls them, thirdly that he cares for his creatures, and fourthly that he is working out a purpose in them. Inevitably these aspects overlap" (*Providence*, ed. Wiles, p. 77). These categories would certainly fit a Victorian definition of providence—and they would overlap there too.

[21]G.A. Starr, speaking of spiritual autobiography in the seventeenth and early eighteenth centuries observes that "to the spiritually minded man, life and literature are equally rich texts on which to enlarge; one could attach as much significance to a tradesman's annual inventory as to the Christian soldier's shield, helmet, and sword. Both life and literature are made up of similitudes, so that things seen and things read equally invite interpretation" (*Defoe and Spiritual Autobiography*, p. 22).

Novels could be structured to reflect the order and method of providential design, and by reflecting that design could, as we shall see, make a powerful claim to the most serious attention.

Another and (as it was perceived) newer emphasis within the providential tradition came from the doctrine of immanence. As Horton Davies puts it:

> In a word, as the older theology had emphasized God's transcendence, so the newer theology emphasized His immanence, His in-dwelling. He was believed to be continually active in human affairs as a dynamic Providence and in continuous creation. Despite the dangers of such an emphasis (among them a certain vagueness, a pantheistic tendency, and a failure to do justice to the specifically "saving" acts of God), it led to a greater sense of the fatherhood and constant care of God, whereas the exclusive emphasis of transcendence had caused God's love to be lost in His sovereignty.[22]

In fact, the devotional literature of the early and mid-Victorian period stresses the presence of God in the world and especially his paternal attention to and care for his creatures. The concept of providence itself becomes progressively less an image of order, regulation, grand planning, and more an intimate solicitude for individual lives. Among the many influences upon this change were late eighteenth- and early nineteenth-century evangelicalism, with its intense preoccupation with a "right state of heart"; the allied and pervasive reaction against "rationalism" in religious thought and practice, most brilliantly articulated by the leaders of the Oxford Movement; and the epistemological legacy of the romantic movement in literature with its emphasis on the particular, the uniquely significant object or person and its vision, especially in Wordsworth and

[22]Horton Davies, *Worship and Theology in England: From Newman to Martineau, 1850–1900* (Princeton: Princeton Univ. Press, 1962), p. 192.

Coleridge, of the sacramental functioning of the natural world.[23] The idea of God as primarily an external judge or "moral Governor," in the words of one Victorian theologian, came to be regarded as "an imperfect, abstract, partial one, needing to be supplemented by a conception more in accordance with the modern doctrine of Divine immanence." For this reason, "the true conception of God's relation to the universe surely is: *God always dwelling in the world and ever active there.*"[24]

The shift of emphasis in religious thought and practice from transcendence to immanence, from general design to immediate participation, has its direct correlation in the changing providential aesthetic of the Victorian novel. The first novels of Dickens and Charlotte Brontë, like most novels that preceded them, reveal providence at work clearly and openly in their representations of the natural order and in the candid poetic justice of the plot. Mr. Pickwick, Oliver Twist, Nicholas Nickleby, and Jane Eyre all live in worlds that would meet their needs and be entirely comprehensible to them if it were not for the machinations of willfully wicked villians and blocking characters. When these are justly disposed of, the harmony of the natural order becomes apparent, and the concatenation of past events reveals a morally lucid pattern. In later Dickens, however, the evidence for an active providence must be glimpsed obliquely in certain shining particularities, in a personal sacrifice, a gratuitous charity, the purity of a virtuous heroine, the courage of a good man. An in Charlotte Brontë's *Villette,* Lucy Snowe develops a desperate private logic to maintain her faith in the providence which she tries to obey

[23]John Henry Newman, among others, considered the influence of romanticism of great importance to nineteenth-century religious feeling and practice, especially in the revival of a Christian vision of God as immanent in nature. See Thomas Vargish, *Newman: The Contemplation of Mind* (Oxford: Clarendon, 1970), pp. 96–108.

[24]Bruce, *The Providential Order of the World*, pp. 183, 56. (Italics, as throughout this study, are the original author's, not mine.) See also his *Moral Order of the World* (London: Hodder and Stoughton, 1899), pp. 244–45.

and which she can only darkly intuit in the delusive realities around her. From the 'middle of the nineteenth century on, the providential aesthetic becomes less a representation of order in the natural and social worlds, less a complementary design in the plot, and more an intimation that divine intention can be found only beyond the immediately obscure or preverse circumstances.

One way of viewing the incorporation of the doctrine of immanence—really a mode of perception, a sensibility—into the providential aesthetic of high Victorian fiction is to think of it as a kind of brilliant temporizing, a sublime stopgap. As we shall see, it became impossible after a certain point (about 1850) for Brontë and Dickens, among others, to write what I will call straightforward providential fiction—novels like *David Copperfield* and *Jane Eyre* that clearly show the divine design, or providential intention, in the complete resolution of the plot and in the representation of a normative benevolence in nature and society. Whatever the causes—and they must have been complex and diffuse—the dictates of realism changed because what seemed real changed. The earlier imperatives of natural benevolence, universal design, and compensatory, or "poetical," justice lost force within fiction as without it. For novelists profoundly affected by this change, like Brontë and Dickens, yet deeply engaged in the providential aesthetic and believing in providence, immanence offered a way out. The world, especially the social world, could be presented as they had come to perceive it—corrupt, indifferent, untrustworthy—and yet, through the darkness, inhabiting the darkness itself (like Florence Dombey alone in the great house), evidence for divine care could be located and represented. Dissociated from the fiction and presented in the abstract, this solution may seem desperate, doomed. In our literary history its decline was signaled (though not completed) by George Eliot's first novels. But just before that, almost at that historical moment, the fictional representation of providence as immanent in nature and society has a last great resistant triumph in *Villette* and all the later Dickens.

In this fiction, then, God's will, the providential intention, can make itself known either through overall design or pattern, as represented in the circumstances and events of the plot, or through certain revelatory glimpses, epiphanies, of immanence. The incorporation of a providential intention is here again essential to the mimetic function of the novel, is inseparable from the representation of reality. Believers in providence, whether the narrators themselves or (as in George Eliot) only characters within the fiction, see reality as necessarily informed by such intention and inseparable from it. The more accurate the representation and the more individualized the characters or particularized the circumstances and events, the more fully this providential intention may be revealed. The underlying premise of a vigorous providentialism is that, as one representative tersely formulates it, "God does not generalize without particularizing."[25]

In individual novels such particularities, often supported by narrative commentary, develop a collective force, a cumulative organization of values and assumptions about the world and the efficacy of human action in it that I will call a *providential decorum*. By this I mean a flexible paradigm of relationships, a sense of the true underlying order of things, a center of value in the narrative. This decorum may vary from novel to novel. It can be as simple as the cosmic sanction awarded to virtue in *Nicholas Nickleby* or as straightforward as the poetic justice meted out in *Jane Eyre*. Or it can be more difficult to locate, as in the resignation and acceptance recommended by *Great Expectations*. It can exist only in the minds of certain principal characters, as in Adam Bede's, or be found in a highly orchestrated exchange of expectation and event as it is secularized in *Daniel Deronda*.

But although the location of such a decorum eludes precise general definition, it nevertheless forms a powerful constituent of the providential aesthetic. In the idea of providence itself there lies an implicit suggestion that the universe contains a right *way*, a kind of historical Tao. If we discipline ourselves

[25]*Encyclopedia of Religion and Ethics*, p. 419, author unidentified.

to stay on the way, everything will seem ordered, significant, suited to our being. If we depart from the way (as Pip does when he engages in great expectations, Jane Eyre when she idolizes Rochester), then the world becomes hostile, delusive, alien. Novels in the providential tradition tend to contain signs and indications that locate and identify the decorum, what H. D. F. Kitto, writing about religious elements in Greek drama, calls "a system of co-ordinates." Kitto's description of the relationship of the "divine background" to the "vividness" of tragic drama is broadly applicable to the providential aesthetic in Victorian fiction; and his formulation has such precision and balance that I want to borrow it here:

> Our business is to see that the divine activity neither controls human activity and suffering nor renders them merely pathetic, but is rather a generalized statement about them. The divine background holds up to us, so to speak, the system of co-ordinates against which we are to read the significance of what the human actors do and suffer. . . . The dramatist does not allow the human actors to do or suffer anything which does not have significance when it is read against the co-ordinates. . . .
>
> Hence comes, in the plays, the combination of lifelike vividness with that "constructiveness" which can be very far from "lifelike" or naturalistic: the persons and their actions must be real, true to life. . . . But the vividness, the "truth to life," was restricted (for good artistic reasons) to what made immediate sense when the audience correlated it, as it instinctively would, with the universal co-ordinates in the background.[26]

In Victorian providential fiction, as in Kitto's religious tragedy, human actions are measured or given meaning by the system of coordinates that constitutes the decorum, the true

[26]H. D. F. Kitto, *Form and Meaning in Drama* (London: Methuen, 1971), pp. 243–44.

enduring order of things. The discovery of this order by principal characters—by Jane Eyre or Arthur Clennam or (in a secular manifestation) Gwendolen Harleth—and its acceptance by readers provide a major movement in the providential aesthetic, and my following chapters offer detailed demonstration of this.

The assertion of a providential decorum is requisite to the development of coherent structure in the Victorian novel and gives it a profound though now often unperceived unity of value, action, and texture. The decorum supplies a presumptive base upon which the varying explicit thematic superstructure can rest. When this is fully appreciated, it seems perverse and inadequate to regard high Victorian fiction as either "loose" or "baggy."[27] It appears rather to be shaped with a stability and conviction that make subsequent English novels, despite the often breathtaking precision of their formal achievement, seem to float a bit vaguely on their appeal to an aesthetics of "life."

Inherent in much English fiction that contains a providential decorum is the convention of poetic justice. On one level of analysis poetic justice means simply what an ingenuous and well-intentioned reader desires as rewards and punishments for the principal characters. The convention throughout its history, however, has been regarded as the literary means whereby the workings of providence are made clear.[28] As literary art heightens and intensifies other forms of social and psychological experience, so it can clarify for the consolation and improvement of its audience the active presence of a divine will in the world. From *Robinson Crusoe* onward the realistic novel in English took the representation of poetic justice to

[27]It is worth remembering that James himself does not attach these adjectives to any of the novels discussed in this study. See his Preface to *The Tragic Muse* (New York: Scribners, 1922), I, x.

[28]See especially Aubrey L. Williams's "Poetical Justice in the World of the Theater," *An Approach to Congreve* (New Haven: Yale Univ. Press, 1979) pp. 37–57. His book also contains valuable sections on the providential tradition in drama and in religion through the seventeenth and into the eighteenth centuries.

be a grave moral and aesthetic responsibility of the artist. When readers of *Clarissa* complained to Richardson that he had betrayed the dictates of "poetical justice" in the heroine's pathetic death, he answered the charge with great seriousness in a long Postscript. He argued that since death for the virtuous as well as for the wicked appears to be a universal dispensation of divine justice, it must be appropriate to representation in fiction. Richardson distinguished between the exemplary punishment meted out to the villains in his novel and the beatific expectations of its heroine. Indeed, he urged, "the notion of *Poetical Justice,* founded on the *modern rules* has hardly ever been more strictly observed in works of this nature, than in the present performance. . . . And who that are in earnest in their profession of Christianity, but will rather envy than regret the triumphant death of Clarissa; whose piety, from her *early childhood*; whose diffusive charity; whose steady virtue; whose Christian humility; whose forgiving spirit; whose meekness, and resignation, HEAVEN *only* could reward?" He argues, in other words, that in representing the action of divine justice he necessarily fulfills the aesthetic obligations of poetic justice.[29]

The sanction given to poetic justice by its alliance with the providential intention kept the convention strong throughout the eighteenth century and most of the nineteenth. Writing of English criticism between 1865 and 1900, Kenneth Graham tells us that "there is obviously little need felt to

[29]*Clarissa; or, The History of a Young Lady* (Oxford: Basil Blackwell, 1930), VIII, 318–19. Melvyn New observes: "That Richardson remained deeply committed to the providential view in spite of his method of characterization, of the radical individualism it entails, does not invalidate his innovation. It does, however, warn us that his fiction can only be understood as a reflection of that moment in Western thought when the antithetical ideas of man as God's creature and man as the radical product of his own autonomous will came together in uneasy and temporary alliance" (" 'The Grease of God': The Form of Eighteenth-Century English Fiction," *PMLA*, 91 [1976], 241). As I demonstrate, however, the "moment" New refers to lasted at least through late Dickens and the tendency to see the autonomy of human will and the pervasiveness of God's paternal care as "antithetical ideas" in providential fiction is a failure of modern historical imagination, what Herbert Butterfield called a "Whig interpretation of history." New's essay is nevertheless bold and suggestive.

re-examine such a time-honored convention. 'We look in a novel for something that shall satisfy the instinct for poetic justice,' says *London Society* in 1869, confident of being understood and approved." Graham goes on to quote Ruskin's important defense of poetic justice in *Fors Clavigera*, where he asserts that "this so-called poetical justice" does not consist in the mere apportioning of "mental peace and spiritual victory" but "in the proportioning also of worldly propensity to visible virtue; and in the manifestation, therefore, of the presence of the Father in this world, no less than in that which is to come." Ruskin adds that failure in a work of fiction to "assert this visible justice" reveals "no power of design" but "merely the consecutive collection of interesting circumstances."[30]

Nevertheless, as early as 1844 certain minority reports attacking the establishment status of poetic justice in the resolutions of English novels had begun to appear.[31] In *Barry Lyndon* Thackeray condemned the "misguided people both in novels and the world, who forthwith set up the worldly prosperity or adversity of a man as standards by which his worth should be tried. Novelists especially make a most profuse, mean use of this pedlar's measure, and mete out what they call poetical justice. Justice, forsooth! Does human life exhibit justice after this fashion?"[32] The answer given by most of his contem-

---

[30]Graham, *English Criticism of the Novel, 1865–1900*, p. 84; Ruskin's observations appeared in letter 83 of *Fors Clavigera* (1877).

[31]The convention was never as strong in French nineteenth-century fiction. For their failure to adhere to poetic justice, Ruskin classes Balzac and George Sand as "good novelists of the second order" (ibid.). Stendhal's plots show satiric contempt for poetic justice and providential intention: "You must never speak of chance, my son, but always of Providence," Father Pirard shrewdly advises Julien Sorel in *Scarlet and Black* (trans. Margaret R. B. Shaw [Baltimore: Penguin, 1964], p. 251; p. II, ch. 1). Emma Bovary is addicted to the shallow sentiment as expressed in the trashy romances she absorbs. In America, Hawthorne, Melville, and Twain show ambivalence or hostility, often veiled because the alliance between the representation of poetic justice and the action of providence was established in the minds of American as of English readers.

[32]Quoted in the Introduction to William Makepeace Thackeray, *Vanity Fair: A Novel without a Hero*, ed. Geoffrey and Kathleen Tillotson (Boston: Houghton, Mifflin, 1963), pp. v–vi.

porary novelists and critics, including at that time Charlotte
Brontë and Charles Dickens, is certainly that, properly perceived and examined, human life does indeed exhibit justice
after this fashion—not perhaps in an exact proportion of wealth
to virtue, but in an equitable distribution of well-being among
the virtuous in the here and now. But Thackeray's novels do
not generally exhibit a consistent providential decorum. Instead
they demonstrate a certain Continental skepticism concerning
the convention of poetic justice and its religious underpinnings, a parodic subversion most brilliantly illustrated in the
double ending of *Vanity Fair* where Dobbin's virtue is about
to be rewarded: "This is what he has asked for every day and
hour for eighteen years. This is what he pined after. Here it
is—the summit, the end—the last page of the third volume."[33]
As we know, this is not quite the last page and Dobbin lives
on to transfer his idolatry from Amelia to his daughter. But
this is a novel wherein, as the narrator puts it, "prosperity is
very likely a satire" (ch. 57).

As the following chapters demonstrate in some detail, both
Dickens and Charlotte Brontë show increasing dissatisfaction
with the convention of poetic justice in their later fiction. In
Jane Eyre providential intention and poetic justice are one, and
no novel concludes with a more cheerfully systematic distribution of rewards and punishments. In exquisite contrast, *Villette* may be read as a radical indictment not only of the
convention itself but of the very forms of thought and modes
of perception it permits. Dickens's work shows a more gradual
turning away from the simple distribution of rewards and
punishments that characterizes his first novels. He never
completely abandons the convention, but beginning with *Martin Chuzzlewit*—where Tom Pinch philosophically rejects the
idea that he should be rewarded "as if I were a character in a
book" and instead aligns himself with "a much higher justice

---

[33]Ibid, pp. 660–61; ch. 67. Walter L. Reed sees Thackeray as "closer to
the myth of moral skepticism and worldliness represented by such French
novelists as Stendhal and Flaubert" than he is to the "moral certitudes of
so many English novelists" (*An Exemplary History of the Novel* [Chicago:
Univ. of Chicago Press, 1981], p. 191).

than poetical justice" that "does not order events on the same principle"[34]—Dickens began to distinguish between providential intention and poetic justice, and to explore the implications of their bifurcation. His later fiction relies less on simple temporal rewards for principal characters and more on symbolic or parabolic manifestations of divine benevolence—more, that is, on the providentialism of immanence than of design.

Dickens and Brontë attempted to preserve the doctrine and function of a providential intention in English fiction while departing from what they came to see as the realistic deficiencies of poetic justice. Some similar adjustment in perspective was suggested by Thomas Arnold in 1866 in reference to a classic of antiprovidential polemic:

> Perhaps no novel ever appeared which seemed at first sight to offend so outrageously against public decency, and the moral sense and sentiment of mankind, as Voltaire's "Candide." And doubtless it has done much mischief. Yet is not mankind the better after all for having learnt the lesson, though coarsely and scoffingly conveyed, which "Candide" was designed to teach? Was it not well that the flimsy and hypocritical optimism, which a certain class of divines and philosophers employed and still employ themselves in fostering, should be rudely pulled to pieces; that we should all see the necessity of including in our analysis a number of awkward and painful facts which seem to be built up in the constitution of the world and of human nature, as a preliminary to the construction of any synthesis that will hold water?[35]

Such a "synthesis" was magnificently achieved in Dickens's later novels, but poetic justice as a convention in serious fiction

[34]*Martin Chuzzlewit*, ed. P. N. Furbank (Harmondsworth: Penguin, 1968), p. 845; ch. 50.

[35]Thomas Arnold, "Recent Novel Writing," *Macmillans Magazine*, 13 (1866), 202–9, reprinted in *A Victorian Art of Fiction: Essays on the Novel in British Periodicals, 1851–1869*, ed. John Charles Olmsted (New York: Garland, 1979), p. 546. This is probably Matthew Arnold's younger brother.

was on the way out. When it lost its traditional status as a manifestation of divine order its aesthetic prestige evaporated. Virtue often meets rewards in later fiction, in George Eliot for example, but it is a human virtue that earns acknowledgment by proven social value in an essentially secular decorum.

Temporality and Interpretation

Inherent in the idea of providence is the concept of *linear time*. Providence means foresight, foreknowledge, anticipation, preparation, plan, pattern, design. Providence is God's will as it makes itself known in realistic time, as it unfolds in the grand pattern of human history and in the particular events of individual lives. Of all literary forms the one with the deepest and most complex dependence on temporal linearity is the realistic novel—with its emphasis on plot or story, its past tense narration, and its premise that time is uniform and continuous throughout the naturalistic world it represents.[36] No literary form could be more congenial to the representation of a providential intention and no thematic content could be better suited to the form. As I have argued, the providential aesthetic in English fiction represents no uneasy and evanescent alliance between the representation of particularized, empirical reality on the one hand and an anachronistic established dogmatic on the other. The providential aesthetic represents a unity of means and ends so seamless that it is difficult to discuss, a unity based upon the apprehension of time as linear, of events as consequences, of actions as causes.

What distinguished the treatment of time in the providential aesthetic from its application in the secular, more formally or naturalistically based aesthetics that followed is the premise that temporal sequence, linear time, reveals and participates in

[36]See Elizabeth Ermarth, "Realism, Perspective, and the Novel," *Critical Inquiry*, 7 (1981), 499–520, especially pp. 516–18.

an order of reality that is transcendent and timeless. The natural order signifies in its degree a true and unchanging divine order; the empirical, transient reality contains signs and intimations of God's will; history acknowledges eternity. The providential novel thus always potentially refers its representation of circumstances and events to some ultimate context that has the power to explain them. This explanation, this constant discovery of transcendent significance in temporal particularity, constitutes the deep resourcefulness of the providential aesthetic. In postprovidential fiction, on the other hand, the power lies in the development of formal unity—masterfully achieved in George Eliot, James, Conrad, Joyce, and Lawrence—in an aesthetic that does not explicitly appeal to a frame of reference beyond its own often richly complex temporal linearity.

In realistic fiction that does not possess a providential aesthetic, time is also the necessary medium for clarification and resolution.[37] But often such clarification and resolution is thematically minimal, ambiguous, or threatening, as for example in *The Mill on the Floss* or *A Portrait of a Lady* or *Sons and Lovers*. Because events are referred to no ultimate context of explanation, there is no appeal in the text to any fixed set of coordinates that can locate a changeless moral or spiritual decorum. For this reason novels that participate in the providential aesthetic offer readers securities and reassurances that those with a wholly secular aesthetic do not. As long as readers feel assured that a novel stands within the older tradition, they can count on a resolution consistent with a providential worldview. "I know," says the poor messenger in Dickens's Christmas story *The Chimes*, "that our inheritance is held in store for us by Time."[38] He knows that time is the medium of restitution and redress, that time will reveal the significance of events and circumstances which presently seem arbitrary and unjust. For characters and readers the consolation of such knowledge is both present and prospective: what happens will represent providence—or at least will represent no violation

---

[37]Ibid., pp. 512—20.
[38]*Christmas Books* (London: Oxford Univ. Press, 1954), p. 151.

of the attributes of the providential intention as they appeared revealed to nineteenth-century readers. It will all turn out cosmically right.

Most English novels before George Eliot's turn out all right in this sense. Even novelists like Austen and Trollope, who do not deal explicitly or deeply with a providential intention in their fiction, do generally make things come round in ways that do no violence to the providential tradition they almost tacitly support.[39] Even when Thackeray presented his readers with the half-jeering parody of poetic justice at the end of *Vanity Fair*, he left "providential" readers with a book they could admire for its compassion for human weakness and for its salutary *contemptus mundi*. Even when one such reader, Charlotte Brontë, wrote her dark ending to *Villette*—almost a sneer at the sensibility that looks for happy endings—she left a work in which the temporal coordinates as Lucy Snowe reads them measure a dark map of divine purpose. If we compare even such deviants as these not just with later English fiction but with certain foreign contemporaries, the satire of *Vanity Fair* with the spiritual radicalism of *The Red and the Black* or the bitter resignation of *Villette* with the nihilism of *Madame Bovary*, we can glimpse how deeply the English novel was invested with providential sanctions. The English Victorian reader could count on not being openly alarmed, and this helps to explain a certain "upholstered" quality in most English nineteenth-century fiction absent from many American and Continental counterparts.[40] Victorian readers, whatever

[39]In reference to Austen's fiction, Alistair Duckworth observes: "By setting her novels in the context of what might be termed 'providential' fiction we may qualify the subversive readings of her moral vision. Then, by briefly looking ahead to the 'contingent' fiction of the nineteenth century, we may suggest ways in which her novels do indeed anticipate later nineteenth century novelistic preoccupations" (*The Improvement of the Estate: A Study of Jane Austen's Novels* [Baltimore: Johns Hopkins Univ. Press, 1971], p. 10). He goes on, however, to minimize the providential elements in later nineteenth-century fiction.

[40]Henry James in "The Art of Fiction" notices this "moral timidity of the usual English novelist" and attributes it to the fact that the English novel is "addressed in a large degree to young people" (*A Victorian Art of Fiction*, p. 304).

personal religious convictions they may have held, could, if they liked, look over God's shoulder into the narrative.

This position is less privileged than it at first appears. The providential world contains its own dangers and risks. Although a reader or character might safely assume that the providential intention would ultimately be fulfilled in the text, nothing could be assumed about individual destiny or the precise relation of individual will to divine order. The element of risk is not cosmological but epistemological, not a matter of ontology but of interpretation. The right action is often far from obvious. Agnes Wickfield may believe that simple love and truth will win, but David Copperfield has good reason to fear that she will achieve filial martyrdom in a marriage to his archenemy because that would not violate known providential precedents. And we as readers may share his distrust. Uriah Heep might get her. After all, Little Nell dies "providentially."

Such suspense arises from the traditional obliquity with which divine intention reveals itself. The obliquity is of course ancient, common to classical tragedy and to the Old Testament. The Book of Job, perhaps the single most significant biblical exposition of the problem, points repeatedly to the difficulty or perhaps impossibility of arriving at a humanly coherent understanding of God's ways. The just and unjust appear to suffer indiscriminately and not in any comprehensible proportion of their degree of righteousness: "He destroyeth the perfect and the wicked" (9:22). In fact, Job seems to argue that God is so much above and beyond human apprehension that any attempt to understand his ways must be pathetically hubristic and doomed to failure—a conviction that would obviate the whole enterprise of interpreting providence and its signs. But if this is the message of the Book of Job, it did not prevent later, especially Christian, apologists from various attempts to establish principles or rules for such interpretation. The most influential of these, Augustine, alludes in *The City of God* to "advantages and disadvantages which often afflict the good and evil alike" and tries to arrive at some conclusions as to "why both good and evil persons are equally afflicted" (I, viii–ix). Augustine's solution is dryly summarized by Henry A.

Kelly: "He draws the conclusion that when manifestly wicked persons suffer great afflictions, they are being punished by God; but when virtuous men suffer similarly, they are being benefited by God." Kelly goes on to observe that the application of such " 'rules' for interpreting the operation of divine providence . . . to actual events must remain largely a matter of conjecture and personal opinion."[41] In other words, the rules encourage the activity of interpretation within the doctrinal framework but they do not solve specific cases. These must be judged on their individual merits.

The realistic novel is the realm of the specific case, and each case contains its own complexities. Jane Eyre, for example, is always being interpreted by the people around her. To Mrs. Reed and Mr. Brocklehurst she is an unredeemed little sinner slated for hell. Rochester, on the other hand, finds her altogether too firm in her adherence to what she believes to be right. St. John Rivers sees her rejection of his proposal of marriage as a dangerous regression into the pride of the flesh. As Jerome Beaty exactly characterizes the necessary act of interpretation:

> Jane Eyre must herself read the providential signs and read them aright, must stand on her principles, use her reason, hearken to her conscience. Since her fate is uncertain, the reader, to participate experientially in her story (and to understand his or her own life in a providentially contingent cosmos), must be kept in the dark just as Jane is. . . .
>
> The individual is always in the position of having to interpret experience and patterns of experience. Leadings and warnings must be both perceived and interpreted and one's own wishes and will must be dissociated from God's will.[42]

---

[41] Henry A. Kelly, *Divine Providence in the England of Shakespeare's Histories* (Cambridge: Harvard Univ. Press, 1970), pp. 3–4.

[42] Jerome Beaty, "*Jane Eyre* and Genre," *Genre*, 10 (1971), 625, 644.

This interpreting, then, is a tricky game and the stakes can be very high. If Jane had decided to stay with Rochester unmarried her spiritual prognosis would not have been good. And what would have become of her if she had confused Rivers's fanatic proposal with a providential leading? What would have happened to Eugene Wrayburn in *Our Mutual Friend* if Lizzie Hexam had done the "right thing" by her brother Charlie and married Bradley Headstone? In *Adam Bede* if Dinah Morris had decided that divine will dictated her perpetual separation from the protagonist?

Although such characters have no doubt that a providential intention exists, they can rarely be certain what it dictates for them at any particular moment. It may not be possible to thwart God's will, but it is possible to destroy oneself and bring misery to others by denying or misinterpreting it at any crisis. This possibility places tremendous importance on seeing things clearly, as free as possible from the distortions of solipsistic inclination, to do what so many of the great Victorians saw as the aim of education and intellect: to be true to one's experience, to see things as in themselves they really are.[43]

Characters in a providential fiction, and readers reading one, must add to this a faithful adherence to the past, to the act of memory.[44] The unfolding of events in linear time, in history, is what reveals the providential, and hence saving, pattern. It is what leads characters to the decorum, the true order of things, not just in the doctrinal abstract but as that order touches them in their necessarily particular circumstances. Successful characters in providential fiction are those who develop a providential habit of mind: one that seeks patterns in apparently random circumstances and concatenations of events, that judges by consequences, that above all remains alert to the

---

[43]See especially David DeLaura, *Hebrew and Hellene in Victorian England: Newman, Arnold, and Pater* (Austin: Univ. of Texas Press, 1969), pp. 66–80.

[44]For a significant distinction between the characters' memory of events and the narrator's (and hence the reader's) see Ermarth, "Realism, Perspective, and the Novel," p. 518; also chapters 2 and 3 of her book *Realism and Consensus in the English Novel* (Princeton: Princeton Univ. Press, 1983).

possibilities of interpretation. Such characters make good readers. They read, as I have said, the text of their experiences. And their act of reading often comes remarkably close to the reader's act of reading. Between a good protagonist in a providential fiction and a good reader of providential fiction an intimate bond is established. They are both at work on the same text.

Except, of course, that the reader has access to a larger, elaborated text, one which may contain events and experiences unknown to characters at the moments of decision and action but which affects and comments on the limited text of a character's individual experience. And the reader's text usually contains a narrative commentary on the characters' actions, either in the third person or in the first person from a perspective of achieved security. This additional commentary, very often an interpretation of the characters' interpretations of events, provides the resonance that gives providential fiction much of its realistic power and credibility. The mature Pip interprets with affectionate, undetached irony the delusions of the young Pip. White-haired Lucy Snowe sets up again and again her own hopelessly calculating youth. The narrator of *The Mill on the Floss*, "in love with moistness," somewhat ostentatiously pities poor Maggie Tulliver.[45] Through the medium of such commentary the reader gains on the interpretations of the characters, distances them, moves closer to the center of meaning, the decorum, of the fictional world.

Finally, this decorum, the true order of things, is ultimately in the control of the author of the providential novel, and narrators have access to it to the degree that they approach the level of authorial control. Narrators are not authors, though in Victorian fiction the distinction is often highly involved and problematic. Critical discussion of such relationships has now evolved into a specialization of its own. My point here is that knowledge of the decorum, of the premises of the providential aesthetic, involves interpretation of the providential intention

[45]*The Mill on the Floss*, ed. Gordon S. Haight (Boston: Houghton Mifflin, 1961), p. 8; ch. 1.

as it operates in any fictional world, and that accurate interpretation represents power in that world. A narrator may be
given tremendous authority—like the third-person narrator of
Bleak House or like the narrator of *Middlemarch*—and yet lack
crucial awareness on a crucial point. In English providential
fiction the narrator engages on a grand scale in a common
action with characters and readers, and this action is the interpretation of events. Only the imagined author may be said to
know what it all means, and this putative knowledge of the
whole distances the author at any given moment of the reading.
The author of the fiction, despite any intimacy of narrative
tone and manner, necessarily maintains an effective opacity,
an obliquity that has its grand precedent and credential in the
"ways of Providence." "The business of art," Dickens observed,
"is only to *suggest*, until the fulfillment comes. These are the
ways of Providence, of which all art is but a little imitation."[46]
The observation contains a humility characteristically under-
cut, one that does nothing to diminish the prestige of his
profession. The author disposes; everybody else interprets.

The Providential
Tradition in the
English Novel

Before I begin my own interpretive chapters on Charlotte
Brontë, Charles Dickens, and George Eliot, it seems appropriate to offer a brief overview of the providential tradition as
developed in representative English novels. Most of these
deserve—and in a few cases have received—more detailed
providential readings than I give them. My aim here is to

[46]*The Letters of Charles Dickens,* ed. Walter Dexter (London: Nonesuch
Press, 1938), III, 124 ff., quoted in Harland S. Nelson, "Dickens' Plots:
The Ways of Providence or the Influence of Collins?" *Victorian Newsletter,*
No. 19 (1961), 12.

indicate some literary-historical perimeters for my three major authors and to suggest the coherence of the tradition they enlarged.

We have already seen that a clear understanding of the providential worldview as it works in the realistic novel requires adjustment of certain accepted critical categories and distinctions. I have argued that the dogmatic content of a novel—its appeal to a providential worldview—may be carried by the realistic elements of the plot: particularity of circumstances and events, psychological credibility of character. This assumption, that God works through the probable and the commonplace, that he is in fact a realist, bears directly on the celebrated but tricky distinction between *romance* and *novel*. Clara Reeve's classical (1785) definition of the romance as "an heroic fable, which treats of fabulous persons and things" has remained useful because on the whole it deals primarily in historical and aesthetic terms and does not intrude significantly into metaphysics or theology.[47] But when we begin to allocate religious, or dogmatic, subject matter to the romance as "that form of fiction best able to contain the activities and characters of a God-ordered world"[48] and claim for the novel some range of empirical reality uninformed by religious or other dogmatic significance, then we have made a critical gesture of debilitating provinciality. We have assigned one view of reality (that it is metaphysically vacant, spiritually neutral) to the novel. But this view of reality is alien to most novelists of the periods for which the distinction is supposed to function. The "God-ordered world" was the common assumption of the romance writer *and* the novelist: only their techniques of representation can be consistently distinguished. It may be correct to say, as Walter Reed does in an important recent history of the novel, that "in romance, the reader's allegiance is finally to some

[47]Clara Reeve, *The Progress of Romance through Times, Countries, and Manners* (1785; reprint New York: Garland, 1970), p. 11. Kenneth Graham alludes to nineteenth-century use of this definition in *English Criticism of the Novel, 1865–1900*, p. 61.
[48]New " 'The Grease of God,' " p. 238.

deeper power, higher ideal, or stronger fulfillment of desire. In the novel, his allegiance is divided, and his perception is directed along a horizontal rather than a vertical axis."[49] But I would add that such division of allegiance would be much more acutely felt in an age like the present when the "horizontal axis" is widely perceived to be exclusively secular than in those periods in which it would often be nothing less than the linear medium of providential intention. Definitions of literary form that arise from assumptions about the nature of what is represented rather than the techniques of representation itself are particularly vulnerable to changes in cultural climate.

Such problems arise wherever we attempt to start our own personal history of the novel. I, like many others, would start mine with *Don Quixote*—largely because of its demonstrated influence on almost all the English writers mentioned in this study. Is *Don Quixote* a romance? Not by most definitions. And yet it contains very strong elements of romance, including the precisely romantic aspirations of the protagonist. No doubt empirical reality dominates in this progenitive novel, but the metaphysical status of that reality has proved very difficult to determine. Don Quixote's commitment to the belief that evil enchanters continually seek to humiliate him by reducing his achievements from the romantic to the mundane is, to "empirical" onlookers, a sign of his madness. The madness, however, is allied to the highest aspirations of the culture, expecially its religious or providential aspirations, which the realists—the priest, the barber, the bachelor, the Duke and Duchess—profess to uphold.

If everything is enchanted then everything means something beyond its empirical weight and measure. Everything is symbolic or allegorical. Everything needs to be interpreted. And Don Quixote does interpret everything, madly perhaps but also with a view to incorporating his romantic ideas with the generally held providential views of the others. Knights are "God's ministers on earth, and the arms by which his justice is executed

---

[49]Reed, *An Exemplary History of the Novel*, p. 42.

here." Sancho believes that his master would make an excellent preacher. Don Quixote tries to teach others to believe in the perfection of Dulcinea without seeing her, and he loves her without hope of reward. "That's the kind of love," says Sancho, "I've heard them preach about. They say we ought to love our Lord for Himself alone, without being moved to it by hope of glory or fear of punishment." Like Christianity, knight-errantry has its scriptures, relics, dogma—and these cannot easily be separated from the scriptures, relics, and dogma of Christianity. Don Quixote occasionally appeals to biblical authority, as regarding the existence of giants for example. He explicitly aligns the parallel allegories of knight-errantry and Christianity: "It is for us to slay pride by slaying giants; to slay envy by our generosity and nobility; anger by calmness of mind," and so on through the deadly sins. In a brilliant defense of Dulcinea's reality against the slyly skeptical questioning of the Duchess, Don Quixote dismisses as effectively irrelevant the kinds of verification that might be accorded to empirical reality: "God knows whether Dulcinea exists on earth or no, or whether she is fantastic or not fantastic. These are not matters whose verification can be carried out to the full. I neither engendered nor bore my lady, though I contemplate her in her ideal form."[50] If we give up Dulcinea as a reality, his discourse implies, then we endanger the reality of the values she embodies—beauty, dignity, love, modesty, courtesy. And not only those values but the habit of mind that believes without seeing, that loves without hope of reward—the habit of mind upon which religious faith depends. If mundane reality seems to contradict these higher, more primary values then we must conclude that mundane reality is enchanted.

It would be difficult to prove that *Don Quixote* contains a thoroughgoing providential aesthetic in the sense that much high Victorian fiction contains it. We would have to accommodate certain strong parodic elements, such as the cave of Montesinos or Sancho's vicarious suffering for the release of

---

[50]Cervantes, *The Adventures of Don Quixote,* trans. J. M. Cohen (Baltimore: Penguin, 1967), pp. 98, 140, 273, 479, 680.

Dulcinea. All I want to show is that the preoccupations and tensions of providential fiction may be found here in some sophistication: " 'You are very philosophical, Sancho,' replied Don Quixote, 'and you talk most wisely. I do not know how you have learnt to. All I can tell you is that there is no such thing in the world as Fortune, and that events here, whether good or ill, do not fall out by chance but by a particular providence of Heaven, from which comes the saying that every man is the architect of his own destiny. I have been so of mine, but have failed in the necessary prudence.' "[51] Don Quixote's logic may strike us as perplexing, but he has made a distinction central to the providential fiction that follows: human freedom exists within a providential framework as it cannot in a universe of fate or fortune. Such freedom makes individuals the architects of their own destiny and places the greatest importance on the interpreting of their particular contexts.

Robinson Crusoe provides the most important early example in English fiction of a protagonist exercising first his freedom and then his powers of interpretation within a providential cosmos, and Defoe's extensive and explicit providentialism has received a good deal of scholarly attention.[52] Briefly summarized, the novel shows a man who follows his own willful inclination against the clear leadings of a providence that repeatedly gives him a "plain and visible token" of its intention. The young Crusoe makes his initial decisions without asking the blessing either of his heavenly or of his temporal father. His obsession with seafaring may, in a providential reading, signify the delusion of radical freedom, the attempt to escape from divine order which Bunyan had treated allegorically in *The Pilgrim's Progress* and *The Life and Death of Mr. Badman* and to which

[51] Ibid., p. 896.

[52] See especially Starr, *Defoe and Spiritual Autobiography;* Hunter, *The Reluctant Pilgrim;* Rodney M. Barrie, *Daniel Defoe and the Supernatural* (Athens: Univ. of Georgia Press, 1968); Viner, *The Role of Providence in the Social Order,* especially pp. 46–47. Viner's account deals with eighteenth-century providentialism generally, as does Norman Goldhawk in "William Paley," *Providence,* ed. Wiles, pp. 51–57.

Marlowe and Milton had given psychological depth in *Dr. Faustus* and *Paradise Lost*. Not surprisingly, Crusoe finds not freedom but slavery, first to a Turkish (non-Christian) pirate and, when that lesson fails to take, to the vicissitudes of his own nature and the natural circumstances of his island. These phenomena as described in all their minute particularity constitute the empirical realism of the text. It may be that they are what make this a novel. But what Crusoe learns at great length and with a good deal of reiteration is that these particularities are God's particularities—lumber, food, tools, seeds, fellow creatures—and that there is no such thing as accident, chance, or escape from the providential order. In the mature Crusoe's ultimate interpretation all events, all circumstances, represent a "chain of wonders" proving that "the Eyes of an infinite Power could search into the remotest Corner of the World."[53] The tension or conflict so often perceived in *Robinson Crusoe* is not essentially profane. It is, as its Preface asserts, essentially providential, though that makes it none the less concrete.

Like Crusoe, Samuel Richardson's Pamela is both tried and rewarded in a context of concrete, material circumstances. *Pamela; or, Virtue Rewarded* offers an unambiguous example of what I have called a straightforward providential fiction— that is, one in which the providential intention and poetic justice are united. Pamela knows that "the unparallel'd Wickedness, and Strategems, and Devices of those who call themselves Gentlemen, and pervert the Design of Providence" may be permitted a temporary conquest, one that involves her own temporal "ruin." But she also knows that once she has done her best to secure her virtue she must, as she puts it, "leave the issue to Providence." Her knowledge of the decorum, the true order of things, allows her to see herself and her enemies in the context of a divine intention, and the consequences of her actions validate her interpretation. She receives her reward

[53]Daniel Defoe, *Robinson Crusoe,* ed. Michael Shinagel (New York: Norton, 1975), pp. 14, 8, 212.

by seeing her master exercise the "Godlike Power of doing Good!" The "once naughty Assailer of her Innocence, by a blessed turn of Providence, is become the kind, the generous Protector and Rewarder of it." This fortunate gentleman, by his decision to marry Pamela, achieves his proper place in the decorum as a protector and provider, and thus as a legitimate temporal agent of the providential government. Eventually he delegates authority by giving Pamela a kind of charity account to draw on in her own good works, and she has no moral difficulty in rewarding the virtue of others with elegantly presented gifts of hard cash. Such beneficence is consistent with the decorum of her world. If virtue can be rewarded by social elevation, then there may be virtue in the five guineas Pamela bestows (along with her praise or forgiveness) on each of her servants. What perhaps distinguishes *Robinson Crusoe* and *Pamela* from the important fiction that follows is the lack of obscurity or subtlety in the extended resolutions of both novels. Here the providential intention is right out front, what Pamela describes as "the blessed Providence which has so visibly conducted me thro' the dangerous paths I have trod."[54]

In partial contrast, *Clarissa* represents a substantial complication and enrichment of the providential aesthetic, especially in the obliquity with which the providential intention is presented and in the consequent ambiguity of its action in temporal sequence and particularity of circumstance. Although, as we have seen, Richardson argued that "poetical justice" was done in this novel, he had to appeal to a frame of reference essentially beyond the temporality of the fictional structure. Since this appeal becomes a convention in later fiction, especially in Victorian providential novels where the death of virtuous heroines, good men, children, and other innocents requires justification or explanation, *Clarissa* serves as an important early example of the separation of temporal reward

[54]Samuel Richardson, *Pamela; or, Virtue Rewarded*, ed. T. C. Duncan and Ben D. Kimpel (Boston: Houghton Mifflin, 1971), pp. 95, 136, 264, 290, 383–85, 234.

from spiritual merit and thus of a more ambiguous, even ambivalent handling of empirical reality.

Like Pamela, once Clarissa has done everything she can to secure her honor, she is driven to "leave to Providence . . . the direction of my future steps." But Clarissa does not possess Pamela's relatively single-minded reliance on a providential design for her ultimate well-being. Letter for letter she mentions providence far less than Pamela does. This may in part be a function of her higher education and social class, but it also represents an acknowledgment of her own more ambiguous role in shaping circumstances. This initiative in turn has been forced upon her by the failure of her immediate social world to reflect a providential decorum. Crusoe's father opposed his errant seafaring; Pamela's father exemplifies virtuous poverty; but Clarissa's father, "who had a right to all my reverence," behaves like a grotesque parody of a wrathful Jehovah (whose authority he apparently believes himself to possess). When she slips into Lovelace's control, Clarissa finds herself in the presence of a masculine egoism aroused by different motives but cosmically analogous to her father's. Lovelace also wants to play God. He believes that he has caused the Harlowe family to do his work against their own will and knowledge; he would have his prospective wife "forgo even her *superior duties* for me"; he assumes the right to *try* Clarissa. Although his pathology is complicated by his repeated association of himself with Satan and his own peculiar providentialism ("I never was such a fool as to disbelieve a Providence"),[55] Lovelace betrays the decorum, the true order of things, in which he would protect and honor the innocent. Like Clarissa's father he betrays his proper identity in the providential design by attempting to arrogate the power of providence.

Before her rape Clarissa frantically attempts to interpret the circumstances and characters that surround her, to discover some escape from her baffling serial imprisonments. After her

---

[55]Samuel Richardson, *Clarissa; or, The History of a Young Lady* (London: Dent Everyman, 1967), III, 265; I, 390; II, 416; IV, 438.

rape, after her sanity returns, *she* becomes the enigma and others attempt to interpret *her*. The creature desperate for a knowledge that will save her becomes the object of that knowledge, the being saved. She achieves this by a single continuous gesture of dismissal and farewell. She transcends her circumstances and their temporal contexts. In effect she leaves the concrete, empirical world, the world of her novel—as Little Nell and Lucy Snowe, in different ways, will do later. Clarissa's deceptive letter to Lovelace announcing her departure for her "Father's House" represents this dismissal eloquently in its assertion that "I cannot spare one moment for any other business"[56] and in its significant resort to allegory, a formal expression quite removed from the realistic practical urgency of her earlier correspondence.

Clarissa escapes, but the other characters, still bound by time and consequence, do not. Nor do we as readers. However we may admire her departure and its flourish, we—as Richardson reminds us in his Postscript—remain behind. Clarissa's salvation presents an appeal to a world beyond the world of the text, but it is nevertheless a palpable event *within* the text. It shows that the providential aesthetic in fiction can accommodate an appeal to a reality, an "aftertext," that realism does not explicitly represent. No doubt this appeal, taken with the heroine's apparent transcendence of her temporal circumstances, somewhat modifies the metaphysical status of the realities described. After the rape concrete particularities seem less significant. But the aesthetic itself remains firmly bound to the temporal conventions, in this case the conventions of an epistolary novel. Clarissa learns that "GOD ALMIGHTY WOULD NOT LET ME DEPEND FOR COMFORT UPON ANY BUT HIMSELF." That knowledge, no doubt, represents the providential intention for Clarissa—and *we* learn of it in a letter from Mr. Belford to Robert Lovelace, concretely placed and dated Soho, Ten o'clock, Sept. 7.[57]

[56]Ibid., IV, 157.
[57]Ibid., IV, 338.

In a major essay on this subject, Aubrey Williams demonstrates Fielding's personal allegiance to the providential tradition and his integration of that tradition in his work.[58] Tom Jones, to take his most celebrated protagonist, believes firmly in providential intervention and design and repeatedly assures the beneficiaries of his noble deeds (such as the Man of the Hill and Mrs. Waters) that he is merely heaven's instrument. He pays attention when Partridge prophesies his prospective reunion with Sophia as patently within the providential plan, and he ultimately subscribes to the doctrine that "time will show all matters in their true and natural colors." In addition the narrative commentary supports these interpretations of Jones, Partridge, and the other providentialists in the text. The coincidences fit the convention of providential interposition by investing the naturalistic juxtapositions with supernatural significance. In fact, the narrator excuses his depiction of certain motives and events that might strike the fastidious as "unnatural" by asserting that "I am not writing a system, but a history," and that in a history "these incidents contribute only to confirm the great, useful, and uncommon doctrine which it is the purpose of this whole work to inculcate"—that good character and prosperity are the reward of virtue.[59] Or, as Williams puts it, "the design of *Tom Jones,* with all of its quite remarkable course of chance encounters and fortuitous mishaps, its long list of extraordinary accidents and coincidences and revelations, is finally artfully contrived to make us see a fictive world that offers a close analogy to that 'real' world wherein, in Archbishop Tillotson's words, 'There are many things, indeed, which to us seem chance and accident; but in respect to God, they are providence and design.' "[60]

The incorporation of such design into Fielding's novels does not conflict with the comic elements of the fiction. The action

[58] Aubrey Williams, "Interpositions of Providence and the Design of Fielding's Novels," *South Atlantic Quarterly,* 70 (1971), 265–86.

[59] Fielding, *The History of Tom Jones* (New York: Random House, 1950), pp. 375–76, 419, 566, 804, 444, 568–69.

[60] Williams, "Interpositions of Providence," p. 281.

of providence is serious, of course, and a "great doctrine." But that does not make it grim. The comic tradition in English literature at least from Chaucer on has been a providential tradition. Reality can be comic primarily because reality is providential.[61] Providence permits the comedy *in* reality as fate or chance would not. Providential fiction becomes tragic—as it does in *Clarissa* or *Villette* or at points in Dickens—chiefly when human volition has failed to achieve the requisite harmony with the decorum, when villain or victim has been separated from it beyond recall. Otherwise and generally the bias of the providential novel is comic. It sustains human expectation and provides a context for the efficacy of human will.

Like the fictional structures of Defoe, Richardson, Fielding (and such others as Goldsmith, Sterne, and Trollope), Jane Austen's fictions rest on an assumption of fundamental cosmic order and design that contains a perceptible moral, perhaps even spiritual decorum.[62] But unlike most providential novels, Jane Austen's rarely make explicit appeal to the divine design as the ultimate source of order. In *Emma*, as Robert Polhemus has observed, the "only serious direct reference to Christian Providence" appears in a fleeting parenthesis as the heroine speculates on the distracting possibility of a union between Mr. Knightly and Harriet Smith: "Was it new for any thing in this world to be unequal, inconsistent, incongruous—or for chance and circumstance (as second causes) to direct the human fate?"[63] As second causes? It almost seems as if the First Cause might be made conspicuous in Austen's works by its absence.

---

[61]Robert M. Polhemus observes that "the basic plot of comic form, I have surmised, grew out of the process and hope of regeneration" (*Comic Faith: The Great Tradition from Austen to Joyce* [Chicago: Univ. of Chicago Press, 1980], p. 17). Polhemus, however, presents a somewhat narrow or selective version of the Christian providential tradition from which he shows a comic tradition asserting freedom and independence.

[62]See Duckworth, *The Improvement of the Estate*, pp. 8, 10.

[63]Polhemus, *Comic Faith*, pp. 31–32; Jane Austen, *Emma* (Boston: Houghton Mifflin, 1957), p. 325.

But absent it seems to be, or at least not visibly present, and Austen's comic fiction, like Trollope's, is broadly secular. Nevertheless, the providential tradition does lend a peculiar force, a moral force, to the action of her novels just as it does to Trollope's. It not only provides the unexamined underpinning (first cause) of her social universe but comments implicitly on the action there. In *Emma*, for example, the heroine's solipsism has often been noticed. What has been often overlooked is that the solipsism is a corollary of Emma's egocentric providentialism, a providential habit of mind by which she sees herself as the provider. In directing Harriet's destiny (writing Harriet's novel) she is repeatedly enchanted by the way events seem to conform to her own "prearrangement," that what she desires "should so immediately shape itself into the proper form." She has to learn the "unpardonable arrogance" of proposing "to arrange everybody's destiny,"[64] an arrogance that Austen's readers would quickly have seen as attempting to usurp the prerogatives of providence and thus as a spiritual as well as a social disorder. The impulse to play providence attacks several of Austen's major characters and is by her time a *type* of egoism in English literature. Emma learns in the end, not that things don't work out (they do), but that they work out mysteriously.[65] When, toward the end of the novel, Emma perceives the inexplicable inequity between the position of Jane Fairfax and that of Mrs. Churchill, she sits "musing on the difference of woman's destiny."[66] Her fresh capacity to be struck by such a disparity signals the acquisition of a saving awareness of her own limitations and the comparable vastness of life's mystery. And our perception of the importance of her

[64]*Emma*, pp. 57, 261, 324.

[65]Though the threat that things may not work out is often pressing. Paul Zeitlow points out that "the disparity between the phenomenal good luck of the characters of *Persuasion*—they seem almost to be protected by the gods—and what their destinies would be if events took their normal course, seems to emphasize the dark possibilities of human life—to emphasize them without actually bringing them about" ("Luck and Fortuitous Circumstance in *Persuasion*," *ELH*, 32 [1965], 195).

[66]*Emma*, p. 301.

discovery can be enriched by seeing it against the latent, tacit imperatives of the providential tradition.

The hubristic impulse to arrogate the prerogatives of providence is more fully explored in Mary Shelley's *Frankenstein*. Here, however, the circumstantial drama of a protagonist reading and misreading the text of experience has been moved still further inside, into the chief character's inner world. Or, as George Levine admirably formulates it, "the transposition of the creator from God to man, the secularization of the means of creation from miracle into science, entail a transposition of the standard of moral judgment from the external world which ought to be reflecting a divine order, to the mind which is somehow forced to establish its own terms."[67] This transposition of the dramatic field from the world of external events that require interpretation to an inner world of motives that equally seem to demand interpretation perhaps excludes *Frankenstein* from the mainstream of the providential tradition, but (as with *Emma*) the existence of that tradition is what gives the story its primary *éclat*. What Mary Shelley in her 1831 Introduction called the "frightful . . . effect of any human endeavor to mock the stupendous mechanism of the Creator of the world" or what Frankenstein sees as his endeavor to "unfold to the world the deepest mysteries of creation"[68] depends for its excitement upon the sense of a fundamental usurpation, the violation of a primeval contract. Frankenstein violates the deeply rooted cultural premise that there can be but one creator because there can be but one providence.

In fact, the novel supports this premise. The horror of the book derives not from Frankenstein's success in bestowing life but from his failure to sustain it. He can create but he cannot

---

[67]George Levine, *The Realistic Imagination* (Chicago: Univ. of Chicago Press, 1981), p. 27. See also Judith Wilt, "Frankenstein as Mystery Play," in *The Endurance of Frankenstein*, ed. George Levine and U. C. Knoepflmacher (Berkeley and Los Angeles: Univ. of California Press, 1979), pp. 31–48.

[68]Mary Shelley, *Frankenstein; or, The Modern Prometheus* (New York: Airmont Books, 1963), pp. 17, 51.

nourish. Physically and emotionally his monster starves. It seems almost as if Mary Shelley, out of her sporting agreement with Byron and her husband each to write a ghost story (*they* failed), devised a telling parable of masculine egoism, grotesque immediate success, and ultimate failure. The monster would prove filial: all he needs is a parent. But his creator lacks the single qualifying emotion, love for his offspring. He cannot do what parents must do: provide, act within the ordained limitations the hieratic role of the providential surrogate. And in his immediate, intuitive, and persistent revulsion from his creature we sense the ghastly parabolic suggestion of cosmic bereavement, a creation destitute of provision.

The parent who plays providence is a familiar type in English drama and fiction from Shakespeare and Richardson through the nineteenth century. Frankenstein's alienation of his monster is a negative of a more familiar domestic image, that of a parent—usually a father—who aims at being all in all to his child. Meredith's Sir Austin Feverel may be the most fully explored example in Victorian fiction of a parent who tries to arrogate providential prerogatives, and he is the creation of a novelist who does not himself subscribe to the providential tradition. Meredith nevertheless exploits that tradition, as Mary Shelley did, to lend force to his representation: Sir Austin "wished to be Providence to his son." Knowing Richard's secrets "allowed him to act, and in a measure to feel, like Providence." He imagines that he knows Richard so well that all his movements are "anticipated . . . and provided for." He not only expects his son to obey but "would have him guiltless of the impulse to gainsay my wishes." Although Sir Austin often prays to his God, he wants to *be* his son's God. He wants to be worshipped by Richard and he wants everyone else to worship Richard: "he had set up an Idol in his house—an Idol of Flesh!"[69]

[69]George Meredith, *The Ordeal of Richard Feverel,* ed. C. L. Cline (Boston: Houghton Mifflin, 1971), pp. 51, 53, 119, 120, 100.

Meredith saw that this classic domestic rigmarole could both parody and be parodied by the Christian mythos of divine paternity and that the parodic elements could lend a kind of demonic force to the psychological drama of masculine egoism. In *The Egoist* he condensed the whole complex into the single character of Sir Willoughby Patterne, who fathers the "flying infant" in himself: "The Egoist is the Son of Himself. He is likewise the Father. And the son loves the father, the father the son; they reciprocate affection through the closest of ties."[70] In *The Egoist* and *The Ordeal of Richard Feveral* the felicity of the exercise comes from the delusive security of apparent self-sufficiency. One of Sir Austin's aphorisms holds that "there is for the mind but one grasp of Happiness: from that uppermost pinnacle of wisdom, whence we see that this world is well-designed." He believes himself to be "the God of the machine," the god of his world, one that can comprehend and control its workings, immune to the vicissitudes common to the lesser beings who remain subject to the comparatively haphazard arrangements of the natural dispensation. And although we know that for Meredith this dispensation was not the more orthodox providentialism of most of his predecessors, the loathing of usurping human systems that Lady Blandish expresses for all of us in the last paragraphs of the book ("he wished to take Providence out of God's hands") conforms to the traditional attack on the arrogation of divine preroga-tives.[71] The attack, in other words, belongs to the convention though in the general dogmatic of this novel "nature" rather than God has been betrayed.

This glance at Meredith's exploitation of the providential tradition brings us well into the historical plane of the chapters that follow. These trace the apogee of the providential aesthetic in English fiction, and I believe that the account is sufficiently

[70]George Meredith, *The Egoist: A Comedy in Narrative,* ed. Lionel Stevenson (Boston: Houghton Mifflin, 1958), p. 321.
[71]Meredith, *The Ordeal of Richard Feverel,* pp. 82, 381, 430.

concluded with an examination of George Eliot's last novels. But before beginning these fuller analyses I want briefly to explain why Hardy's work does not form a part of this study, especially since his well-known obsession with what might be called cosmic disjunctiveness seems to qualify him so naturally for inclusion.

For many readers Hardy's cosmically alienated protagonist has come to seem *the* Victorian protagonist. It is a credit to his immense influence that this should be so, and in part he benefits from the widely felt temptation to modernize the Victorians. J. Hillis Miller, for example, employs Kierkegaard in what aims at being a general description of the nineteenth-century type:

> In eighteenth-century England the stability of the social order, sustained by divine Providence, is a guarantee of the stability of selfhood. For more writers at least God is still immanent in society. But in nineteenth-century literature the protagonist is usually in the condition of the central character of Kierkegaard's *Repetition.* "My life," says Kierkegaard's hero, "has been brought to an *impasse.* I loathe existence. . . . One sticks one's finger into the soil to tell by the smell in what land one is: I stick my finger into existence—it smells of nothing. Where am I? Who am I? How came I here? What is this thing called the world? What does this word mean? Who is it that has lured me into the world? Why was I not consulted, why not made acquainted with its manners and customs . . .? How did I obtain an interest in this big enterprise they call reality? Why should I have an interest in it? Is it not a voluntary concern? And if I am compelled to take part in it, where is the director? I should like to make a remark to him. Is there no director? Whither shall I turn with my complaint?"[72]

[72]J. Hillis Miller, *The Disappearance of God: Five Nineteenth Century Writers* (Cambridge: Harvard University Press, Belknap Press, 1963), p. 9.

The image of alienation moves us. To us it is familiar. But the protoexistential protagonist complaining here is not the one "usually" found in nineteenth-century English literature, especially not in fiction. Neither Emily nor Charlotte Brontë's characters find *reality* alien in this sense though they often choose among realities. Dickens's characters stick their fingers into existence all right, but they don't usually complain that it smells of nothing. Even George Eliot's principals tend to find ways out of the "impasse" to which they are regularly brought and find life profoundly relevant though not of course in conversation with a divine "director."[73]

In English fiction this Kierkegaardian experience, experience of the absurd, really becomes typical and dominant only in Hardy's novels. His characters stick their rough, or dainty, or sensitive fingers into existence, and the experiment tells them nothing definite. Yeobright, Henchard, Tess, Jude, and their offspring, lovers, and spouses feel the weightlessness of life in a universe essentially bereft of meaning because it has been abandoned by the source of meaning. Exiled by their "modernism" from a coherent apprehension of events and circumstances, outraged by a suffering that has become nonconsequential, they desperately posit a malicious or an indifferent or a vacuous first cause. For a time they tend to search eagerly for clear signs, divine leadings, the footsteps of justice. They passionately long for a providential vision. Like

[73]In his highly suggestive lectures *The Form of Victorian Fiction*, Miller makes similar claims specifically for the nineteenth-century novel, that in it "each person comes into existence as a self only in relation to others" (unsustained, that is, by a relation to God) or that "Victorian fiction may be said to have as its fundamental theme an exploration of the various ways in which a man may seek to make a god of another person in a world without God, or at any rate in a world where the traditional ways in which the self may be related to God no longer seem open" (Notre Dame, Ind.: Univ. of Notre Dame Press, 1968, pp. 45, 96). I am not inclined to take potshots at so stimulating and influential a critic, one to whom I feel intellectually indebted; but in this case his generalizations seem to me to be broadly contradicted by the majority of the texts in question. Of course his observations could have pertinence to carefully chosen characters in Thackeray, George Eliot, Meredith, and others. Again, they apply exactly to most of Hardy's.

Hardy himself they are denied it. The universal malice or indifference (depending upon the operative metaphor of the moment) wears out their aspirations, their faith, sometimes (as in *Jude*) their love for each other. And, unlike George Eliot, Hardy seems to offer no secular decorum that does for the fiction what the providential decorum used to do.[74]

The failure of Hardy's protagonists to find a providential vision and the absence of a coherent providential aesthetic from his novels does not mean that the characters or the novels fail aesthetically. It means that his novels do not participate coherently in the providential aesthetic. They are haunted by it, they protest against it, they even play around with it. But they are not in that tradition. Indeed, the fact of their persistent success as novels in which the explicit disjunction from the providential tradition provides a major element of their thematic unity demonstrates the distance which English fiction had traveled between *Jane Eyre* and *Daniel Deronda*. That is the movement discussed in what follows.

---

[74]Hardy's work is not sustained even by a consistent inversion of the decorum, as I at first supposed it might be. His novels do not prove to be structured by antiprovidential systems of punishment or reward. Although he makes free use of traditional metaphors, and often for the purpose of ironic inversion, his break from the tradition is more fundamental and more thorough. He saw that the reverse of providentialism was not a cosmic countersystem but a denial of perceptible order.

2

CHARLOTTE BRONTË
The Range of the
Providential Intention

WE HAVE SEEN that the forms in which a providential intention makes itself known in the English novel are various and diverse and that they become richer and more complex as the genre develops. In broad generalization, however, it may be said that a major thematic occupation from *Robinson Crusoe* through *Jane Eyre* lies in the reiterated formal assurance that virtue will be rewarded and vice punished. Such assurance may sometimes be ironic, sometimes parodic, sometimes unconvincing; but the collective emphasis of the major fiction during this period fosters a dominant expectation of poetically just resolutions in a divinely ordered cosmos. When Charlotte Brontë began to write her serious fiction, English readers expected novels to show them that poetic justice and providential intention are one.

Jane Eyre met this expectation and *Villette* did not. Between these two novels an impressive and, for the future cheerfulness of English fiction, a philosophically ominous rift was opened. The cheerful conventions of *Jane Eyre* seem, by the time we reach *Villette*, to have suffered a kind of shock or, to employ the operative metaphor, a "shipwreck." The distance between the two novels suggests a radical thematic discontinuity, prophetic and emblematic of the fiction to come later in the century. The achievement seems the more remarkable when we realize that the failure of poetic justice in *Villette*, calculated as it certainly is, represents no breakdown of Charlotte Brontë's religious faith but an investigation of what it means to keep that faith in a world from which the visible signs of divine mercy have been withdrawn, a fictional world that has become somehow as sealed off from providential rewards as *Jane Eyre* is replete with them. *Villette*'s metaphysical silence and mystery, its rejection of poetic justice, have been sources of confusion and anxiety from the time of its publication. And yet behind its apparent reserve, its protested reluctance to discuss the matter, a providential intention may be found at work in *Villette*; and in its treatment of the attendant disconsonance between human aspiration and the ultimate ordering of circumstances, the novel serves as a kind of outer limit for the fictional representation of divine will in the world.

Jane Eyre

Jane Eyre is Charlotte Brontë's brightest, happiest book. Its energy, clarity, and cheerfulness were praised from the first month of its publication, and a reading of the early reviews shows the approval which met the novel to be deeper and more general than the well-known censure of the heroine's social and sexual daring. Charlotte Brontë's contemporaries found her book to be powerful, moral, vigorous, healthy, fresh, true, improving, pure, sound, straightforward, and comprehensible. These are among the words they used to describe what they called the "thought," the "moral," the "spirit," as well as the style of *Jane Eyre*. Certainly the actions and sentiments of the heroine seemed to some writers inappropriate or even wrong; but in general the reviews convey a sense of moral cheer and wholesomeness and even a kind of gratitude for a work that manages to combine these qualities with power and honesty. For most contemporary reviewers the book clearly complemented and sustained those providential assumptions about life which were important to early Victorian readers and which they expected to see celebrated in their literature. It cheered them by showing the providential intention vigorously at work in their world.[1]

[1]See "The Early Reception of *Jane Eyre*," in *Charlotte Brontë*: Jane Eyre *and* Villette, *a Casebook*, ed. Miriam Allott (London: Macmillan, 1973),

In our day as well the providentialism of *Jane Eyre* has received extensive acknowledgment. In 1960 Joseph Prescott found that "Jane's autobiography becomes an illustration of divinity's ends" in which "romance and exemplum blend." In 1964 Barbara Hardy conducted an extended unraveling of the threat of divine intention, showing that the novel's essential character is religious, that in it nature is "the expression of God," and that "the happy ending is not merely the resolution of the rough course of true love but a justification of God's ways to Man." R. B. Martin sees *Jane Eyre* as "largely a religious novel, concerned with the meaning of religion to man and its relevance to his behavior" wherein the perfected hero and heroine "become a microcosm of man's striving for Christian reward." William Marshall testifies to the degree to which Charlotte Brontë "clearly exploited the dramatic possibilities of Providentialism" and the ways in which Jane Eyre intensifies and sophisticates her childhood impressions of a providential world. Lawrence Dessner sees *Jane Eyre* as a novel that "expresses an unquestioning faith in Divine justice," a faith absent in his view from *Shirley* and *Villette*. Jerome Beaty describes the novel as "essentially the story of Jane's increasing awareness of the role of Providence in her life," and a book in which "Divine Providence is the ultimate reality of human life."[2]

---

pp. 50, 53, 66; and *The Brontës: The Critical Heritage,* ed. Miriam Allott (London: Routledge, 1974), pp. 69, 75, 76, 79, 81, 87, 103. See also Queen Victoria's judgment ("fine religious feeling") quoted in *Brontë Society Transactions,* 59 (1949), 247; and reviews in *The Tablet.* 23 Oct. 1874; Oxford and Cambridge Magazine, June 1856; *Tait's Edinburgh Magazine* ("unexceptional and instructive"), NS 15 (1848), 348; and *Howitt's Journal* ("perfect womanhood"), 2 (1847), 333–34. A good account of the reception of the Brontë's novels, one that does full justice to the "coarseness" issue, may be found in Tom Winnifrith's *The Brontës and Their Background* (London: Macmillan, 1973), pp. 110–38.

[2]Joseph Prescott, *"Jane Eyre*: A Romantic Exemplum with a Difference," *Twelve Original Essays on Great English Novels,* ed. Charles Shapiro (Detroit: Wayne State Univ. Press, 1960), pp. 93, 95; Barbara Hardy, *Jane Eyre,* Notes on English Literature Series (Oxford: Basil Blackwell, 1964), pp. 68, 29; and Hardy, *The Appropriate Form,* pp. 67–70; R. B. Martin, *The Accents of Persuasion: Charlotte Brontë's Novels* (London: Faber, 1966), pp. 81, 83;

The unusual breadth of agreement between current critics and Victorian reviewers is made possible by the relatively straightforward nature of *Jane Eyre*'s providentialism. It is hard to miss and hard to doubt. To see it we need no more than a brief summary of the providential design for Jane and Rochester, their pattern of opportunities. The heroine's childhood and education equip her with the fortitude and reserve to withstand temptation while her ardent temperament makes her peculiarly susceptible to it. She errs in idolizing Rochester and is punished. She appeals to providence to sustain her, wanders in pain, and is finally reunited with her lover. Rochester tries to shape divine law to his own needs, is thwarted, appeals to providence for a remission of his anguish, and receives Jane. Prayers are answered with a promptness and consistency worthy of attentive omnipotence. If the suffering of the principals is acute and, at least for Jane, out of proportion to the guilt incurred, it is of a salutary variety, perfecting and purifying them. In the end the mystery of divine intention clears away, and lovers and readers alike are permitted to see that, as Rochester puts it, "divine justice pursued its course" and, as Bessie's song foretold, "God is a friend to the poor orphan child."[3]

Such bald review of the providential design lends itself to ridicule and does little to endear *Jane Eyre* to current sensibilities. It also underplays the powerful rebellious energies that recent feminist criticism properly emphasizes in this text. In fact, our experience of the providential design is varied and developed as we read by a web of incidents, images, allusions, and foreshadowings—and we will look briefly at some of these. For my present purpose, that of contrasting the straightforward providentialism of *Jane Eyre* with its inversion in *Villette*, it makes sense to move directly to the implicit assumptions

William Marshall, *The World of the Victorian Novel* (London: Thomas Yoseloff, 1967), pp. 130, 158; Lawrence Dessner, *The Homely Web of Truth: A Study of Charlotte Brontë's Novels* (The Hague: Mouton, 1975), p. 79; Beaty, "*Jane Eyre* and Genre," pp. 624, 651.

[3] *Jane Eyre*, ed. Jane Jack and Margaret Smith (Oxford: Clarendon, 1969), p. 571 (ch. 37 in most editions) and p. 21 (ch. 3).

behind the structure of the earlier work. What are the conditions of life in the world of *Jane Eyre*? What laws govern a fictional universe in which a providential intention can be perceived in the pattern of events and in the destinies of the various characters? What is its providential decorum?

The first assumption of the traditional providential aesthetic is that circumstances have a direct and proportional relationship to the aspirations of the protagonist. What Jane is, and what she wants, strikes a kind of harmony with the natural world of which she perceives herself to be a part. Here nature is the expression of divinity, and one great source of communion with nature and with the goodness it embodies is human love. Jane's romantic impulses toward Rochester, even when they are excessive and idolatrous, involve her deeply in the natural world, as in the famous proposal scene in the garden. What Jane desires bears a direct relation to what she will receive (as soon as she learns to desire it properly); her being has a place in the decorum of circumstances in a way that Lucy Snowe's decidedly does not. In loving, Jane becomes pertinent to her world, a world that accommodates someone who loves with a kind of natural approbation.

The relationship between romantic love and natural benignity is a highly achieved quality in *Jane Eyre*. It was not present in the earlier world of the Angrian legends, the extended fictive structure of Charlotte Brontë's long literary apprenticeship, a structure from which the action of providence was generally excluded. In Angria despairing maidenhood demonstrates a fatal propensity to throw itself at the feet of peremptory masculine egoism. The fantasy matches slavish masochism with imperious mastery, and in such stories as those of Mina Laury and Caroline Vernon the narrator broods over the humiliation and longing that result. When Charlotte Brontë turned her writing to representation of the everyday world, however, this indulgence was denied; and from that time onward her fiction aimed at celebrating love's power to promote social and emotional equality. Sexual love in the world of *The Professor* and of *Jane Eyre* becomes a source of virtue rather than of corruption, of reciprocity rather than of exploitation. When Charlotte

Brontë made her famous longing renunciation of Angria, it was for the sake of *reality,* a real everyday world of which providence was the animating principle, a world where human love and longing had cosmic significance, a world of apprehensible correspondences between the protagonist and her circumstances.

A second major assumption of *Jane Eyre*'s straightforward providentialism, closely connected with the proportional relationship between character and circumstances, concerns the efficacy of the human will. *Jane Eyre,* like *The Professor,* is largely devoted to the balancing and contrasting of individual wills. The theme of the power struggle is so pervasive as almost to define all social relationships not based on the reciprocity of mutual romantic love. The "Professor," William Crimsworth, presents himself as a kind of master technician of willpower, one who knows from self-examination that "human nature is perverse" and who uses that knowledge to gain the upper hand over everyone, however disposed toward him, who falls in his way.[4] Jane Eyre, far less disagreeable and much more fallible, also has his habit of speaking about "my powers," "what I like," "my position," "my time," "what suits me," and his persistence in seeking the opportune moment in which to seize the ascendancy. She has, indeed, too few other means to power, and what is important here is not the asperity of her watchfulness but the affirmation behind it. The struggle can be won. The individual will can be controlled, and its control can lead to lasting happiness. God helps those who—with patience, endurance, hard work, and self-respect—help themselves.

This is an affirmation promoted by the providential worldview in its straightforward form. Helen Burns tells Jane that "it is weak and silly to say you *cannot bear* what it is your fate to bear" (p. 63; ch. 6); and Jane goes on to bear what is

---

[4]*The Professor,* Shakespeare Head Brontë (SHB) Edition (Oxford: Basil Blackwell, 1931), p. 47; ch. 6. Even of his kindly Dutch benefactor, Crimsworth has the heart to claim, "My mind having more fire and action than his, instinctively assumed and kept the predominance" (p. 222; ch. 22). Terry Eagleton has explored the social importance of power brokering in *Jane Eyre* and *The Professor (Myths of Power: A Marxist Study of the Brontës* [London: Macmillan, 1975], pp. 15–44).

required of her. She will learn to modify her expectations, to work and to live with heartache. Rochester too learns that he must accept God's law and that the proper exercise of the will is not to attempt to bend the law to his own desire but to accept it and own it.[5] His repentance should not be seen as a feeble submission to circumstances or as a hopeless collapse under the incessant blows of the divine rod, but as a characteristic though tentative redirection of his large and generous impulses and thus not a failure of will but its proper and effectual mastery.

But the most important implicit assumption in the providential world of *Jane Eyre* and the one that most distinguishes it from *Villette* and certain other important later novels is that the divine intention is distinctly perceptible as it works in the world. The principal characters can eventually see the outline of the divine plan, where they went wrong and where they were given the opportunity to go right. They can see as well that the secondary characters, the Mrs. Reeds, the Blanche Ingrams, and also the Miss Temples and Misses Rivers, have all received what they deserved. Sinners are punished, saints crowned, shallow natures earn a pedestrian happiness, the greathearted and much-suffering enjoy a proportionate bliss. Divine justice makes sense in this novel: no conflict exists between what happens to the characters and what the well-meaning reader hopes for them. In *Jane Eyre* providential intention and poetic justice are one.

This may be illustrated by comparing the final allotments accorded to Jane and to Rosamond Oliver. To Rosamond much has been given: "All advantages, in short, which combined, realize the ideal beauty, were fully hers. I wondered, as I looked at this fair creature: I admired her with my whole heart. Nature had surely formed her in a partial mood; and forgetting her usual stinted step-mother dole of gifts, had endowed this, her darling, with a granddame's bounty" (pp. 463–64; ch. 31). Jane, as we are often told, lacks not precisely beauty but particularly the "ideal" kind of beauty.

---

[5]This was clear to the novel's first readers. See for example the review in the *Era* (1847), quoted in *The Brontës: The Critical Heritage*, pp. 79–80.

The individuality of her physical characteristics, much noticed by Rochester, as well as the individuality of her mind "suits" her to her lover. Only with each other can Jane and Rochester be fulfilled. Rosamond, a flower whom all the world can admire, will find no such special happiness. The very fact that she possesses the qualities so generally acknowledged allows her to give up the immovable St. John and after two months' acquaintance engage herself to someone else. We are permitted to assume that Rosamond will partake of a moderate happiness as "the connection is in every point desirable" (p. 505; ch. 34), but this is properly distinguished from Jane's hard-earned marriage, "blest beyond what language can express" (p. 576; ch. 38). In contrast with Rosamond's uneventful well-being, we see that the very hardships, deprivations, and apparent injustices of Jane's original condition have been transformed into blessings, into sources of fulfillment.

The straightforward agreement between poetic justice, the meting out of merited punishments and rewards, and providential intention, the completion of God's design in the novel, allows Jane at the end to combine love for Rochester with Christian rectitude. St. John Rivers observes that "propensities and principles must be reconciled by some means" (p. 455; ch. 30); but he "reconciles" them by trying to subdue the propensities in the interest of the principles, creating an apparent dichotomy between temporal love and love for God. This dichotomy is the challenge to Jane in her undying love for Rochester. It lies behind the altercation over the value of "domestic endearments and household joys," which for Jane are "the best things the world has" but for St. John "the selfish calm and sensual comfort of civilized affluence" (p. 499; ch. 34). His proposal is not a call to married love but a call to sacrifice, an invitation to take sides in what he sees as the unending conflict between propensities and principles.[6] Jane's rejection

---

[6]St. John does not propose a celibate relationship, as many commentators have assumed. He speaks of "our physical and mental union in marriage," and Jane wonders whether she could endure "all the forms of love (which I doubt not he would scrupulously observe)" (pp. 520, 517; ch. 34).

of him represents an intuitive affirmation of the integrity of
being and the divinity of nature.[7] In her concluding paragraph
she acknowledges St. John's heroism with a eulogy that movingly asserts her own wholeness of being: "The last letter I
received from him drew from my eyes human tears, and yet
filled my heart with Divine joy" (p. 578; ch. 38).

We can see here how closely Brontë's perception of providence at work in the temporal world is bound up with her
mildly heterodox assumption that nature and human virtue
are complementary in their action. The concept of an apprehensible providential intention gains tremendous force from
the romantic sense of the immanence of God in nature. These
unities as they exist in *Jane Eyre* have an emblem in Ferndean.
The nature of Rochester's retreat suggests something like
"nature's ministry"—in marked contrast to "Thornfield"—and
Jane describes it as a kind of natural cathedral: "Iron gates
between granite pillars showed me where to enter, and passing
through them, I found myself at once in the twilight of close-
ranked trees. There was a grass-grown track descending the
forest-aisle, between hoar and knotty shafts and under branched
arches." She tells us that "all was interwoven stem, columnar
trunk, dense, summer foliage—no opening anywhere." She
enters "a portal, fastened only by a latch," to find the house
"as still as a church on a week-day." Of this sacred place Jane
will be the "dean" and her "soft ministry," as Rochester has
it, "will be a perpetual joy" (pp. 550, 551, 570; ch. 37).

As nature's minister Jane works at Ferndean to restore Rochester to physical and mental health, to renew him as a man
and as a lover. The once fashionable view that Charlotte Brontë
rejoiced in "castrating" Rochester and in otherwise cutting
him down to Jane's size betrays not only ignorance of the
author's attitude toward masculine sexuality (to the degree

---

[7]John Hagan observes that "Jane can attain her goal of freedom only if
her service of God and man are reconciled. This is what finally happens
when she is reunited with the chastened Rochester at Ferndean"; marriage
to St. John "would have destroyed that vital wholeness of being in which
throughout the book she struggles so heroically to keep herself alive" ("Enemies of Freedom in *Jane Eyre*," *Criticism,* 13 [1971], 353, 376).

that she reveals it in her writings) but a shallow and somewhat perverse exploitation of certain insights of twentieth-century psychology. More important for my purposes here, it leads to false ideas about the values of Jane Eyre's world. Whatever Charlotte Brontë may be working out unconsciously (and that we can never know), Jane Eyre does not object to the imperiousness of Rochester's passion. His impulsive attachment is what, in her eyes, makes him lovable. There is no reason to doubt her assertion that when she sees him blind and maimed, "rapture was kept well in check by pain" or that his avowal of dependence brings her to tears (pp. 551, 562; ch. 37). Rather than celebrating her ascendance and the suspension of his mastery, she will do what she can to raise him from despondency and return him to power.[8]

The moment when Jane ceases to torment Rochester with the false vision of her union with Rivers gives rise to one of the most characteristic Victorian love speeches: "Oh, you need not be jealous! I wanted to teaze you a little to make you less sad: I thought anger would be better than grief. But if you wish me to love you, and could you but see how much I *do* love you, you would be proud and content. All my heart is yours, sir: it belongs to you; and with you it would remain, were fate to exile the rest of me from your presence for ever" (p. 568; ch. 37). Here the teachings and uncertainties are swept away, and what follows, though far from flawless, contains no subversive negations. "Be proud and content," she tells him; and he reaches his true nobility in learning to claim her help "without painful shame or damping humiliation" (p. 577;

---

[8]See the sympathetic discussion by Sandra M. Gilbert and Susan Gubar in *The Madwoman in the Attic: The Woman Writer and the Nineteenth-Century Literary Imagination* (New Haven: Yale Univ. Press, 1979), pp. 368–71. Helene Moglen asserts that "Rochester's mutilation is, in terms of this nascent feminist myth, the necessary counterpart of Jane's independence: the terrible condition of a relationship of equality" (*Charlotte Brontë: The Self Conceived* [New York: Norton, 1976], p. 142). Her argument is powerful and, to me, convincing—but it need not contradict the providential view that Rochester's punishments are necessary to his spiritual salvation and therefore to his *rise* toward spiritual equality with Jane.

ch. 38). The jockeying for position, the power play that infests *The Professor* and many of the earlier chapters of *Jane Eyre,* is resolved in a temporal equality of nature and grace.

The erring Rochester had called Jane his "Mustard-Seed," thus identifying her with the biblical parable concerning the kingdom of God in which an infinity of bliss may be contained in the smallest of things (p. 325; ch. 24).[9] The prophecy is fulfilled when she leads him home, serving "both for his prop and guide." "God bless and reward you," he has said. "I am rewarded now," she answers. "To be your wife is, for me, to be as happy as I can be on earth" (p. 569; ch. 37). In that "now," in that happiness "on earth," in the palpable waxing of the mustard tree, we see the providential intention at work in its most apprehensible and humanly gratifying form.

Shirley

Direct contrasting of *Jane Eyre* with *Villette* is an effective way of pointing to what I take to be an inversion of the central structuring theme of English fiction up to this time, an inversion that has interesting implications for the future of the providential aesthetic. What makes Charlotte Brontë so valuable a subject for the study of providentialism in fiction is that she explores its possibilities from disparate perspectives. In the development of her art, however, she covered the distance between them through an intervening work, *Shirley,* and began there to raise questions and confront problems that become central for Lucy Snowe. Before turning to an analysis of the providentialism of *Villete,* I want to take a passing look

---

[9]See Matthew 13:31–32, Mark 4:30–32, and Luke 13:18–19. The editors of the Clarendon edition of *Jane Eyre* content themselves with noting that "Mustard-seed is one of the fairies in *A Midsummer Night's Dream.* Mr. Rochester often refers to Jane as a fairy, as in Chapter xiii" (p. 599, n. for p. 325). Joseph Prescott on the other hand shows that Rochester is made to fulfill literally the Biblical injunction "If thy right eye offend thee, pluck it out" (in *Twelve Original Essays,* pp. 94–95). See also Hardy, *Jane Eyre,* p. 28.

at certain preoccupations of Charlotte Brontë's third novel, preoccupations that provide the most significant kind of transition.

Like *The Professor* and *Jane Eyre, Shirley* ends in domestic happiness for the principal characters. In each of the first three novels personal independence unites harmoniously with personal fulfillment in sexual love. As we move from novel to novel, however, the happy resolutions seem more and more seriously threatened, the protagonists progressively more vulnerable to fate or circumstance. In *Shirley* this is made possible by a shift in narrative perspective from that of the earlier works (personal recollection from a position of domestic prosperity) to a comparatively distant, rather acrid voice in the third person. The complex single protagonist splits and becomes two, with Shirley Keeldar wielding and representing health, money, and power, and Caroline Helstone playing the harried victim of circumstances. This separation of roles frees the exceptional and idealized Shirley from most of the constraints that fetter every other Brontë protagonist. It also allows the author to focus on the inequalities of earthly allotments and Caroline's response to them—and in Caroline we have Charlotte Brontë's first exploration of a character who finds life's conditions irreversible, who cannot by her own efforts subdue self or circumstances and continue to live. Caroline's attempts to sublimate her passion for Robert Moore by devoting her energies to charitable acts show courage and resignation but not lasting strength. Unlike the professor, Jane Eyre, or Shirley, she lacks the fortitude to triumph over circumstances and personalities by an act of will or an assertion of self. Her potential is that of a tragic character. She can only hope to live for that providential event that ultimately and almost gratuitously saves her.

The theme which attaches itself to Caroline is not that of the struggle for independence, equality, and fulfillment but that of justice, and of divine justice in particular. She begins to collect for us the questions and assertions that lie at the center of *Villette*: "What was I created for? . . . Where is my place in the world?"[10] "I have been mocked, and Heaven is cruel!" (I, 210; ch. 11). "Truly, I ought not to have been born" (I, 257; ch. 13). "God surely did not create us, and cause us to live, with the sole end of wishing always to die" (II, 81; ch. 22). She suspects that "there is something wrong some-where" (II, 82; ch. 22).

Caroline's complaint does not lead her to rebel against prov-idence (though the novel deals explicitly with civil and domes-tic insurrection). Instead the author has her criticize society for its shortsighted treatment of women, their limited edu-cation and oportunity. Beyond this Charlotte Brontë begins to develop that doctrine of resignation and endurance which, as we have seen, is evident in the two earlier novels primarily as a kind of self-control that is rewarded with power over others. As Caroline begins her suffering, the narrator makes a recommendation: "Take the matter as you find it: ask no ques-tions; utter no remonstrances: it is your best wisdom. You have expected bread, and you have got a stone; break your teeth on it, and don't shriek because the nerves are martyrized. You held out your hand for an egg, and fate put into it a scorpion. Show no consternation: close your fingers firmly upon the gift" (I, 114; ch. 7).

The bitterness of this doctrine is finally qualified in *Shirley* by the happy resolutions, but such qualification seems neither very deep nor very carefully developed. The novel's thematic structure is formed throughout by a peculiar rhythmic fluc-tuation between suffering and happiness, weakness and strength, sickness and health. For long sections the hand of providence seems to have been at least partially withdrawn, leaving the fictional world to "fate" and resignation. There is no carefully prepared development toward the revelation of a providential design at the moment of fulfillment. The happy but somehow flat resolutions seem twisted arbitrarily from refractory circumstances. When Robert Moore has given up hope of financial success, he hears of the repeal of the Orders

[10]*Shirley*, SHB ed. (Oxford: Basil Blackwell, 1931), I, 193; ch. 10.

in Council and his fortune is made. "Oh! Providence is kind," Caroline exclaims. "Thank him, Robert." "I do thank Providence," he answers (II, 355; ch. 37). Coming from Robert Moore, this sounds a bit glib, one more indication that the providentialism of *Shirley* is neither as deep nor as consistent a structuring principle as that of *Jane Eyre*. And although *Shirley* finally serves up a kind of perfunctory poetic justice, Caroline's questions—Why was I born? What is my place in the world?—are not met on the metaphysical level where they sometimes appear to be asked. Her union with Moore offers us the traditional resolution of marriage, but the lack of resonance suggests again how far from traditional providentialism Charlotte Brontë had come. In *Jane Eyre* the heroine's marriage seemed an almost completely gratifying resolution; in *Shirley* it lacks conviction; in *Villette* it never arrives.

Villette

Villette's refusal to provide the accustomed answers to such questions as Caroline's troubled its early reviewers, and their uneasiness is a valuable measure of the extent to which the novel disappointed the conventional expectations of providentialism. It is not the case, as Mrs. Gaskell asserted and as most commentators since have assumed, that Charlotte Brontë's contemporaries received her last completed work "with one burst of acclamation."[11] The novel's reception in 1853 was actually a cacophony of admiration and anxiety. The *Observer* called *Villette* "half atheistical and half religious." The *Edinburgh Guardian* found in Lucy "a certain pagan strength" and "a degree of irony and impatience in her tone, when she is forced to speak of characters shaped in a different mold, which is, to say the least, neither very just nor very Christian." The *Athenaeum* commended Charlotte Brontë for her superiority to "the nonsense and narrowness that call themselves religious

[11] *The Life of Charlotte Brontë*, Introduction and Notes by Clement Shorter (London: Smith, Elder, 1900), p. 594.

controversy" but warned that "her books will drive many minds out among the breakers,—they will guide few to safe havens." The *Spectator,* in a passage worth quoting at length, provided an accurate account of the heroine's final position and an intelligent summary of the problems early readers had with the providentialism of *Villette*:

> Faith is indeed a very prominent feature in Miss Snowe's mind; more a religious than a theological faith; more a trust, a sentiment, and a hope, than a clearly-defined belief that could be stated in propositions. But truth is another feature, and she will not sacrifice truth to faith. When her experience is blank misery, she does not deny it, or slur it over, or belie it by shamming that she is happy. While her eyes turn upward with the agony that can find no resting-place on earth, she indulges no Pagan or Atheistical despair—she does not arraign God as cruel or unmindful of his creatures—she still believes that the discipline of life is merciful; but she does not pretend to solve God's providence—she rather with a certain sincerity cries aloud that her soul is crushed, and drinks the bitter cup with the full resolve not to sweeten the bitterness by delusion or fancy. She seems to think that the destiny of some human beings is to drink deep of this cup, and that no evasions, no attempts to make it out less bitter than it is, will turn aside the hand of the avenging angel, or cause the cup to be taken away one moment the sooner. We doubt the worldly philosophy of this view, as much as we are sure that it is not in any high sense Christian. It may, however, be a genuine effusion from an overstrained endurance—a sort of inverted Stoicism, which gives the sufferer the strength of nonresistance and knowing the worst.[12]

[12]*Observer,* 7 Feb. 1853, p. 7; *Edinburgh Guardian,* 3 Dec. 1853, p. 5; *Athenaeum,* 12 Feb. 1853, p. 186, quoted in *The Brontës: The Critical Heritage,* pp. 187, 189; *Spectator,* 12 Feb. 1853, p. 155, quoted in part in *The Brontës: The Critical Heritage,* p. 183.

Villette strikes the *Spectator*'s reviewer neither as true to his experience of the world nor as very deeply Christian. Lucy Snowe's view of things is too parochial to be accurate and too dark to be religious "in any high sense." And this indeed typifies much of the contemporary reaction. A diffuse awareness of the book's intimate power is linked to a troubling doubt about its meaning. It puts itself forward as a Christian, even as a Protestant work. But what is one to make of the catastrophe at the end, the temporal prospering of evil self-interest and the apparent inefficacy of good will, the gratuitous suffering, the noble endurance of the heroine unrewarded?

The cheerful assumptions that characterize straightforward providentialism, the conditions of life in *Jane Eyre* and in most novels that preceded it, have lost their primacy in the world of *Villette*. In the first place, that relationship of significant proportion between protagonist and circumstances, that decorum, has suffered a radical distension and defacement. What happens to Jane seems to have something to do with what she is, what she has done, what she can bear, and what she hopes for. The arrangement of circumstances has a direct and positive relation to the nature of the protagonist. If this is true of *Villette*, it is true only in a bitterly ironic way, one that has more to do with passive frailty than with erring strength, more with an apparently limitless capacity for suffering than with a potential for fulfillment, more with individual deprivation than with equity of allotment. Secondly, as we shall see, there is little in *Villette* to persuade us that the individual will can emerge victorious from a struggle against fate or circumstances. *Jane Eyre* seems to show us that such struggles can be won, that God will in this life help those who have achieved self-mastery. In *Villette* the rules have undergone some sinister modifications, and the individual will is not only deprived of its power to control circumstances but has become a kind of double agent, capable of conspiring with events to increase the protagonist's pain. Finally, the third condition of life in a traditional providential novel, that the divine intention is clearly perceptible as it works in the temporal world, perceptible to characters as God's will and to readers as God's will in the form of poetic justice, has been replaced in *Villette* by a portentous silence and mystery.

Because the conditions serving poetic justice in the English novel had long been associated with the working out of a divine plan for the protagonists, their defection in Villette appeared to early readers to leave the action of the providential intention ambiguous and obscure. The ending especially threatened their sense not only of the way things ought to be in novels but of the way things really are, if properly observed, in life. We on the other hand tend to like *Villette* in part because it denies the workings of poetic justice and therefore satisfies our sense of the way things ought to be in serious novels— the literature which began to establish itself after Charlotte Brontë's death—and of the way things really are in a world without providence. Some of the present critical popularity of *Villette*, I suspect, is owing to that canon of aesthetic seriousness that holds we do *not* get what we deserve and that characters in novels shouldn't either, that (for example) Pip should not wind up with Estella and that Hetty Sorrel and Tess Durbeyfield show us something more real than Jane Eyre.

But whatever our prejudices about happy endings might be, *Villette* still raises critical problems for us now. The novel drops the convention of poetic justice, but it steadily and with an admirably controlled increasing insistence evokes and maintains the workings of a providential intention. Closer in many ways to *Jane Eyre* than to *Shirley, Villette* is constantly informed with portents and signs of a divine plan for the protagonist. These portents and signs, and the plan itself, are kept dark throughout—almost as if Charlotte Brontë had reversed the affirmations of *Jane Eyre* and then asked what had become of our idea of providence. But since, as we shall see, the presence of some kind of providential intention is undeniable in *Villette*, the question for us is not so different from the question raised by Charlotte Brontë's contemporaries: What kind of dispensation is this, what kind of world where vice is permitted to prosper and where virtue suffers by divine mandate?

There is no short answer to this question. Early Victorian readers did not know what to make of the absence of poetic justice; we do not know what to make of the presence of the providential intention.[13] According to the narrator (and she is, as we shall see, coherently supported by the events she narrates) God's will in her world is in continual process of fulfillment. Providence is immanent even in Labassecour. It was a step of great importance for Charlotte Brontë to have relinquished the aesthetic felicities and ethical prestige of poetic justice. That she did so without surrendering the authority of a providential intention at work in her text strikes me as necessarily conservative in conviction and as brilliantly radical in form. Most novelists to come when they dispense with poetic justic will dispense with providence as well. Charlotte Brontë does not, and this makes *Villette* a kind of pivotal point, a transitional work of importance in the development of the English novel. In the remainder of this chapter I would like to examine the peculiar providentialism of *Villette,* in part for the sake of understanding the central movement of this remarkable book, but chiefly in order to see just how a major thematic transition in the providential aesthetic was effected.

Providential intention in *Villette* is established not by a single denouement, fulfillment, or catastrophe, but by the reiteration of a pattern in the heroine's experience. This pattern is one of disciplined and prudential calm blasted by unforeseen and inescapable storm, of resolute forbearance rendered valueless by emotional riot. The movement establishes itself in the first chapters of the novel. There we are introduced to a young Lucy who takes pains to assert a calm, philosophical, orderly view of life's visissitudes. She pretends to enjoy the precarious

---

[13]Carol Ohmann sees Lucy abandoned to a cosmos "unrelieved" by divine interposition: "The cosmos as Lucy experiences it is willfully, terrifying naturalistic." Brontë "renders a world in which some people suffer intensely and unfairly and attributes inequity to an austere cosmic design . . . [but one in which Lucy] earns through her suffering the treasure of wisdom. That, along with her faith, is her temporal glory" ("Historical Reality and 'Divine Appointment' in Charlotte Brontë's Fiction," *Signs,* 2 [1977], 777). These perceptions take us a long way into the book, but I will go on to show that the cosmos of *Villette* is far from naturalistic in the exclusive sense, and that the terror for Lucy is precisely that she suffers by divine appointment.

complacency of late childhood, affecting to wonder at the maternal partiality of Mrs. Bretton and the passionate attachments of little Polly. Her very insistence on her superiority to such emotions, however, makes us suspicious of her sincerity, or of her self-knowledge, or at least of her stability. There are hints of potential disturbances beneath the surface. When a letter causes Mrs. Bretton some evident concern, Lucy trembles in expectation of a "disastrous communication" from home.[14] Polly's stifled ecstasy when her father arrives distresses Lucy Snowe in a decidedly unphilosophical way: "I wished she would utter some hysterical cry, so that I might get relief and be at ease" (I, 13; ch. 2). Charlotte Brontë shows us a Lucy Snowe presenting a partial Lucy Snowe—masked, quiet, sustaining a brittle illusion of inner order.

If this illusion comes of hubris, the nemesis is quick and harsh. A metaphor of storm and shipwreck veils the actual horrors: "All hope that we should be saved was taken away. In fine, the ship was lost, the crew perished" (I, 39; ch. 4).[15] Later the memory of this suffering returns to Lucy in the *allée défendue*: "Oh, my childhood! I had feelings: passive as I lived, little as I spoke, cold as I looked, when I thought of past days, I *could* feel. About the present, it was better to be stoical; about the future—such a future as mine—to be dead. And in catalepsy and a dead trance, I studiously held the quick of my nature" (I, 134; ch. 12). What exactly did happen to Lucy in late childhood we are never to know. When she tells Mrs. Bretton at La Terrasse, the reader is put off with vague generalities. This mysteriousness about the particular nature of early sorrows is not what we would expect from the author of *Jane Eyre*; but we do know that the suffering has been great—so great, this reticence suggests, that she will not inflict the history of it upon us. If young Lucy's evasive complacence

[14]*Villette*, SHB ed. (Oxford: Basil Blackwell, 1931), I, 2; ch. 1.
[15]The rhetorical parallel is to the last paragraph and M. Paul's death. The biblical allusion is appropriately to the shipwreck which the apostle Paul survived: "All hope that we should be saved was then taken away" (Acts 27:20). The significance of the persistent association of Paul Emanuel with St. Paul is explored later in this section.

at Bretton earned a punishment, the debt has been fully paid even before she arrives in Villette.

Life's first great storm leaves Lucy stranded, and she becomes Miss Marchmont's companion and nurse. Miss Marchmont's sudden early loss of her lover foreshadows Lucy's loss of M. Paul, and her final words suggest the deep affirmative passivity that Lucy must learn. On the eve of her death Miss Marchmont sees that the ways of God are not comprehensible: "I do not know . . . I cannot—*cannot* see the reason; yet at this hour I can say with sincerity, what I never tried to say before—Inscrutable God, Thy will be done!" (I, 45; ch. 4). To arrive at this affirmation has cost Miss Marchmont a lifetime of suffering. Lucy admires her strength because she too has suffered acutely; but to adopt the lesson, to take it into herself in its fullness, will require wave after wave of new experience.

In her service to Miss Marchmont, Lucy seeks to make a characteristic bargain with life. "I had wanted to compromise with Fate: to escape occasional great agonies by submitting to a whole life of privation and small pains. Fate would not so be pacified; nor would Providence sanction this shrinking sloth and cowardly indolence" (I, 43; ch. 4).[16] In her desire to achieve a plateau of resigned isolation we detect a subdued analogue to her childhood inclination to substitute order and calm for feeling and love. These attempts to give up the hope of real happiness in return for an escape from great suffering, and the ultimate failure of each attempt, provide the rhythm of the heroine's development and much of the novel's structural power.[17] What is more important thematically, these attempts

---

[16]Helene Moglen calls such words as *fate* and *providence* the "language of passivity" (*Charlotte Brontë: The Self Conceived*, p. 203), leaving this an unfinished point in her valuable study. As Lucy sees it, providence forces her into life and action; but the ironies are complex: to be forced to reject a chosen passivity is still to be forced.

[17]Andrew Hook points to what he considers the novel's "essential internal movement . . . of rising and falling rhythms of inner passivity and acceptance on the one hand, emotional excitement and turmoil on the other" ("Charlotte Brontë, the Imagination, and *Villette*," *The Brontës: A Collection of*

and failures begin to suggest what providence has in mind for the protagonist.

Alone in Villette during the ghastly vacation period, weeks that culminate in her bizarre confession and collapse, Lucy Snowe learns that, like the rest of humanity, she cannot survive in utter isolation. Graham Bretton rescues her and brings her to La Terrasse where she can recover amid the furniture of childhood associations, almost as if disaster had not broken in and she might join her present life to the relative peace of her Bretton days. But Lucy has learned something from the rhythms of her suffering. In the very coincidence of her rescue and her reunion with the Brettons, she spots the divine trap:

> "Do not let me think of them too often, too much, too fondly . . . let me be content with a temperate draught of this living stream: let me not run athirst, and apply passionately to its welcome waters: let me not imagine in them a sweeter taste than earth's fountains know. Oh! would to God! I may be enabled to feel enough sustained by an occasional, amicable intercourse, rare, brief, unengrossing and tranquil: quite tranquil!" (I, 224; ch. 16)

But in this novel knowing her liabilities does not protect the protagonist from their consequences. The negative answer to this prayer is Lucy's rapidly increasing and finally complete dependence upon Dr. John and his letters. The quality of her devotion is balanced with admirable delicacy somewhere between romantic love and the neurotic attachment of an

---

Critical Essays, ed. Ian Gregor [Englewood Cliffs, N.J.: Prentice Hall, 1970], p. 147). In an early review of *Villette*, Eugène Forçade diagnosed Lucy's fear of happiness as a general peculiarity of the author's Protestantism: "Curieuse résistance de cette âme souffrante aux premieres brises du bonheur! Il y a là un singulier phénomène de psychologie Protestante" (*Revue des Deux Mondes*, 15 Mar. 1853, p. 1094).

isolated soul who has nowhere else to turn. Against all premonition she cultivates a "new creed," "a belief in happiness" (II, 1; ch. 23). She becomes an embodiment of those propensities she tried to despise as a child—reduced, at last, to a "grovelling groping monomaniac" (I, 312; ch. 22).

As Dr. John draws away from her, as he turns naturally and easily to Paulina, Lucy attempts again to give order to her life and reason to her expectations. She buries his letters. She replaces the belief in happiness with what she takes to be honest emotional bookkeeping. Henceforth she will not try to cheat the "mighty creditor." She will call anguish, anguish; despair, despair. "Offer to the strongest—if the darkest angel of God's host—water, when he has asked blood—will he take it? Not a whole pale sea for one red drop" (II, 141; ch. 31). She learns and can tell Paulina that "deeper than melancholy, lies heartbreak" (II, 224; ch. 37).

This knowledge does not prevent Lucy from falling in love with M. Paul. She seems to realize that it cannot so prevent her, and she appears to have relinquished that faith in the efficacy of the human will that distinguishes Jane Eyre. Instead of bargaining with "fate" as before, Lucy now attempts to embrace it. In so doing she sets her inner stage for what seems to me the cruelest, or at least the most ironic, reversal of all. This Charlotte Brontë achieves when the enamored, despairing, drugged heroine rises to explore Villette by night, seeking salvation of some kind, some solace, some assuaging coolness. There she sees M. Paul with the second Justine Marie and mistakes her for his future wife. On what she feels to be a presentiment, she knows a truth that is not true, suffers a fate that is not a fate. Embracing what she takes to be her destiny, Lucy Snowe caps circumstances in a self-imposed ecstasy of gratuitous jealousy and loss. She has been driven to create her own tragic ironies in a last frantic attempt to read a pattern in her text of experience. And the perversity of the delusion provides her with one more proof of the subtle opacity of her world, a sign that the appointed destiny of suffering carries with it the condition that all attempts to deflect the onslaught through anticipation are doomed to fail; or, what is worse, that the anticipation itself may provide the otherwise unnecessary pain. It is almost her last lesson.

The final movement of the novel, Lucy's scrupulous preparation for M. Paul's return and his death in the storm, confirms that pattern of forebearance and self-discipline mocked by circumstances that I have been tracing. The shipwreck seals the design in the novel and reinforces retroactively its importance in Lucy's history. Its providential significance, however, the crucial assurance that this is indeed a divine plan for the protagonist, is offered in part through certain supporting evidence. The providential elements are pervasive but diffuse, and it is their cumulative force that matters at the end. To illustrate this, I would like to glance briefly at a few of these elements, at certain characters in *Villette* and at part of the symbolic stage on which they act. The patterns of Lucy's pilgrimage have religious meaning, providential meaning, in the context of a world where ordinary things can become spiritual portents and signs and where even minor characters provide a kind of intimate spiritual commentary on her actions.

We know for example that Charlotte Brontë used the architecture and setting of the Pensionat Heger in *The Professor* and in *Villette*. In both we have the garden with its *allée défendue* and the window overlooking it. In *The Professor* the setting is used chiefly for purposes of plot and action rather than for symbolic staging. In *Villette,* with its deeper metaphysical resonance, the *allée défendue* becomes Lucy's special path, her *way*, a different way from that of the Roman Catholics and "foreigners," different from that of anyone else in the novel. To the garden is added an ancient blooming pear tree, and beneath the tree legend has it that a nun was buried alive "for some sin against her vow" (I, 131; ch. 12). Among the roots of the tree Lucy ritualistically buries Dr. John's letters in a sealed bottle, interring an emotion that refuses to stay dead. For Lucy, as perhaps for the erring nun, the need to love is a corollary of life: "I thought the tomb unquiet, and dreamed strangely of disturbed earth, and of hair, still golden and living, obtruded through coffin-chinks" (II, 141; ch. 31). Lucy's self-conscious affinity to the buried nun threatens her symbolically with the emotional consequences of humanly insupportable repression.[18]

Another and spiritual antithetical option appears in the actress Vashti.[19] Shortly after Lucy adopts her creed of happiness and immediately after a second visit from the nun, Dr. John takes her to the theater. In Vashti, Lucy sees a creature torn by passion and defiance. "I found upon her something neither of woman nor of man; in each of her eyes sat a devil. . . . Hate and Murder and Madness incarnate, she stood." Lucy compares the actress with a painting of Cleopatra in the style of Rubens, representative of simple concupiscence, and finds her a "different vision." She means to tell us that Vashti's rebellion goes beyond the assertion of sexual passion, that she resists providence, rejects the conditions of mortality. "Scarcely a substance herself, she grapples to conflict with abstactions. . . . Fallen, insurgent, banished, she remembers the heaven where she rebelled." Vashti "resisted to the latest the rape of every faculty, *would* see, *would* hear, *would* breathe, *would* live, up to, within, well-nigh *beyond* the moment when death says to all sense and all being—'Thus far and no farther!' " (I, 7–8, 11; ch. 23).

[18]See E. D. H. Johnson, "Daring the Dread Glance: Charlotte Brontë's Treatment of the Supernatural in *Villette*," *Nineteenth-Century Fiction*, 19 (1966), 325–36.

[19]The original of Vashti is of course the famous actress Rachel, whom Charlotte Brontë saw in the spring of 1851. Vashti, the rebellious queen in the Book of Esther, is alluded to twice in the first part of Thackeray's *Henry Esmond*, which Charlotte Brontë read while she was writing *Villette*. There may be other connections with Thackeray's works, as suggested in a letter of 31 Dec. 1847: "I have received the 'Scotsman' and was greatly amused to see Jane Eyre likened to Rebecca Sharp—the resemblance would hardly have occurred to me." Perhaps Mme Beck owes her name, with its French pun, in part to *Vanity Fair's* Becky Sharp, of equal guile and more spectacular career. More important, the theme of *vanitas vanitatum* lies close to the center of *Villette*: In a letter of 14 Aug. 1848 she writes: "There is something, a sort of 'still profound,' revealed in the concluding part of *Vanity Fair* which the discernment of one generation will not suffice to fathom" (*The Brontës: Their Lives, Friendships, and Correspondence*, ed. T. J. Wise and J. A. Symington [Oxford: Basil Blackwell, 1932], II, 170, 244).

Vashti's reaction to suffering is resistance, rebellion, defiance. Lucy finds her frightening, horrible, and intensely interesting. We are invited to suspect that she feels within herself impulses that could lead her to a similar response to the conditions imposed upon her. In Vashti, Charlotte Brontë offers Lucy and the reader an embodied antithesis to resignation and repression, an alternative her heroine refuses to adopt because it is the posture of the damned.[20] Vashti makes a kind of ultimate tragic comment on the human condition, but Villette is a world where the exercise of individual will, however indignant or humanly appropriate, can become radically impertinent when opposed to fate, to the ineluctable thrust of the providential intention.

Between burial alive in conventual self-repression and damnation through the rebellious assertion of will, other possible paths, other options, are represented in the lives of other characters. A career of candid vanity and selfishness gives Ginevra Fanshawe little suffering. Mme Beck prospers through pluck and guile. Mme Walravens preys on the flesh and blood of others. But Lucy's most telling comparison is with Paulina Home de Bassompierre.

Paulina really has two careers in *Villette,* a childhood of passionate attachment and subsequent suffering and an adult life of passionate attachment and subsequent fulfillment. (The fact that neither the suffering nor the fulfillment can be termed *consequent* reinforces the arbitrary quality of this moral universe.) Young Lucy takes pains at first to dissociate herself from a creature so strange, so intense, so evidently vulnerable. She sees Polly as a being almost supernatural, associated with sainthood and martyrdom, "some precocious fanatic or untimely saint," consumed with a monomania for "Papa; my dear Papa!" When Polly's father leaves her, her cry seems "a sort of 'Why hast thou forsaken me?' " Lucy emphasizes the religious quality of the child's devotion by observing that she

---

[20]Lucy's rejection of Vashti is a version of Charlotte Brontë's fascinated horror upon seeing Mme Rachel. See *Lives,* III, 245, 251, 253, 290.

"must necessarily live, move, and have her being in another" (I, 10; ch. 2 and I, 22, 26; ch. 3).[21]

When Paulina reappears in Villette, to be saved from the crowd by Graham at the Vashti performance, she retains some of her preternatural qualities but she is no longer associated with saints and apostles and the passion of Christ. Her apparent destiny of suffering has been lifted. The young Lucy had misread the signs of Paulina's story. Her childish vulnerabilities have become graceful and beautiful strengths. A more perceptive Lucy Snowe now discovers curious affinities with Paulina, similar thoughts and habits of mind: "There are certain things in which we so rarely meet with our double that it seems a miracle when that chance befalls" (II, 33; ch. 24). Lucy and Paulina remember the past with accuracy and interpret it in the same way. They undertake the same studies and evince an English superiority to the Labassecourian girls. It may be that Paulina represents what Lucy might have become had she too been endowed with beauty, wealth, and, above all, a fortunate star. This last, the novel unceasingly reiterates, is what Lucy most lacks. As Paulina rises her unlucky counterpart takes on the sufferings that had once seemed inevitable for the young countess.

Paulina and Lucy discuss the inequality of their lots on more than one occasion. Paulina offers her friend a share in her happiness, but Lucy knows that such sharing is not possible. The nobility of her nature rejects it too, without rancor and without envy. Her hard-earned knowledge of the disparity in temporal allotments makes her a prophet of the happiness of others. "Providence has protected and cultured you. . . . In all that mutually concerns you and Graham there seems to me promise, plan, harmony. . . . Some lives *are* thus blessed: it is God's will: it is the attesting trace and lingering evidence of Eden (II, 160; ch. 32).[22] In this Lucy not only foretells Paulina's

---

[21]This is another paraphrase from St. Paul: "For in him we live, and move, and have our being" (Acts 17:28).

[22]Paulina has just given a little thanksgiving speech in which she acknowledges that higher and better spirits than she have "sowed in tears" and "died

happiness but acknowledges a providential intention at work there. She sees that Paulina is not merely lucky: she is chosen. She shows what providence *can* design for us in the order of things.

Charlotte Brontë took great care in the creation of Lucy's exquisite counterpart, and not least in effecting a transition important to the novel's providential structure. We have seen that Paulina's troubled childhood is described in terms of Christian suffering. When she returns to the novel as a woman and settles into her destined happines with Graham she incurs a tempered reduction in aesthetic stature. She becomes the diminutive her name suggests while the religious associations are transferred to Lucy and her lover. The movement is from Paulina to Paul; and unlike Paulina, M. Paul has unmistakable associations with his great namesake. Like St. Paul, he undergoes storm and shipwreck. The name of his confessor, Père Silas, invokes the disciple Silas whom St. Paul chose to accompany him to Macedonia and Corinth. Paul Emanuel's enthusiastic unscheduled lectures at the pensionat evoke St. Paul's dynamic preaching in the synagogues, and his letters, like the inspired epistles of the saint, are in Lucy's words "real food that nourished, living water that refreshed" (II, 311; ch. 42).[23]

"I lie in the shadow of St. Paul's," Lucy thinks before leaving

---

of utter want" (II, 158; ch. 32). She is more acute than her father, who voices the shallow expectations of conventional providentialism when he looks at Lucy's hardships: "This lot has, I imagine, helped her to an experience for which, if she live long enough to realize its full benefit, she may yet bless Providence" (II, 44; ch. 25).

[23]Much of the language used to treat Paul Emanuel hints at a greater than St. Paul: "He was come" (II, 248; ch. 38). "Be ready for me" (II, 249; ch. 38). " 'I will be your faithful steward,' I said, 'I trust at your coming the account will be ready' " (II, 303; ch. 41). The audacity of the parallel is confirmed when M. Paul proposes to his virgin on the Feast of the Assumption. Jane Eyre also identifies herself with the Virgin: "I kept these things then, and pondered them in my heart" (II, 278; ch. 37: paraphrase from Luke 2:19); and Jane compares the effect of Rochester's call for her to "the earthquake which shook the foundations of Paul and Silas's prison" (II, 243; ch. 36). Barry Qualls notices M. Paul's association with the apostle and with "Isaiah's prophesied Messiah" (*The Secular Pilgrims*, p. 80).

London (I, 54; ch. 5). In fact, the entire novel lies in the shadow of Pauline doctrine as set forth in the English Bible. Especially pertinent to Lucy's fate are St. Paul's assertions about the apparently arbitrary nature of God's judgments: "For he saith to Moses, I will have mercy on whom I will have mercy, and I will have compassion on whom I will have compassion. . . . Shall the thing formed say to him that formed it, Why hast thou made me thus?"[24] St. Paul's own conversion taught him that for some human beings salvation and suffering are inseparable: "For the word of God is quick, and powerful, and sharper than any twoedged sword, piercing even to the dividing asunder of soul and spirit, and of the joints and marrow, and is a discerner of the thoughts and intents of the heart." Indeed, for St. Paul suffering is the mark of a special grace: "For whom the Lord loveth he chasteneth, and scourgeth every son whom he receiveth."[25]

Lucy's destiny is to support this assertion, to suffer deeply and in a special way. When she leaves London, when she boards the *Vivid,* when she enters Mme Beck's pensionat, she feels the direction of a "fate" or "Providence." She learns, forgets, and learns again that her lot must be a peculiar and a dreadful one: "How I used to pray to Heaven for consolation and support! With what dread force the conviction would grasp me that Fate was my permanent foe, never to be conciliated. I did not, in my heart, arraign the mercy or justice of God for this; I concluded it to be a part of his great plan that some must deeply suffer while they live, and I thrilled in the certainty that of this number, I was one" (I, 198; ch. 15). Hers is a kind of inverted election, a variation of Protestantism in which divine favor reveals itself through a logic of reversal. Lucy Snowe's suffering is no accident, and Charlotte Brontë takes care to emphasize that her heroine's experience at times transcends the natural. When she has Lucy describe an agony in a dream, it is an agony that goes beyond mortality: "Between

---

[24]Romans 9:15, 20.

[25]Hebrews 4:12, 12:6. These words are also invoked with regard to Caroline's trials in *Shirley,* II, 36; ch. 20.

twelve and one that night a cup was forced to my lips, black, strong, strange, drawn from no well, but filled up seething from a bottomless and boundless sea. Suffering, brewed in temporal or calculable measure, and mixed for mortal lips, tastes not as this suffering tasted" (I, 200–201; ch. 15).

From these repeated onslaughts, culminating in M. Paul's death, Lucy learns at last that her isolation is inalterable. This is the meaning of the great concluding paragraphs of *Villette*. Poetic justice belongs not to life but to the romance of human wishes, to the novels of the past. God's judgments are a mystery, a mystery Lucy acknowledges in her use of the word *fate*. What happens to her is "the result of circumstances, the fiat of fate, a part of my life's lot, and—above all—a matter about whose origin no question must ever be asked, for whose painful sequence no murmur ever uttered" (II, 19–20; ch. 24). She knows that what God wills is fate, and "long are the 'times' of Heaven" (I, 225; ch. 17).

Lucy's courage and strength permit her to accept her allotment without Vashti's apostasy and without the moral depravity of Mme Beck or Père Silas. In her final isolation she transcends the weaknesses and the strengths of Charlotte Brontë's earlier protagonists. Lucy Snowe will ask no more questions, make no more denials. But for this grim integrity there can be no compensation in the form of temporal happiness, no balm of resignation. She will not cease to be angry, bewildered, bereaved. To mitigate the suffering would be a mockery and a contradiction. To reward Lucy at the end would be to deny the primary validity of her history and the peculiar fulfillment granted to those who, like Job, embrace pain as divinely sent and who embrace it not from choice but from compulsion.

The reason for Lucy's special destiny must of course remain mysterious. And yet Charlotte Brontë allows a hint to escape, a speculation, not satisfactory as a solution to the mystery of providential intention but perhaps helpful as a way of providing a kind of answer to the problems raised by the absence of poetic justice in *Villette*: "His will be done, as done it surely will be, whether we humble ourselves to resignation or not.

The impulse of creation forwards it; the strength of powers, seen and unseen, has its fulfillment in charge. Proof of a life to come must be given. In fire and in blood, if needful, must that proof be written. In fire and in blood do we trace the record throughout nature. In fire and in blood does it cross our own experience" (II, 240; ch. 38).[26]

Lucy has seen in the happiness of Paulina and Graham evidence of God's benevolence, an aftertaste of Eden. Now, in reading the text of her own story, she achieves and surpasses the wisdom of Miss Marchmont. She sees what Charlotte Brontë had seen in the death of her sisters, that exceptional suffering implies an afterlife.[27] Despite everything, because of everything, Lucy refuses to do without providence; and the last irreducible, perhaps even vestigial demand of a belief in providence is that somehow, somewhere, the inequities be set right. God's benevolence and justice demand it. The very inequities provide a proof for the few who can follow it. Lucy Snowe's life thus becomes a kind of extended secret sacrifice or martyrdom. The destiny that seemed to threaten others descends upon the divinely chosen surrogate. Lucy, with her

[26]A radically different vision of nature from that of *Jane Eyre* is presented here. Lawrence Dessner observes that *Villette* refuses to follow conventional demonstrations of poetic justice and that although conventional expectation would have Lucy and M. Paul receive their reward in the hereafter, "the text offers little support for that belief." Divine justice, according to Dessner, is not necessarily denied, "but *Villette,* in the end, can bring only silence to its support" (*The Homely Web of Truth,* p. 107). As the passage just quoted shows, however, the narrator is not silent on this point. And the facts of her world (though we are of course dependent on her perception of them) seem to support her conclusion. The question of her reliability as a narrator is, I think, less disturbing than post-Jamesian criticism tends to make it. I take some assurance from the fact that she is nothing if not reflexive and self-questioning.

[27]"Had I never believed in a future life before, my sisters' fate would assure me of it. There must be a Heaven or we must despair" (To W. S. Williams, 13 June 1849, about two weeks after Anne's death, *Lives,* II, 339). See also the "Autobiographical Notice of Ellis and Action Bell," (19 Sept. 1850), p. 7, bound at the end of the SHB ed. of *Wuthering Heights.*

Paul, assumes the burden and the glory, endowed with a kind of sacramental importance, earned by an agonized passivity.[28]

Thus the providential intention is hard at work in *Villette* in a form that readers of such cheerful predecessors as *Jane Eyre* could hardly have anticipated. *Villette*'s departures from the tradition of straightforward providential fiction depend finally on a displacement of the context of gratification, of rewards and punishments, a relocation of the sphere where justice is possible to somewhere mysteriously beyond the frame of the novel. In this life, in this world, the wicked inherit the earth. At the bottom of the spiritual hierarchy are the schemers and time-servers, those who in the book's last lines become the survivors—Mme Beck, Père Silas, Mme Walravens. At this level they possess Villette, the "little city," the mundane setting of worldly hypocrisy and greed. No earlier providential fiction had abandoned the lower world to evil so completely as this. Higher up are the Brettons, whose dwelling and refuge, La Terrasse, serves as a kind of halfway house where the pilgrim Lucy rests before continuing her journey.[29] They are enriched

---

[28]"She is where I meant her to be, and where no charge of self-laudation can touch her" (Letter of 22 Mar. 1853, *Lives*, IV, 53). There is, of course, no necessary implication that salvation will be denied those who, like Graham and Paulina, practice a measured human goodness. It should be clear that Lucy does not see her exceptional suffering as necessary to *her own* salvation. When a pupil of hers suggests this view—"Pour assurer votre salut là-haut, on ferait bien de vous brûler toute vive ici-bas"— Lucy laughs, "as, indeed, it was impossible to do otherwise" (I, 103; ch. 9). She also rejects a more sophisticated version of the same doctrine from Père Silas (I, 204–05; ch. 15). Her story is, rather, a "proof" for herself and others, a text "written" "in fire and in blood," for the attentive reader.

[29]When Lucy rests at La Terrasse she hears the noise of the great storm— the storm which becomes a metaphor for the most fully lived spiritual life, but there it sounds like a tempest in a distant upper world, "a world so high above that the rush of its largest waves, the dash of its fiercest breakers, could sound down in this submarine home, only like murmurs and a lullaby" (I, 228; ch. 17). The Terrace recalls the arbor on the Hill of Difficulty in the *Pilgrim's Progress*, where Christian slept the sleep that cost him dear.

by Paulina, the "little Paul," blessed with temporal prosperity, fortitude, delicacy, and a saving breath of spiritual refinement. Finally, Lucy and her Paul belong to the highest sphere. Their history can have its meaning only in that context. "But ye are come unto mount Sion," writes St. Paul in his epistle to the Hebrews, "and unto the city of the living God, the heavenly Jerusalem, and to an innumerable company of angels. . . . For here we have no continuing city, but we seek one to come."[30] What the title of this novel really says is that only in the continuing city, the heavenly city, will the providential intention make sense—a sense it stubbornly refuses to yield in Villette, in the earthly city, which is the place novels are about.

The conditions of the straightforward providentialism of *Jane Eyre* and of most earlier English novels no longer have force in *Villette*. That essential decorum of the protagonist in her world has been washed away: what Lucy gets has little to do with what she is, what she wants, what she can do. The protagonist's pertinence to her world has become emblematic rather than organic. Secondly, the power of her will in the world has become nugatory, not only to control events but even to control herself in such ways as will help her to grow or to enlarge her powers. Finally, although Lucy arrives at a reading of her experiences—that she is doomed to a special and immeasurable suffering—the meaning, the *justice,* of the pattern is withheld, at least while she inhabits Villette. And indeed, the intricacies of the pattern are so subtle that the times for suffering and for rejoicing can never be accurately anticipated, and any attempt to anticipate helps tighten the closing spiral of pain. This last condition lends *Villette* an irony of peculiar suggestiveness and modernity: that ultimate power will be demonstrated not by the orchestration of harmonies or by the creative drive toward unity, but in the arbitrary, the abrupt, the disconsonant.

---

[30]Hebrews 12:22, 13:14. Winifred Gérin associates the childhood fantasy city of Verdopolis with Bunyan's image of the Heavenly City (*Charlotte Brontë: The Evolution of Genius* [Oxford: Clarendon, 1967], pp. 45–47).

3

CHARLES DICKENS
The Completion of the Providential Aesthetic

CHARLOTTE BRONTË'S WORK creates a frame for the providential aesthetic in nineteenth-century fiction. Most novels in which the assumption of a providential design dictates the overall narrative structure may be located within the thematic boundaries set on either side by *Jane Eyre* and *Villette*. This is true of all of Dickens. Although no single Dickens novel deals as intensively as Brontë's with the relation of poetic justice to providential intention, the immense range of his complete work comprises the fullest extended exploration of the possibilities inherent in the tradition of English providential fiction. All Dickens's novels deal with justice and providence; he explores the vast middle ground of the subject with an animation, subtlety, and deepening awareness unequaled elsewhere. He fills in the orchestration of this theme for the English novel, and in so doing confirms its importance and centrality for students of the form.

Each of Dickens's novels supports in some degree those coordinates of a straightforward providentialism, those conditions of life in a providential world, elicited during the foregoing examination of *Jane Eyre*: that circumstances bear a direct and proportional relationship to the nature of the protagonist, that individual human will has a redemptive power in the world, and that the divine intention is ultimately perceptible in the text of personal history and experience.

Although the radical threats to the decorum that these coordinates identify increase in intensity and pervasiveness in certain of the later novels, they never overcome or dictate the structure of the fiction with the authority they develop in *Villette*. In the first place, that proportional relationship between protagonists and their circumstances, that essential decorum of individual nature and its context, always in Dickens subsists somehow to the end. Even when prominent characters prove too ethereal or too battered to withstand the onslaughts of the world, a palpable heaven (as we shall see) descends into the text to enfold them and bear them away. The grotesque and monstrous thrive in Dickens as they thrive in no other English novelist, but his heroes and heroines inevitably return to some sense of the fitness, propriety, congruity of their relation to what happens to them. This may be largely because (to take up the second coordinate) they find ultimate evidence for a basic responsiveness in their surroundings to the action of their own wills. Dickens's good protagonists are never finally helpless, never fatally duped as Lucy Snowe or Tess Durbeyfield are duped. However self-deluded they may have allowed themselves to become, in the end their earnestness and courage receive acknowledgment. They can alter their lives. Finally, these lives make sense to them: they can read a pattern in their experience. The "times" of earth, the temporal medium in which the text of this experience can be written and interpreted, is adequate for the purpose. The "times of heaven" that freeze and age Lucy Snowe are, in Dickensian narrative perspective, accommodated to human endurance.

The body of Dickens's work asserts for us, with an assurance that even Charlotte Brontë's does not, the existence of a providential order. The chief and most obvious reason for this superior assurance lies in his dominant use of third-person narration. Speaking very generally, we can say that he conceives of a context in his fiction that precedes and encompasses individual perspective, and our undertaking as readers is not isolated and troubled by the limitations of first-person narration to the degree that the perspectives of Jane Eyre or, much more powerfully, Lucy Snowe isolate and trouble us. This primacy of context in relation to individual viewpoint is evident even when Dickens employs first-person narrators, as in *David Copperfield, Bleak House,* and *Great Expectations*; we are encouraged to see past the narrator's consciousness with a challenging but nevertheless reassuring constancy to a world beyond.

In both Brontë and Dickens narrative subjectivity, the dangerous tendency of the narrating consciousness to lose accurate perception of the world in solipsistic retreat, is explicitly acknowledged by the first-person narrators. The explicitness of their acknowledgments is in fact what reassures readers that they and the narrator are still seeing the same world. When Jane Eyre tells us that in her early love for Rochester she lost sight of God, she does so from an established perspective of knowledge and maturity that we trust. She can see how her view of things was once twisted, and if she can see that (this logic proceeds), then she must be at least moderately reliable *now*. When in *Great Expectations* Pip, hopelessly enamored of Estella and still living out his fairy tale of being destined for her by Miss Havisham, looks around the old woman's bizarre room with its stopped clock and decaying bridal dress, he tells us: "I saw in everything the construction that my mind had come to, repeated and thrown back to me" (p. 293; ch. 38). He too is speaking from a perspective of knowledge and maturity, and he *now* knows what he was then. But he is also saying what is still more reassuring as to his reliability as narrator of external events: he is saying, as he often does, that he knew *then* what he was then. With all this self-knowledge, then and now, we as readers are apt to trust him.[1]

Lucy Snowe is a more difficult case as to reliability than Pip or the other first-person narrators in Dickens. Lucy suffers from an apparent disjunction or lack of decorum between events and her reaction to them. She makes confessions to an alien priest, grovels over a friendly letter, succumbs to moral paralysis at a crucial moment. Although her world cannot be called ordinary with its occasional ghostly masquerades, legends,

---

[1]We trust Pip despite such arguments against his reliability as those advanced by Julian Moynahan in "The Hero's Guilt: The Case of *Great Expectations,*" *Essays in Criticism*, 10 (1960), 60-79. We don't doubt the narrating Pip because he has done the doubting for us, but we don't expect him to know everything.

and carnivals, it nevertheless seems commonplace compared with her fiery imagination and passion-tossed mind. Readers educated in the problematic of the unreliable narrator, readers nowadays, sometimes wonder whether she can be trusted to narrate events accurately and to tell the truth about other characters. Her inner life seems much more exceptional than her circumstances. But with Pip, as in a lesser degree with David Copperfield and Esther Summerson, this condition is reversed. As narrators they seem limited but comparatively stable. It is their world that is crazy, monstrous, bizarre. Pip's tone of wistful, gentlemanly, urbane irony contrasts, much to his credibility, with the characters and settings of his past— with Jaggers, Miss Havisham, Magwitch, Little Britain, Satis House, Newgate. In Dickens it is circumstances that are strange and unreliable. The Dickensian narrators, first and third person, tend to sympathize with our astonishment.

These distinctions are important in making a transition from Charlotte Brontë's intense, almost obsessive concern with temporal allotment and divine justice in her two major novels to Dickens's gradual, more diffuse development of the theme throughout his work. For Charlotte Brontë's heroines the question is necessarily more self-referential: How can I account for and accommodate the radical disparity between what I know myself to be and need and what I perceive the apprehensible dispensation of circumstances to require and offer? Dickens's protagonists ask a much simpler question based on less clearly defined premises: What is the true order of things and where do I fit in? When Jane Eyre and Lucy Snowe glimpse the true order of things, the providential decorum, they are at first appalled. Their real work begins with the development of this perception. In Dickens, when the true order of things can be apprehended, the protagonists' struggles are almost over.[2] They then affirm the things they find.

Thus the question that leads to the definition of a providential aesthetic in Dickens's fiction, reduced to its simplest

---

[2]An arguable exception here is Pip. But his moral development after Magwitch presents himself and destroys the fairy tale does not take long and in fact forms a part of his discovery of the true order.

form, seems to be: What is the true order of things? How do I find the decorum? To reduce the question to these terms helps to acknowledge Dickens's speculative boldness, a metaphysical daring revealed in the fact that in most of his novels the existence of providence itself is explicitly challenged. This challenge is usually first offered by certain nihilistic villains, and it appears as an assertion that there is no divine order or any reflection of it in the moral world (beyond, perhaps, improvisation by the fast and loose).[3] Ralph Nickleby, Quilp, Sir John Chester, Jonas Chuzzlewit, Uriah Heep, Skimpole, Rigaud, Riderhood, and the rest all suggest that virtue and justice are illusory, either by active and explicit negation or, more often, by the invention of some spurious and parodic countersystem ("Do other men, for they would do you"). Nor is the threat to the existence of a decorum limited to the villainous nihilists. Heroes and heroines have moments of doubt. Even Nicholas Nickleby has one as he wonders in discouragement why Madeline Bray's life "should not form an atom in the huge aggregate of distress and sorrow." Esther Summerson in her illness has a dream of existence as endlessly repetitive suffering (a parallel to the workings of Chancery) that leads her to pray for release in death, and her guardian claims at one point to see the universe as "rather an indifferent parent."[4] Little Dorrit sees Venice as a vast social reflection of the Marshalsea prison. And in *Our Mutual Friend* the lovelorn Mr. Venus sums up his state of mind and the case against significant order itself in a brilliant catalog of the realities about him:

[3]That *human* wickedness is the primary source of evil in the world is a theme so pervasive in Dickens that I hardly know how to cite a single reference. But the Spectre in "The Haunted Man" says it succinctly in distinguishing the spiritual conditions of Redlaw and the Baby Savage: "He is the growth of man's indifference; you are the growth of man's presumption. The beneficent design of Heaven is in each case overthrown" (*Christmas Books*, pp. 378-79).

[4]*Martin Chuzzlewit* (p. 181; ch. 11); *Nicholas Nickleby*, ed Michael Slater (Harmondsworth: Penguin, 1978), p. 791, ch. 53; *Bleak House*, ed. George Ford and Sylvère Monod (New York: Norton, 1977), p. 432, ch. 35; p. 68, ch. 6.

"You're casting your eye round the shop, Mr. Wegg. Let me show you a light. My woking bench. My young man's bench. A Wice. Tools. Bones, warious. Skull, warious. Preserved Indian baby. African ditto. Bottled preparations, warious. Everything within reach of your hand, in good preservation. The mouldy ones a-top. What's in those hampers over them again, I don't quite remember. Say, human warious. Cats. Articulated English baby. Dog. Ducks. Glass eyes, warious. Mummied bird. Dried cuticle, warious. Oh dear me! That's the general panoramic view."[5]

But these illustrations represent the views of individual characters, often passing and always partial. More threatening to the endurance of a providential order in Dickens's novels are descriptive intimations in the third-person narrators that things have got out of hand, that they are not right any longer and may never be right again. These are more frequent and pressing in the later novels where they accompany and support the often remarked darkening vision of society, but they surface in the early fiction as well. The description in *The Old Curiosity Shop* of the river as seen from Quilp's wharf suggests a world of refractory aimlessness. The confused and bumping barges look like "lumbering fish in pain," the steamship coming through "wanted room to breathe," dogs and boys run to and fro, and on the shore the Tower and the church spires "seemed to disdain their chafing, restless neighbor." The descriptions of the mob in *Barnaby Rudge* and of a society in which the only solution found for social ills is more hanging, a world where the younger generation is, as Edward Chester puts it, "repelled at every turn, and forced to disobey," poses the same kind of threat in a novel where the social poison is even at the end only partially neutralized.[6] In *Bleak House* Jo looks up at the

[5]*Our Mutual Friend*, ed. Stephen Gill (Harmondsworth: Penguin, 1971), p. 121; bk. 1, ch. 7.

[6]*The Old Curiosity Shop*, ed. Angus Easson (Harmondsworth: Penguin, 1972), pp. 86-87; ch. 5; *Barnaby Rudge*, ed. Gordon Spence (Harmondsworth: Penguin, 1973), p. 312; ch. 32.

cross of St. Paul's and we are told that "from the boy's face one might suppose that sacred emblem to be, in his eyes, the crowning confusion of the great, confused city" (p. 243; ch. 19); but the viewpoint seems only putatively Jo's, for the language certainly belongs to the narrator, a kind of cynical prophet who speaks in the present tense and who ridicules the notion of "things coming round!" (p. 249; ch. 20).

Many more examples of this kind of pessimism could be offered. My point is that in Dickens's fiction a kind of tension is created largely independent of the views of the characters, a drama of circumstances between the unifying, harmonizing forces of providential design and the alienating, self-consuming disorder of apparent randomness or chance.[7] Certain social institutions align themselves with one side or the other as do certain characters, but the drama is cosmic in its ultimate implication. As readers we are led to seek a confirmation of the true order of things—confirmation that such an order exists beyond or above our own lonely endeavors.

In Dickens this search is always rewarded. The drama of circumstances always resolves itself with at least a glimpse of the divine order. This does not mean that there are no casualities along the way—Nancy in *Oliver Twist* for example or Magwitch in *Great Expectations*—but beyond the consequences of human wickedness and neglect we perceive telling intimations of a providential intention that human benevolence and love reflect aspects of the higher order and that connections can be made which show it to us.

In *Bleak House* Dickens asks: "What connexion can there be, between the place in Lincolnshire, the house in town, the Mercury in powder, and the whereabout of Jo the outlaw with the broom, who had that distant ray of light upon him when he swept the churchyard step? What connexion can there have

---

[7]W. H. Harvey observes in *Bleak House* an "extreme tension set up between the centrifugal vigour of its parts and the centripetal demands of the whole" ("Chance and Design in *Bleak House*," *Dickens and the Twentieth Century*, ed. John Gross and Gabriel Pearson [Toronto: Univ. of Toronto Press, 1962], p. 146). He does not deal with providential design explicity.

been between many people in the innumerable histories of this world, who, from opposite sides of great gulfs, have, nevertheless, been very curiously brought together!"(p. 197; ch. 16). The quick answer to this question—at least as regards Jo and Lady Dedlock—could be "smallpox." That sinister organic filament lashes out from him to her daughter Esther, and such "connexion" is certainly in keeping with the tone of the third-person narrator, the most threatening and cynical of Dickens's narrative voices. But smallpox is not the final answer given by the novel. Instead its narrative structure meets the question by bringing the third-person narration (the "pessimistic" present tense) closer and closer to Esther's (the "optimistic" past tense), until finally they intersect or *connect*. Chapter 56, told in the third-person historic present, brings Inspector Buckett on his errand of forgiveness to John Jarndyce's house in order to enlist Esther's help in the search for her mother. The benign first-person narrator is thus sought and incorporated into the design of the third-person narration —or, more exactly, the narration of events is transferred from third to the first person, Esther, who takes over with chapter 57. She is needed by Inspector Buckett to strengthen this errand of mercy, and she is needed by us as readers because her vision of the world is an assertion of benevolent connectedness, a vision of mercy. As Ada Clare says, "It rained Esther" (p. 61; ch. 6). No doubt it can be objected that forgiveness and mercy do not save Lady Dedlock. *Bleak House* is a grim novel, the one in which the threats to divine order are most radically posed. But the connection has been made. The initially disparate and disdainful third-person narration has sought Esther out, acknowledged her, and in the acknowledgment credited her with an apprehension of realities.[8]

---

[8]Peter Garrett believes that "The fictiveness of Esther's providence emerges when it is confronted by Harold Skimpole's. . . . For all their obvious moral differences, both versions of providence emerge as individual creations and imply the fictiveness of all objectified moral orders. . . . But one can hardly reconcile the orders of providential design and human effort except by an

Bleak House, with its double narration, has peculiar strengths and liabilities. One of the strengths lies in its ability to offer a glimpse of the true order of things with peculiar force and subtlety—which is why I have used it here. It reveals with disarming openness, hidden on the surface of its surface, that the tension between cosmic absurdity and providential order is central to Dickens's sense of fictional form. In this context the movement I have just traced may serve as an emblem for the other novels where other devices—plot, metaphor, allusion, characterization, setting, direct narrative instruction—carry the burden of asserting the promise or offering the glimpse of a divine order in human affairs.

Such promises and glimpses may of course be indirect or veiled. We have seen that the providential tradition comprehends a certain mystery or obscurity or obliquity in God's dispensation. This obscurity demands careful interpretation if the will and design of providence are to be discerned. Dickens belongs to this tradition.[9] His characters read and interpret the texts of their experience; his narrators comment on the interpretations of the characters; his readers must interpret the interpretations and the commentary. In a letter to Wilkie Collins, Dickens wrote, "I think the business of art is to lay all that ground carefully, not with the care that conceals itself—to show, by a backward light, what everything has been working to—but only to *suggest*, until the fulfillment comes. These

act of faith that begs the question of the relation" (*The Victorian Multiplot Novel: Studies in Dialogical Form* [New Haven: Yale Univ. Press, 1980] pp. 67, 68). But, as I have argued, the business of the providential aesthetic is in part to demonstrate precisely that relation—and in *Bleak House* the demonstration validates Esther's version of providence, not Skimpole's (his is parodic in any case). Nevertheless, Garrett's sensitivity to the possibilities here is original and acute.

⁹Though not without some qualification. As Steven Marcus puts it, "Dickens was of course a Christian—Dostoevsky called him 'that great Christian'—which is to say that, living when he did, his involvement with Christianity was by nature profound, passionate, contradictory and, as frequently as not, adverse" (*Dickens: From Pickwick to Dombey* [New York: Basic Books, 1965], p. 68).

are the ways of Providence, of which all art is but a little imitation."[10] A providential aesthetic is one that imitates not only the unities of divine dispensation but also the indirection by which these unities are revealed. Dickens's narratives imitate the "ways of providence" in these respects while they anticipate, in their comic insistence upon the connectedness of things, the providentially potential "fulfillment" to come.

These introductory remarks are intended to suggest the general direction of my discussion. What follows represents an attempt to organize the very large volume of material that constitutes Dickens's significant development of the providential aesthetic. We have seen that themes and structures of this magnitude exercise a strong centripetal influence on aspects of the fiction at some distance from their evident centers of origin and that the assertion of a providential intention in most novels is designed to exert such influence. This on the one hand justifies our attention to it and on the other poses extraordinary problems of critical discrimination. Some limitation comes easily from the fact that I am dealing not with all order in Dickens but with providential order—order identified in the texts as divine in source— and its explicit moral reflection in characters and social institutions. Nevertheless, to prevent the discussion from becoming either diffuse and formless or excessively reductive and abstract, I have chosen to isolate certain subthemes or categories, to treat them individually, like spokes to a wheel, and then to demonstrate in brief readings of five novels how they turn together. These categories are arbitrary in the sense that they are mine and organic in the sense that they represent preoccupations which extend throughout the range of Dickens's fiction.

[10]*Letters*, III, 125 (6 Oct. 1859). Four years later Dickens wrote to Cerjat that "nothing is discovered without God's intention and assistance, and I suppose every new knowledge of His works that is conceded to man to be distinctly a revelation by which men are to guide themselves" (p. 352). E. D. H. Johnson writes that "in Dickens' world. . .the apparent randomness of existence conceals an underlying providence" (*Charles Dickens: An Introduction to His Novels* [New York: Random House, 1969], p. 101).

Specious Providentialism:
Gambling, Hypocrisy, and Solipsism

We have seen that in the drama of circumstances in Dickens's novels the conflict lies between the harmonizing, unifying forces of providential design and the alienating, disparate, self-referential fragmentation of apparent randomness or chance. What it means to yield to or to trust in chance is in fact a theme of the novels; and this theme is chiefly embodied in characters who in one way or other become gamblers. The decision to gamble amounts in Dickens to a willed submission to the arbitrary vicissitudes of an action by definition cut off from the true order of things, or at least from its reflection in moral life. Gamblers are guilty of denying the efficacy of individual will to participate in personal destiny, their own or that of someone for whom they are responsible. Ralph Nickleby rationalizes the abandonment of his niece Kate with the formula, "She must take her chance" (p. 418; ch. 26). He gambles with her innocence, and his betrayal is harshly punished in the destruction of his own child. Richard Carstone loses his life in *Bleak House* by playing at Chancery with "the careless spirit of a gamester" (p. 204; ch. 17). Mr. Micawber never gets anywhere while he shoots craps with life, hoping for something to turn up, expecting to be the guest of providence. He succeeds only when he unmasks Heep by means of his own careful exertions, the exercise of his own will. In *Little Dorrit* Clennam ruins himself by speculating in the Merdle bubble and is saved only by his past steadfastness and the love of his friends.

In *Hard Times* the hypocritical Mrs. Sparsit tries to teach the loathsome Bitzer that "It's immoral to Game." "It's ridiculous, ma'am," he returns, "because the chances are against the players" (p. 94; bk. II, ch. 1). They are both right. It is immoral because it denies the cosmic decorum, and it is ridiculous because the order of things works against the gambler. Perhaps the most interesting example of this in Dickens is the obsessive gambling of Little Nell's grandfather in *The Old*

Curiosity Shop. He bases his expectations on a kind of specious providentialism, and its failure is central to the action of the novel. According to his calculations Nell's virtues merit a tangible reward in the here and now:

> "I call Heaven to witness that I never played for gain of mine, or love of play; that at every piece I staked, I whispered to myself that orphan's name and called on Heaven to bless the venture, which it never did. Whom did it prosper? Who were those with whom I played? Men who lived by plunder, profligacy, and riot, squandering their gold in doing ill and propagating vice and evil. My winnings would have been from them, my winnings would have been bestowed to the last farthing on a young sinless child whose life they would have sweetened and made happy. What would they have contracted? The means of corruption, wretchedness, and misery. Who would not have hoped in such a cause—tell me that; now who would not have hoped as I did?" (pp. 126-27; ch. 9)

The apparent reluctance of heaven to sanction the venture has left the grandfather bitter and enraged: "God knows that this one child is the thought and object of my life, and yet he never prospers me—no, never" (p. 49; ch. 1). When the old man experiences his grandson's importunity and ingratitude he sarcastically exclaims, "And this is Heaven's justice" (p. 58; ch. 2).

Nell's grandfather is not just a crazy old codger but a spiritual pervert—as the repellent description of his night theft of her little stock of money strongly implies.[11] He illustrates what becomes of characters inhabiting a providential universe who

---

[11]Though he *is* also a crazy old codger. Leonard Manheim offers a clinical diagnosis of his case as "that of advancing senility accompanied by some paranoid trends and by a compulsion to gamble rationalized by his concern over his granddaughter's future" ("Dickens' Fools and Madmen," *Dickens Studies Annual*, 1 [1970], 90). Just so, and perfectly acceptable as describing the naturalistic manifestation of Trent's spiritual perversion.

attempt to dictate the outcome of events over which they have no proper control but to which they have entrusted themselves or their charges. Nevertheless, Nell's grandfather destroys her not because his reasoning is formally bad throughout—the virtuous schoolmaster also believes her virtue merits success ("The cause is too good to fail")—but because he deprives her of the tools of survival. The significant difference between Nell's grandfather and the schoolmaster lies in the latter's inclination to find Nell " some humble occupation" (p. 435; ch. 46). He offers her a way to help herself, an active commonplace of providentialism. The grandfather's gaming had, on the contrary, put her at the mercy of chance, thereby undermining her proper security in the temporal order of things. He believes that her "image sanctifies the game" (p. 306; ch. 31), but the game cannot be sanctified. Chance is not to be confused with providential order. To abandon oneself or others to chance means to deny personal responsibility and personal freedom and by implication to derogate the efficacy of the human will. The only reliable counter to the random threats which human depravity and indifference have loosed on human innocence is, in Dickens, the discipline of willed human benevolence. When providence strikes on its own, it strikes in its own good time.

Gamblers and hypocrites both attempt to exploit the order of things, to harness its energies in the service of their own aspirations. This is an inherent liability (as George Eliot will show us) of the providential habit of mind. Although Dickens believed in a benevolent providence, he saw very clearly that its interpretation is highly susceptible to corrupt and self-serving distortion. Much of his treatment of the theme incorporates an extensive satirical attempt to extricate it from hypocrisy and indifference, to identify and isolate venal usage of the conception and affected mouthing of the word. In the *Pickwick Papers* Tony Weller initiates—as he initiates so much else in Dickens— the satire of the long line of temporizers and hypocrites who would enlist the divine intention in their special service. After hearing the account of his stepmother's death, Sam Weller seems to experience a rare moment of mental lassitude in which he attempts to offer his father some traditional consolation:

> "Vell, gov'ner, ve must all come to it, one day or another."
>
> "So we must, Sammy," said Mr. Weller the elder.
>
> "There's a Providence in it all," said Sam.
>
> "O' course there is," replied his father with a nod of grave approval. "Wot 'ud become of the undertakers vithout it, Sammy?"
>
> Lost in the immense field of conjecture opened by this reflection, the elder Mr. Weller laid his pipe on the table, and stirred the fire with a meditative visage.[12]

The ancient riposte shines forth from its pleasant frame. Death benefits the undertaker. But the twaddle about providence into which Sam has uncharacteristically lapsed benefits nobody and finds itself consigned to the comic obscurity of Tony Weller's meditations.

Sam Weller leaves the word alone after this. So for the most part do Dickens's other morally sound characters. It is the wicked and the weak who refer often to providence. Gashford and Miggs employ it in *Barnaby Rudge*, and Sir John Chester, really a believer in chance, provides a satirical commentary: "It was a good stroke of chance (or, as the world would say, a providential occurrence)" (p. 671; ch. 75). Uriah Heep, of course, is the classic example of special pleading ("With the blessing of Providence, Master Copperfield").[13] Podsnap nationalizes the word in *Our Mutual Friend* in behalf of Britain, the young person, and himself: "It is not for me to impugn the workings of Providence. I know better than that, I trust,

---

[12]*The Posthumous Papers of the Pickwick Club*, ed. Robert L. Patten (Harmondsworth: Penguin, 1972), p. 830; ch. 52.

[13]*David Copperfield*, ed. Nina Burgis (Oxford: Clarendon, 1981), p. 201; ch. 16.

and I have mentioned what the intentions of Providence are"
(p. 188; bk. I, ch. 11).

Pecksniff in *Martin Chuzzlewit* looks forward to Podsnap
in specializing his definition of providence, but he makes more
elaborate and effective use of it. He sees himself as the center
of a cosmos which, with the help of hypocrisy and deceit, will
order itself to the service of his avarice and lust: "Providence,
perhaps I may be permitted to say a special Providence, has
blessed my endeavors" (p. 393; ch. 20). According to Pecksniff it lies with providence, when not occupied in promoting
his own aims, to pick up social loose ends, like the poor: "Mr.
Pecksniff said grace: a short and pious grace, invoking a blessing on the appetites of those present, and committing all persons who had nothing to eat, to the care of Providence; whose
business (so said the grace, in effect) it clearly was, to look
after them" (p. 204; ch. 9). The fate of those who have nothing
to eat does not touch him personally, for, as he observes to
his daughter, Charity, "There is nothing personal in morality,
my love" (p. 65; ch. 2). The phrase in its bogus decency sums
up the credo of the providentializing hypocrites in Dickens.[14]

Evident in his treatment of Pecksniff is Dickens's rejection
of providential explanations for social and personal inequities.
Podsnap justifies starvation in the London streets by the assurance that "Providence has declared that you shall have the poor
always with you" and that serious inquiry into the source of
social ills is to "fly in the face of Providence" (p. 188; bk. I,
ch. 11). Skimpole, meeting the disfigured Esther for the first
time after her illness, tells her that he "began to understand
the mixture of good and evil in the world now; felt that he
appreciated health the more, when somebody else was ill; didn't

---

[14]Dickens goes on to associate the idea of a "special Providence," the
tendency to consider oneself as "specially licensed to bag sparrows," with
British complacency in general, a national license for what Matthew Arnold
was to call "doing as one likes." Pecksniff in his nationally representative
role looks forward not only to Podsnap but in his "special" providentialism
to Bulstrode in George Eliot's *Middlemarch*, for whom "God's cause was
something distinct his own rectitude of conduct" (*Middlemarch*, ed.
Gordon S. Haight [Boston: Houghton Mifflin, 1956], p. 453; ch. 61).

know but what it might be in the scheme of things that A should squint to make B happier in looking straight; or that C should carry a wooden leg, to make D better satisfied with his flesh and blood in a silk stocking" (pp. 459-60; ch. 37). Mr. Spenlow applies a similar line of argument when David Copperfield questions the justice of certain Doctors Commons' practices: "He said, Look at the world, there was good and evil in that; look at the ecclesiastical law, there was good and evil in *that*. It was all part of a system. Very good. There you were!" (p. 408; ch. 33). Clearly such characters have made their good thing into the order of things.

As an object of satire self-serving providentialism adopts an impressive range of philosophical positions in Dickens. Those temporizers who profit from the social status-quo find the system providential. But there exists an equally degenerate minority who explain their position and that of their victims by arguing that the true order of things has been lost and that the universe itself may be functioning badly. Wackford Squeers in *Nicholas Nickleby* has devised an explanation which he finds adequate to justify the sufferings of others and which is one of the comic achievements of the novel: "A wisitation, sir, is the lot of mortality. Mortality itself, sir, is a wisitation. The world is chock full of wisitations; and if a boy repines at a wisitation and makes you uncomfortable with his noise, he must have his head punched. That's going according to the scripter, that is " (p. 839; ch. 56). Squeers can expand this comfortable conviction into a pedantic vision of philosophy as a disease of the flesh and a disorder of the spheres: " 'Measles, rhumatics, hooping-cough, fevers, agers, and lumbagers,' said Mr. Squeers, 'is all philosophy together, that's what it is. The heavenly bodies is philosophy, and the earthly bodies is philosophy. If there's a screw loose in a heavenly body, that's philosophy, and if there's a screw loose in a earthly body, that's philosophy too; or it may be that sometimes there's a little metaphysics in it, but that's not often. Philosophy's the chap for me' " (pp. 849-50; ch. 57). The loose-screw theory of evil in the world is picked up by Montague Tigg in *Martin Chuzzlewit*: "I do feel that there is a screw of such magnitude loose somewhere, that the whole framework of society is shaken, and the very first principles of things can no longer be trusted. In short. . .when a man like Slyme is detained for such a thing as a bill, I reject the superstition of ages, and believe nothing. I don't even believe that I *don't* believe, curse me if I do!" (p. 159; ch. 7). This is as close to an avowal of agnosticism as we get in Dickens, and even here the comic *reductio* covers its seriousness. In the later novels wicked or indifferent or ambiguous characters may act as if there is no God and no true order, but they don't talk much about it.

Miss Wade for example at the beginning of *Little Dorrit* uses a covering metaphor of preordination to mask a paranoid vision of a universe of exploitation and deceit: "In our course through life we shall meet the people who are coming to meet *us*, from many strange places and by many strange roads. . .and what it is set to us to do to them, and what it is set to them to do to us, will all be done." Madame Defarge in *A Tale of Two Cities*, has a putatively political viewpoint, but the tone and the motives are similar to Miss Wade's: "Her husband's destiny," she portentously announces, "will take him where he is to go, and will lead him to the end that is to end him. That is all I know." She evades the personal responsibility for the injustice to Darnay by pretending to be a mere scribe of fate, encoding his destiny (and that of all his race) into her knitting.[15] Revolution, in this novel becomes the act not of taking political responsibility but of abdicating moral responsibility and thus enlists the motive of revenge in perpetuating the inversion of values begun under the old regime by the misuse of privilege.

Jaggers in *Great Expectations*, the novel that follows *A Tale of Two Cities*, bears certain interesting resemblances to Madame

---

[15]*Little Dorrit*, ed. Harvey Peter Sucksmith (Oxford: Clarendon 1979), p. 173; bk. I, ch. 2; *A Tale of Two Cities,* ed. George Woodcock (Harmondsworth: Penguin, 1970), p. 215; bk. II, ch. 16. Mme Defarge's motives are of course personal—she is the sister of the girl Darnay's father raped and killed and whose fate Dr. Manette was imprisoned for protesting. But while she never lets go of her injuries, Mme Defarge has no capacity for gratitude: "I care nothing for this Doctor, I" (p. 388; bk. III, ch. 14).

Defarge. Like her he justifies his moral withdrawal by reference to the evil and injustice that surround him.[16] By attending chiefly to the wicked and self-interested, he has come to see chiefly wickedness and self-interest in the world. Like Madame Defarge, he washes his hands of the suffering in which he is implicated. He too has made himself into a kind of false providence—here to the criminal population of London—and, without taking direct responsibility for it, acts the part of a superhuman hunter (*Jäger*) who preys on human guilt. "Mind you, Mr. Pip," says Wemmick as they emerge from a visit to certain "clients" in Newgate prison, "I don't know that Mr. Jaggers does a better thing than the way in which he keeps himself so high. He's always so high. His constant height is of a piece with his immense abilities. That Colonel [a prisoner condemned to death] durst no more take leave of *him*, than that turnkey durst ask him his intentions respecting a case. Then, between his height and them, he slips in his subordinate—don't you see?—and so he has 'em, soul and body" (pp. 253-54; ch. 32). This has the appearance of a kind of hectic allegory, with Jaggers as a dark providence figure from whom even the moribund have something to fear, and it places him firmly in the thematic structure of a novel to which false or inadequate surrogate providence figures are central: Pumblechook, Miss Havisham, Magwitch (later called *Provis*).

Although Jaggers does possess a high degree of ambiguity—he has saved Estella from the street by transferring her to Satis House—his cynical manipulation of the law seems based on a moral nihilism. This quality finds wider expression in a familiar Dickensian type, the bored gentlemen. Sir John Chester begins the tradition in *Barnaby Rudge*: "The world is a lively place enough, in which we must accommodate ourselves to circumstances, sail with the stream as glibly as we can, be content to take froth for substance, the surface for the depth, the counterfeit for the real coin. I wonder no philosopher has ever established that our globe itself is hollow. It should be, if Nature is consistent in her works" (p. 145; ch. 12). This

[16]See, for example, p. 399, ch. 51.

third-rate Voltaire comes to a violent end, exactly as specified in the valedictory curses of his condemned bastard son Hugh. Skimpole, casually interested in everything, carries on the type in *Bleak House*. His remark "I have no Will at all—and no Won't—simply Can't" (p. 385; ch. 31) suggests the danger Clennam is in at the beginning of *Little Dorrit* ("I have no will," p. 20; ch. 2). Harthouse in *Hard Times* believes that the easy formula "what will be, will be" is "the only truth going" (p. 99; bk. II, ch. 2). He provides Coketown with an example of "a thorough gentleman, made to the model of the time; weary of everything, and putting no more faith in anything than Lucifer" (p. 91; bk. II, ch. 1). This also seems to be Eugene Wrayburn's problem in *Our Mutual Friend* and, as with Hart house, it leads him to try to corrupt the innocent: "I am in a ridiculous humor. . .I am a ridiculous fellow. Everything is ridiculous" (p. 213; bk. I, ch. 13)[17] If this is true, then everything—including the seduction of Lizzie Hexam—may be permitted. But as we will see, providence interposes to show him otherwise.

Taken without qualifying reference to context and character, the extent of Dickens's satire of cheap, self-serving providentialism as represented in the Squeerses, Heeps, Pecksniffs, Podsnaps, Skimpoles and their superior but solipsistic colleagues (Sir John Chester, Madame Defarge, Harthouse, Wrayburn) could suggest a general depreciation of the concept of providence itself throughout Dickens's work. I have already offered some partial demonstration that this is far from the case. In the following I attempt to show more precisely and specifically the important providential elements at work. To clear the way

[17]Eugene has a forerunner in Dr. Jeddler in "The Battle of Life," who begins by holding that life is a "farce," and the world "a gigantic joke . . . something too absurd to be considered seriously." Jeddler learns through loss and suffering that "the scheme" is a "serious one," that the world is full of "sacred mysteries, and its Creator only knows what lies beneath the surface of His lightest image!" The loss of "one little unit in the great absurd account, had stricken him to the ground" (*Christmas Books*, pp. 243, 245, 308, 309).

for this, I have emphasized that Dickens was intent on distinguishing what he saw as specious providentialism from an active, willed affirmation of the true order of things.

Virtuous Heroines:
Immanence

When in my introductory chapter I outlined the elements of the providential aesthetic, I argued that credibility of character in this fiction does not necessarily conflict with the representation of divine order. Although characters can exercise no ultimate independence from the providential decorum of their world, psychological individuation—the illusion of completeness and uniqueness of discrete characters—may be seen not as a departure from but as a constituent of the providential aesthetic. "Personality" is a dispensation, and the richer and more credible it is, the more fully it supports the providentialism of Victorian realistic fiction. But Dickens's virtuous heroines, with their heavy allegorical cargo, may seem to contradict or qualify these assertions. They are often hard to believe in, and especially at those moments when they seem to be most angelic, most the representatives of divine mercy and truth. As a type, however, the virtuous heroine in Dickens undergoes an important development, a progress toward the integration of psychological credibility with the representation of divine immanence. This development is central to the completion of a providential aesthetic in his novels.

"Young, Beautiful, and Good" were the words Dickens caused to be inscribed on Mary Hogarth's tombstone.[18] All Dickens's heroines are young and beautiful—and in the end they all wind up good. Their goodness shows itself in the qualities of modesty, reserve, attentiveness, and patience. As a type the virtuous

[18]Edgar Johnson, *Dickens*, I, 197.

heroines probably constiute for present–day readers the single greatest obstacle to taking Dickens seriously.[19] Not only do most of them appear to be born with supernatural goodness—thus offending our sense of the condition in which people come into the world—but they seem never to lose it no matter what life subjects them to—thus running afoul of our paradigms for the way people develop. Unconscious of internal contradiction Dickens's angelic heroines insist on celebrating their domestic humanity, in the sevice of which they spend their lives by biding their time, keeping house, and ultimately rearing children. They suffer in silence every kind of danger to themselves but speak out eloquently against a wide range of personal and social evils. Worst of all they are, at least in the early novels, hard to tell apart. "If you have seen the picture-gallery of any old family," says the Single Gentleman in *The Old Curiosity Shop*, "you will remember how the same face and figure—often the fairest and slightest of them all—come upon you in different generations; and how you trace the same sweet girl through a long line of portraits—never growing old or changing—the Good Angel of the race—abiding by them in all reverses—redeeming all their sins" (p. 637; ch. 69). From this tribute to Little Nell it might have been deduced as early as February 1841 (when the last installment of this novel appeared) that the virtuous heroine was here to stay.

Nell's first typological offspring of importance appeared as Florence Dombey in 1846, harder to believe in than Little Nell herself. Florence, "so young, so good, and beautiful," as Walter Gay puts it, was in fact meant to be a grown-up Nell,

[19]Dickens's virtuous heroines have always given some readers trouble. "We are bound to admit that Boz's young ladies are awful" (Review of 1839, *Dickens: The Critical Heritage*, ed. Philip Collins [New York: Barnes and Noble, 1971], p. 62). Chesterton complained that "it is not the death of Little Nell, but the life of Little Nell, that I object to" (quoted in George Ford, *Dickens and His Readers* [New York: Norton, 1965], p. 62). See also Collins, "The Decline of Pathos," *Listener*, 81 (1969), 635-37. Alexander Welsh provides excellent cultural and historical background on "the bride of heaven" in *The City of Dickens* (Oxford: Clarendon, 1971), pp. 164-95.

existing on a more rarefied plane then the rest of the characters in *Dombey and Son*:[20] "Floy, are we *all* dead, except you?" asks Little Paul on his deathbed (p. 223; ch. 16). The devout Captain Cuttle, himself an angel in the rough, "converted the little dressing-table into a species of altar" for her service (p. 643; ch. 48). The etherealization, however, becomes problematic in characterizing a wife and mother, and readers find Florence's mercurial emotional transition from feelings of sisterhood to those of romantic love for Walter hard to believe. Even more twisted is her return to her father to beg forgiveness, not just for herself but for her equally innocent husband—a scene to which she brings an apparently unchanged adherence to Dombey's own former sense of himself as a god: "Papa, dear, I am changed. I am penitent. I know my fault. I know my duty better now. Papa, don't cast me off, or I shall die!" (p. 801; ch. 59). When we remember that Dombey had himself cast her off, that he had struck her and "told her what Edith was, and bade her follow her, since they had always been in league" (p. 637; ch. 47), then we may feel that Florence is indeed sacrificed at the end of the novel and that Dickens has wielded the knife. What, after all, has she to be repentant about, and why should she need Dombey's forgiveness in order to go on living? Perhaps children who suffer as Florence has *do* behave in this way. Humiliation breeds dependency. But this can scarcely be a subject for admiration or rejoicing.

Florence as a credible character, or at least as an admirable one, is sacrificed to the theme of Dombey's redemption. She becomes the agent of his spiritual resurrection, and to this function her viability and interest as a discrete character become secondary. Like other virtuous heroines from Little Nell on, her primary role is to provide a kind of solution to a deepening problem in the providential aesthetic of Dickens's fictional

[20]*Dombey and Son*, ed. Alan Horsman (Oxford: Clarendon, 1974), p. 669, ch. 50. See John Forster, *The Life of Charles Dickens* (New York: Scribners, 1900), II, 43. Steven Marcus calls Florence "Dickens's first important representation of female *caritas*" (*Dickens: From Pickwick to Dombey*, p. 355).

structures: how among refractory circumstances can we recognize, what proof do we have, that the true order of things
is benign? If, as in *Dombey and Son*, the world is a world of
trade, of buying and selling, where wealth and temporal power
seem inseparable, what can show us that these activities and
values have limits even in the temporal sphere? Dickens's answer
seems in part to be the aggressive assertion of an inalienable
goodness, goodness so radical that it threatens conventional
concepts of selfhood and defies even minimal requirements for
credibility of character in fiction.

The goodness of the virtuous heroine is a form of immanence, of divinity radiating from within the human form. This
is seen with exceptional clarity in Dickens's next portrait of
the type, Agnes in *David Copperfield*. David associates Agnes
("Lamb") with "a stained glass window in a church"(p 191;
ch. 15) with "goodness, peace, and truth" (p. 198; ch. 16),
with "Hope embodied" (p. 435; ch. 35), and even with Can-
terbury Cathedral (p. 481; ch. 39). At the end of the novel he
hopes that on his deathbed he will see her near him, "pointing
upward!" (p. 751; ch. 64). The image grotesquely suggests a
gothic figure in a cathedral porch, and such distortion may be
in some ways psychologically appropriate. The abstract quality
of these associations may help explain the difficulty David has
in bringing himself to think of Agnes as a marriagable lover—
along with other difficulties such as the fraternal character of
his regard for her and his infatuation with Dora (surely one
of the few girls in the England of Dickens's fiction by whose
side this young hero can look manly). Agnes functions in the
novel to prove, as she says, "that real love and truth are stronger
in the end than any evil or misfortune in the world" (p. 436;
ch. 35). But the young David's problem bears affinities to ours
as readers: how to make a vessel of divine goodness an object
of sexual love?

It is worth observing that Uriah Heep, who is incapable of
perceiving goodness anywhere, suffers from no such inhibition. He wants Agnes with an undeniable lasciviousness. Quilp
in *The Old Curiosity Shop* wants Nell in the same way. Carker

once had his eye on little Florence. Mr. Turveydrop pays unpleasant attention to Esther Summerson. There is usually a lustful villain somewhere around the virtuous heroine, ignoring the immanence she radiates, insisting upon her sexuality, her humanity, her subjection to the common imperatives of life.[21]

Indeed, this counterpoint was part of Dickens's original conception of the type. In a preface to *The Old Curiosity Shop* he tells us that "in writing this book, I had it always in my fancy to surround the lonely figure of the child with grotesque and wild, but not impossible companions, and to gather about her innocent face and pure intentions associates as strange and uncongenial as the grim objects that are about her bed when her history is first foreshadowed" (p. 42).[22] Master Humphrey, when he first glimpses Nell, "surrounded and beset by everything that was foreign to [her] nature," allows that "she seemed to exist in a kind of allegory" (p. 56; ch. 1). The allegory is essentially that of *The Pilgrim's Progress*, read by Nell on the road, the tale of the Christian soul traveling through the world, fleeing temptation and guarding its purity. Nell's story, a Victorian version of the myth and common in varying degrees to all Dickens's heroines, derives its poignancy from its representative quality. When we see Nell among the artifacts of the old curiosity shop, among the dancing dogs, giants, dwarfs, punch-and-judys of the traveling showmen, among the quasi-historical figures of Mrs. Jarley's waxworks, we are meant to see the pure human spirit beset by the evils and absurdities of the temporal sphere, holding fast to the way of its true home.

---

[21]Alfred Harbage notices that "the virginial quality of the girls is often stressed by. . .a Gride, Quilp, or Uriah Heep slavering in their vicinity, like the monsters at the feet of the angels in medieval statuary" (*A Kind of Power: The Shakespeare-Dickens Analogy* [Philadelphia: American Philosophical Society, 1975], p. 57).

[22]This represents the sophistication of an idea central to *Oliver Twist*, of showing embodied in the child the principle of good "surviving every adverse circumstance and triumphant at last" (Preface to 3d ed., quoted by Edgar Johnson, *Dickens*, I, 281). The work of Dickens's virtuous heroines, it could be argued, was begun by a small boy.

We can see as well Florence Dombey outcast in the world, Agnes Wickfield beset by Uriah Heep, Esther Summerson contending against disease and disorder, Little Dorrit strange in Venice, Lucy Manette assailed by the revolution, Lizzie Hexam hounded by false lovers.

This mythic association provides some explanation for the trying similarities among Dickens's virtuous heroines. Whether it makes them more acceptable will depend upon a given reader's tolerance for allegory in realistic fiction. What the mythic identification does not explain are certain important dvelopments in the heroines after Agnes Wickfield. With *Bleak House* Dickens seems to have begun a more critical testing of his ideas about the capacity of human goodness, however transcendent in its source, to survive amid the sinister circumstances of a spiritually alienated world and still to remain recognizably human. This novel begins Dickens's extended attempt to unify the demands of the heroine's authentic psychological development with her emblematic goodness.

Esther Summerson chirps busily away in her narrative, cheerful and loving, but what that narrative consists of is a series of ordeals, of tests, of assaults on her psychic and physical frame that, to borrow a phrase from Hardy, are "like the moves of a chess-player."[23] Her illegitimate birth exposes her in childhood to Old Testament predestinarian loathing on the part of her aunt, and she acquires the feeling that it would have been better if she had never been born; after her arrival at Bleak House she is given a series of pet names so that her "own name soon became quite lost among them" (p. 90; ch. 8); she develops what seems to her in her illegitimacy a hopeless love for Allen Woodcourt; she contracts smallpox, which temporarily and symbolically blinds her and which ravages or at least changes her face ("It was not like what I had expected; but I

---

[23]Thomas Hardy, *Tess of the d'Urbervilles*, ed. Scott Elledge (New York: Norton, 1979), p. 239; ch. 43. Alex Zwerdling gives a good psychological analysis of Esther's "progress" in "Esther Summerson Rehabilitated," *PMLA*, 88 (1973), 429-39.

had expected nothing definite, and I dare say anything definite would have surprised me," p. 445; ch. 356); she soon sees her illness as something to thank God for because no one can now associate her with her mother; she receives a proposal from Mr. Jarndyce, whom she regards as a father, accepts it, and with exquisite ambivalence tries to make it do; she receives (too late, she thinks) a proposal from Woodcourt whom she still loves; she finds her mother dead, and (again symbolically) at first takes her for "the mother of the dead child" (p. 113; ch. 59). Throughout these trials she records her reactions circumspectly, but her record leaves no doubt that they are having an effect on her character. Finally, she endures, as a kind of pleasant surprise, a sudden change in prospective mates. Kindly John Jarndyce *surprises* her with the news that she is not destined for him but for Allen Woodcourt.[24] At this point readers have a right to feel that the time has come for any healthy Englishwoman to have (at least) a nervous breakdown.

Not Esther. All along she has distracted herself from her own condition by immersing herself in the care of others. She continues to do so. "You're a pattern, you know, that's what you are," Bucket tells her, "you're a pattern" (p. 704; ch. 59). It is as if Dickens had determined to make a radical assertion about psychological survival in a world of indifference and self-indulgence, much as he had made similar assertions about moral purity in *Oliver Twist* and *The Old Curiosity Shop*. Esther's mind does not prey upon itself as Ridley's and Carstone's do; she does not endlessly re-create her own image like Skimpole and Mrs. Jellyby. Instead, Esther loses sight of herself completely. She has, properly speaking, no independent selfhood. The maddening ambiguity of her conclusion, that her friends "can very well do without much beauty in me—even supposing" (p. 770; ch. 67), shows, if it shows anything, that she does not know what she looks like, that the events of her life have made her goodness incompatible with self-knowledge. Her

---

[24]Dickens's contemporaries also found Esther's sudden marriage surprising: "It is said matches are made in heaven: and certainly if this is a specimen, strange processes are carried on in the celestial laboratory" (*Eclectic Review*, NS 6 [1853] 672).

chirpy, busy, sunny style—with its insinuating references to what others say about her (her sole margin of reference for self definition)—represents a penetrating though not completely winning attempt to show us how someone might sound who had endured what Esther has endured and who has kept her goodness, who has been able to stay alive in the world despite everything.[25] If Esther's private hollowness is disconcerting, grotesquely at odds with her joy in her own condition, this is a comment on the price goodness pays for survival in a world of otherwise meaningless self-consumption, spontaneous combustion, Chancery. It is the psychological corollary of transcendence of the self.

Esther's survival in her world depends on her ability to escape the full emotional consequences of her experience by keeping herself undefined. She accepts her lot and even manages to affirm it by adopting whatever role, name, position, destiny the people she loves and trusts assign to her. As a psychic entity—I hesitate to call her a "self"—she has for her personal resources no pertinent history, no past. She can certainly be called selfless, but her selflessness is as much a form of survival as it is a moral quality—and this lends it a degree of credibility.

Amy Dorrit, Dickens's next major exploration of the immanence theme, provides a healthy or at least a refreshing contrast.

---

[25]There was a good deal of contemporary criticism of Esther's tone, and an awareness that part of her difficulty emerges from her role as narrator. The reviewer for the *Ecclesiastic and Theologian*, for example, observed that "her humility is constantly evincing itself in depreciation of the attention and praises lavished upon her by all with whom she comes in contact, but an autobiography is ill-suited for this purpose" (17 [1855], 471). The *Dublin Review* found her "fussy and vulgar . . . vapid and tiresome. . . . She is, in reality, an affected, self-seeking, self-conscious egoist, recording every compliment paid her with the air of an *ingénue*, but not hiding the smirk of self-satisfaction, and perpetually jingling her household virtues about our ears with those everlasting keys" (NS, 17 [1871] 347). In our time critics like Robert Garis have agreed: "No one has ever thought Esther a success as a realized character. . . . She has been both actively detested and quietly ignored" (*The Dickens Theatre: A Reassessment of the Novels* [Oxford: Clarendon, 1965], p. 141).

Despite strong similarities to Esther, especially in the care she extends to others, Little Dorrit possesses herself with a decision and awareness entirely beyond Esther's reach. Little Dorrit does not float with the present, she does not easily accept new names or new forms of address, she does not like giving up old forms of contact and habits of thought, she cannot take a new surface, she does not forget, she believes in herself, she wills her own destiny.

In *Little Dorrit* the power and paralysis of the will is a major theme, and it is closely bound up with the concept of truth to the past. After his enrichment William Dorrit finds his daughter Amy a constant reminder of his years in the Marshalsea: "You alone and only you—constantly revive the topic, though not in words. . . . I say, sweep it off the face of the earth and begin afresh. Is that much? I ask, is *that* much?" (p. 464; bk. II, ch. 5). For her it is everything, and she tacitly refuses. Her next letter to Clennam asserts her allegiance, approaching an obsession, to the past, to her life in the Marshalsea. It seems strange to her that the ancient Italian cities "should have been in their places all through those days when I did not even know of the existence of more than two or three of them, and when I scarcely knew of anything outside our old walls." The beauty of Pisa moves her not for itself but in the fact of its existence "when the shadow of the wall was falling on our room." She dreams of herself always as a child learning needlework. She longs for England, "so dearly do I love the scene of my poverty and your kindness." She concludes her letter by unconsciously echoing the motto (inscribed "D.N.F.") in Clennam's father's watch, "Do not forget" (pp. 537-38; bk. II, ch. 11).

Although such passages show a rooted attachment to her former life, Amy Dorrit's concern for others and her love for Arthur prevent her from lapsing entirely into the solipsistic imprisonment in the past which Mrs. Clennam has chosen and from which William Dorrit never really escapes. Instead she assumes a kind of responsibility toward it that without enslaving her provides her with a self-definition stronger than that of any of her predecessors among the virtuous heroines. "I have always been strong enough," she tells Flora Finching, "to do what I want to do" (p. 279; bk. I, ch. 24). Probably no other female principal in Dickens except Lizzie Hexam could say that truthfully. Little Dorrit loves her father as devotedly as Florence Dombey does hers, but she sees the distortion in his nature with a clarity that Florence lacks. There is nothing grotesque in the way she gives herself to Clennam as there is in Esther's abrupt transference to Allen Woodcourt with John Jarndyce's admonition to "blot [her engagement to himself] out of your memory" (p. 753; ch. 64). Little Dorrit is not, as Clennam observes to himself, "a kind of domesticated fairy" (p. 252; bk. I, ch. 22). The phrase has a reassuring self-consciousness about it, especially when we think of Dickens's earlier heroines, those to whom it might very well apply. At any rate when Amy Dorrit gives herself to Arthur Clennam, she does it *for* herself with a candor unprecedented in Dickens's romantic episodes: "I am yours anywhere, everywhere! I love you dearly! I would rather pass my life here with you, and go out daily, working for our bread, than I would have the greatest fortune that ever was told" (p. 792; bk. II, ch. 34). We can believe it: she has tried the alternatives and we know that she does not forget.

In the novels before *Little Dorrit* the providential aesthetic seems to entail a limit to or loss of credibility, of vitality and humanity, for the virtuous heroine. But *Little Dorrit* advances beyond these, beyond *Bleak House* in the sophistication with which it unites the protagonist's domestic and allegorical functions. In the preface to *Bleak House* Dickens had written that there he "purposely dwelt upon the romantic side of familiar things" (p. 4). Esther participates in the romantic element by providing a local emblem of cosmic immanence: "Little old woman, and whither so high/ To sweep the cobwebs out of the sky" (p. 90; ch. 8). Little Dorrit, although she is alternatively either too poor or too rich to be quite as tidy as Esther, also embodies the power to give us a glimpse of the true order of things. We hear that she is "inspired to be something which was not what the rest were" (p. 70; bk. I, ch. 7), that her tears are like "the rain from heaven" (p. 736; bk. II, ch. 29). At the end of the novel she counters Mrs. Clennam's Old Testament creed of retributive justice with New Testament forgiveness, and the narrator takes pains to associate her with Christ and his doctrine: "In the softened light of the window, looking from the scene of her early trials to the shining sky, she was not in stronger opposition to the black figure in the shade [Mrs. Clennam], than the life and doctrine on which she rested were to that figure's history" (pp. 770-71; bk. II, ch. 31). And her initials, A.D. (*anno Domini*—in the year of the Lord) help to set her at the center of the novel's providential structure.

Little Dorrit contains the last full-length portrait of the virtuous heroine in Dickens's novels, and it represents a major achievement in the providential aesthetic of his art. Amy Dorrit's important predecessors—Little Nell, Florence Dombey, Agnes Wickfield, Esther Summerson—all bear their double burden of humanity and immanence somewhat uneasily. Little Nell, perhaps, gets away with her allegorical function best because we are not asked (except by the omnivorous Quilp) to imagine her as sexually available or romantically aroused, and somehow our present expectations as readers of fiction still allow more freely for the symbolic or allegorical use of child characters.[26] The others borrow from their credibility as women to serve the spiritually renewing function of immanence figures, to show that there exists a larger system than the corrupt social one, to suggest a glimpse into the true order of things. This is the case even though Esther Summerson, as I have argued, contains a peculiar developmental logic of her own to help account for her use as a vehicle for such meanings and so gains in aesthetic dignity over Florence and Agnes.

But with Little Dorrit, however inadequate she may be as a realistic or naturalistic representation of womanhood, Dickens found a way to harmonize the immanence with the facts or

---

[26]Amy Dorrit is little, like Nell, but she is decidedly not a child. This is strikingly emphasized in her chance encounter with a prostitute: " 'Why, my God!' she said, recoiling, 'you're a woman!' 'Don't mind that!' said Little Dorrit" (p. 170; bk. I, ch. 14).

data or experiences of a character's history, and he did so by adjusting the circumstances of that history. From her birth through her childhood and into young womanhood, the sources of power and gratification are very limited for Amy Dorrit. But she does discover sources of gratification and power. When her father's rise in fortune obviates these, she misses them profoundly and remains true to them. She can be an angel of mercy to Clennam when he goes to debtor's prison because her importance in her own person has been derived from such a role, and she can be true to the self she has become in taking it again. When she loses her fortune she can bear it nobly because wealth has meant nothing but harrassment and indignity to her and because she loves Clennam, whose maturity, earnestness, and sincerity all suit him to her in readily understandable ways. Her virtue at the end coincides with truth to her life, to her past and present. This makes it none the less virtue, and Dickens's ability to realize this conjunction in *Little Dorrit* marks a considerable advance over his earlier handling of the type. The emblematic heroine is now also a woman.

In the three novels that follow *Little Dorrit* the duties of immanence are more diffused and the theme itself is somewhat muted. *Great Expectations*, although it deals profoundly with acceptance and rejection of personal history, contains no virtuous heroine (Biddy and Estella are both disqualified on different grounds). In *A Tale of Two Cities* Lucy Manette can scarcely be said to have a character of her own, and she is in this sense a regression. But she does pick up the theme of a continuity from the past through the present, especially for her father. "She was the golden thread that united him to a Past beyond his misery, and to a Present beyond his misery" (p. 110; bk. II, ch. 4). The metaphor of a golden thread linking past and present ("The Golden Thread" is the title of Book Two), a thread Lucy spins by her care and love, contrasts formally with the coded knitting of Madame Defarge, a design for the future wrought out of past indifference and outrage. The metaphorical question raised by the novel is that of which fabric will prove strongest, and the domestic solution as usual seems much more hopeful than the broader institutional one. But as we will see, the strong providential elements in *A Tale of Two Cities* and in *Great Expectations* are not borne by the heroines.

In *Our Mutual Friend* Bella Wilfer has almost nothing to offer in the way of immanence. She is, as her name suggests, an Estella gone too straight. But Lizzie Hexam's goodness, although it is not celebrated in obvious allegorical or symbolic allusion to Christ and New Testament doctrine like Esther Summerson's and Amy Dorrit's, stamps her in the tradition of the virtuous heroine as the novel's most intensely engaged agent in the providential design. She is a good witch, and her integrity serves as a kind of moral touchstone. Contact with her brings out Bella's good nature and her brother's selfishness. Her effect upon her lovers, in the mad pun her name suggests, is to "hex 'em" into a kind of moral polarity, Bradley Headstone toward evil and Eugene Wrayburn, who can see a little way past himself, eventually toward good.

More important, Lizzie Hexam picks up the theme of inner truth to the past celebrated in *Little Dorrit*. What practically qualifies her to save Eugene Wrayburn from drowning in the Thames is a skill learned as a waterman's daughter. It is part of her strong parallel to Amy Dorrit that she qualifies herself to save the man she loves by not forgetting, by staying close to the river. As she rows out to save Wrayburn she prays, "Now, merciful Heaven be thanked for that old time, and grant, O blessed Lord, that through thy wonderful workings it may turn to good at last!" (p. 768; bk. IV, ch. 6). Earlier she had said that she did not love the river, that she could not be far enough away from it to please herself, that some mysterious force kept her close to it: "It's no purpose of mine that I live by it still" (p. 278; bk. II, ch. 1). The force that keeps Lizzie by the river is love, first for her father and then for Jenny Wren. Her spiritual qualifications for saving Wrayburn grow out of this fidelity to those she has loved and the obligations she acknowledges in her memory of the past. Her brother Charley, like William Dorrit with his daughter Amy, would like her to get away from the river and "let bygones be bygones." When he asks her why she bothers with a "little witch" like Jenny, she points to the river and says, "Any compensation—restitution—never mind the word, you know my meaning. Father's grave" (p. 277; bk. II, ch. 1).

The Thames is symbolic throughout Dickens of time flowing out into eternity, and Lizzie's unwilled fidelity to the river represents her willed truth to the past. She does not forget; and her refusal to forget and get away forms a central part of the providential design of *Our Mutual Friend*. It belongs as well to Dickens's great and penetrating dramatic exploration of time and timelessness, an exploration that forms in one way or another the central thematic figure in each of his last four novels.

Immortality and the Decline of Poetic Justice

"Proof of a life to come must be given," says Lucy Snowe in *Villette*. "In fire and in blood, if needful, must that proof be written. In fire and in blood do we trace the record throughout nature. In fire and in blood does it cross our own experience" (II, 240; ch. 38). We have seen that Lucy regards the otherwise inexplicable inequity of her life as a part of this proof, that in the logic of the novel the only possible human explanation for her unmerited suffering—given her insistence on the existence of a divine order—lies in the necessity of a life to come. The history of her suffering, therefore, becomes a text for those who can read it, a text of fire and blood that "proves" the afterlife. But what makes *Villette* a radical departure from other and earlier novels that also premise a divine order of things is that Lucy's personal salvation has no explicit place in the text of the novel. It can only be deduced by means of an arcane logic accessible to people like Lucy herself, those who possess the keenest awareness of injustice combined with an unwavering belief in God's goodness, a persistent refusal to accede to the apparent absurdity of experience.

This does not mean that Lucy Snowe is the first character in English fiction to experience injustice, but that she may be the first principal character in English providential fiction to find no compensatory logic in her own suffering for her own sake. She discovers no motivating reward in it. The strangeness of this becomes clear when we look at such earlier victims of temporal injustice and unmerited suffering as Clarissa Harlowe. This heroine has a strong sense, especially after her rape, of being in the cosmic mainstream. Her example benefits those around her and she sees this and encourages it. She prepares elaborately for her own death with full regard for herself and with entire confidence in her own salvation. As Richardson put the question in his Postscript, "who that are in earnest in their profession of Christianity, but will rather envy than regret the triumphant death of Clarissa?" Her salvation is, in Christian terms, poetically just. It is a palpable event in the text; it allows Richardson to argue that there can be no true conflict between "Poetical Justice" and the providential intention as it works in the Christian history of his heroine.

Dickens's treatment of immortality, although it runs through the full course of his work from *Oliver Twist* to *Our Mutual Friend*, lies well within the range of possibilities set on either side by *Clarissa* and *Villette*. On the whole he employs the convention in ways traditional to providential fiction, though with his own boldness and emphasis. Nevertheless, his handling of the theme undergoes a development important to the deepening providential structure of his novels and therefore draws our attention here.

"A list of the killed, wounded, and missing amongst Mr. Dickens' novels," wrote Fitzjames Stephen in 1855, "would read like an *Extraordinary Gazette*. An interesting child runs as much risk there as any of the troops who stormed the Redan."[27] Readers hard pressed by the sentimental demands

---

[27]Stephen, *Cambridge Essays*, p. 174n.

of Dickens's moribund innocents still find relief in this kind
of ironic dismissal, and their reaction has not been qualified
by the fact that in most cases the text guarantees salvation for
the little victim.[28] The nameless and purposeless human casualties of the Crimean debacle (to adopt Stephen's clever comparison) must be lost to us gratuitiously and forever. But Little
Dick, Smike, Little Nell, little Paul Dombey, Jo, and Johnny
the orphan each ascend with varying degrees of ceremony to
their reward. Little Nell receives a baroque apotheosis, little
Paul drifts down the river of time to an oceanic eternity that
contains the explicit promise of immortality, Jo the outlaw
with the broom dies when "the light is come upon the dark
benighted way" (*Bleak House*, p. 572; ch. 47).

These characters receive "poetical justice" as Richardson represented it: their deaths are to be envied by those who "are in
earnest in their profession of Christianity" with its doctrine
of an afterlife. In this sense Little Nell's death is her real gain
and a celebration of the providential order. As the good schoolmaster says, "It is not on earth that Heaven's justice ends.
Think what it is compared with the World to which her young
spirit has winged its early flight, and say, if one deliberate wish
expressed in solemn terms above this bed could call her back
to life, which of us would utter it!" (p. 654; ch. 71). But this
kind of consolation, however richly supported by textual assertions that the heroine has seen her salvation, does not quite
do justice to our response, either to the fate of Little Nell or
to that of Clarissa Harlowe. If most readers, well-intentioned
readers as opposed, say, to the Oscar Wildes and the G.K.
Chestertons, wanted Nell or Clarissa to go directly to heaven
as painlessly as possible, there could be no pathos and no
novel.[29] So the death of innocents in Dickens and elsewhere

---

[28]See, for examples of this reaction, *Dickens: The Critical Heritage*, p. 85;
Ford, *Dickens and His Readers*, ch. 4; and Collins, "The Decline of Pathos."

[29]"According to Oscar Wilde, one must have a heart of stone to read the
death of Little Nell without laughing" (Ford, *Dickens and His Readers*, p. 55).
Chesterton said that "the death of Little Nell is not pathetic. It is perhaps
tragic; it is in reality ironic" (*Criticisms and Appreciations of the Works of
Charles Dickens* [London: J.M. Dent, 1933], p. 54).

only partially fulfills the injuction of poetic justice as I have formulated it: what a well-intentioned reader hopes for the characters.

But beyond this the heaven-bound victims in Dickens's providential aesthetic have a special and peculiar significance. They present an indictment of human justice, an expression of social outrage. Heaven takes over and gives them what they deserve when the world is through with them, when circumstances have sapped their last earthly hope and strength. The theme of immortality becomes an indictment of the way things are, of the way of the world. Immortality in the later novels is strongly linked to indignation. It shows divine benevolence, certainly; but it also tells us that we have acquiesced in a social order where human justice can no longer provide adequate protection and redress, that without powerful and benevolent friends innocence does run a terrible risk.[30] Dickens's use of immortality thus cuts two ways: it provides a traditional means of giving the moribund innocents what, according to the dictates of poetic justice, they deserve, and at the same time it denies that poetic justice as an aesthetic principle can be a formula adequate to represent temporal dispensation. It is a wedge that increasingly serves to separate the structural principles of poetic justice and providential intention in Dickens's novels.

Poetic justice, we have seen, is a kind of decorum. It premises a balanced relation between human beings and their circumstances. What they need, it suggests, has a great deal to do with what is available, and, on the other hand, what the world

[30]This, of course, goes not only for children but for certain adult characters. Sydney Carton in *A Tale of Two Cities* choses a death he does not deserve; so does Betty Higdon in *Our Mutual Friend*. They strike us as less sympathetic than the martyred children because they do choose, and they are sustained by a more controlled awareness of Christian resurrection and rebirth. More troubling than these are a handful of casualties in the Dickens canon who appear to fall through both nets, who do not meet with poetic justice or whose salvation is not a palpable event in the text. In what sense, for example, does Nancy the prostitute get what she deserves in *Oliver Twist*? Or Gridley the poor suitor in *Bleak House*? As we shall see, Dickens confronted this problem of apparent human waste directly in *Great Expectations* and offered the lesson of a proper response to it in the character of Magwitch.

offers them is suited to what they can be. Poetic justice assures us that we are not alien in our universe, that our human ethos lies at the heart of an ethical cosmos, and that when we reduce our perception of the world to a formal structure, like a novel, it is this relationship that stands out. It is therefore no accident that most English novels before Brontë and Dickens in which a providential intention can be discerned rely on the structural securities of poetic justice and that (for example) Richardson categorically refused to surrender them in his Postscript to *Clarissa*. Dickens, like Charlotte Brontë, did not rest with this but went on to make the distinction between poetic justice and divine justice that his apprehension of the temporal order entailed.

He made it explicitly in *Martin Chuzzlewit*:

> "You think of me, Ruth," said Tom, "and it is very natural that you should, as if I were a character in a book; and you make it a sort of poetical justice that I should, by some impossible means or other, come, at last, to marry the person I love. But there is a much higher justice than poetical justice, my dear, and it does not order events upon the same principle. Accordingly, people who read about heroes in books, and choose to make heroes of themselves out of books, consider it a very fine thing to be discontented and gloomy, and misanthropical, and perhaps a little blasphemous, because they cannot have everything ordered for their individual accommodation. Would you like me to become one of that sort of people?" (pp. 845-46; ch. 50)

Tom Pinch does not marry the person he loves and deserves. In fact he doesn't marry anybody. It must have seemed strange to read these words in 1844 in a novel that seems to be all about the use and misuse of fictions—Mrs. Gamp and her imaginary Mrs. Harris, Montague Tigg and his fraudulent assurance company, Mr. Pecksniff and his special providence. It must have been enough to make many readers wonder where the gratification of reading novels was going to come from.

The Good Man: Locating the Decorum

Tom Pinch is a good man, a good man who wakes up to the existence of evil in the world, to the fact that human goodness does not always right itself, that innocence left to itself does not always triumph. As he points out in the foregoing passage, he learns that poetic justice and the "much higher justice" do not necessarily correspond. This, for Pinch, is hard-won knowledge. He likes books—books in which the characters get what they deserve—and he likes to believe in a world where every man is a capital fellow. While he believed in Pecksniff as a being of transcendent virtue, a kind of surrogate providence, he could allow himself to be morally passive. When Pecksniff turns out to be a hypocrite, and one who preys on innocence, that world, the world animated by poetic justice, turns out to be an illusion: "An uneasy thought entered Tom's head; a shadowy misgiving that the altered relations between himself and Pecksniff were somehow to involve an altered knowledge on his part of other people, and were to give him an insight into much of which he had no previous suspicion" (p. 654; ch. 37).[31] The measure of Tom Pinch's goodness lies in his ability to accept his new awareness without the kind of bitterness that has poisoned the life of old Martin. He does not adopt the monstrous inversion of Jonas Chuzzlewit's "rule for bargains": "Do other men, for they would do you" (p. 241; ch. 11). Pecksniff has done him, but he does not go forth and do others. Instead he becomes morally active in the world— begins to protect himself and those he cares about—even while he continues to accept the conditions of his life. Of his hopeless

---

[31]There is a suggestive and parodic parallel between Tom's discovery that there exists no such Pecksniff as he had dreamed of and Betsy Prigg's malevolent but probably accurate assertion that "there's no sich person" as Mrs. Harris (p. 756; ch. 49), refuted by Mrs. Gamp by means of a flood of biographical detail.

love for Mary Graham he can tell his sister, "The realities about me are not to blame" (p. 846; ch.50).

Tom Pinch's "progress" is characteristic of that undergone by the good men in Dickens's fiction: a sense of harmony with the world is shattered or troubled by some experience or series of experiences, some *imposition* which ultimately leads to greater wisdom and caution and which forms the basis of their moral action. Mr. Pickwick, Gabriel Varden, Mr. Peggotty, Dr. Strong, John Jarndyce, Arthur Clennam, Dr. Manette, Mr. Boffin, and others all participate to varying degrees in this pattern. In some, like Clennam and Manette, the scars are deep and the changes profound. Others, like Pickwick and Boffin, emerge almost unaltered. In some cases we follow their development all the way through; others, like Jarndyce, come before us with most of the crucial experience behind them. In each case, however, the lesson learned is what to make of a world which is devoid of the laws of poetic justice but which nevertheless shows signs of supreme significance, which contains goodness, and which therefore demands moral engagement. Or, to put the question strictly in terms of this study, the good man in Dickens shows how we can locate the fictional decorum, that reciprocal action of oneself and the world essential to the novel's providential structure.

In *David Copperfield* the two good men, Mr. Peggotty and Dr. Strong, serve as models for the protagonist in his development toward moral autonomy and self-discipline. Although they cannot be said to develop in the sense that David does—they come before us initially at too high a level for that—they both participate largely in the pattern set by Tom Pinch. Dr. Strong, wrenched from his domestic harmony by the machinations of Uriah Heep, realizes acutely the grave emotional risks in the apparent disparity between himself and his young wife, remains nevertheless true to his own honor by steadfastly refusing to credit the aspersions on hers, and ultimately finds himself rewarded by means of Mr. Dick's benign intervention. Mr. Peggotty loses Little Emily at his moment of rejoicing in her engagement to Ham, takes upon himself the task of seeking her through the world, and finds her at last with the help of the formerly despised Martha. He is sustained throughout his search by a supernatural assurance: "I doen't know where it comes from, or how 'tis, but *I am told* as she's alive!" (p. 576; ch. 46). When she has been found, he says, "I thank my Heav'nly Father as my dream's come true! I thank Him hearty for having guided of me, in His own ways, to my darling!" (p. 618; ch. 50).

The pattern of David Copperfield's own development is drawn much more elaborately than these models, but in general it conforms to them. His marriage to Dora contains dangers to which he is blind, dangers of "unsuitability of mind and purpose." David sees a troubling application to himself in this phrase of Annie Strong's and in her allusion to her childhood infatuation with Jack Maldon as "the first mistaken impulse of an undisciplined heart" (p. 567; ch. 45). David's spiritual growth entails the disciplining of his heart, the strengthening of a quality his aunt sees as nascent in him. She calls it learning to be a "fine, firm fellow, with a will of your own," developing "resolution," "determination," "character," "reliance upon yourself" (pp. 234-35; ch. 19). She sees that he lacks earnestness of some kind, "deep, downright, faithful earnestness" (p. 430; ch. 35).

The development of this quality of earnestness—*David Copperfield* asserts at the high noon of Dickens's career the transcendent importance of being earnest—is what all of David's experience aims at. He must learn that somewhere between the "firmness" of the Murdstones and the urgent self-indulgence of his own romance with Dora (too similar in motive to Steerforth's infatuation with Emily) lies that responsibility to the deep seriousness of life represented for him by the figure of Agnes. He approaches this condition through suffering, through a masterfully contrived combination of bereavement and disillusion. He goes abroad to cope with what has happened to him, spiritually dismantled. "As a man upon a field of battle will receive a mortal hurt, and scarcely know that he is struck, so I, when I was left alone with my undisciplined heart, had no conception of the wound with which it had to strive" (p. 696; ch. 58). His depression is summarized in two unmemorable pages and his recovery begins with an awakening to the beauty of the human and natural landscape: "Great Nature spoke to me." He opens a letter and sees "the writing of Agnes" who tells him that his own nature will "turn affliction to good" and that through suffering he will "gain a firmer and higher tendency" (p. 648; ch. 58). He follows her advice: "I sought out Nature, never sought in vain; and I admitted to my breast the human interest I had lately shrunk from" (p. 699; ch. 58). He begins to think of Agnes as a woman. The natural world operates, as it does in *Jane Eyre*, to help awaken the protagonist to romantic love, although in this case with a domestic angel. He contracts the illusion that she has set her heart on another and in the generosity of his mature earnestness disciplines his heart to selfless affection ("There is no alloy of self in what I feel for you," p. 737; ch. 62), thus proving that he has come at last to deserve her, that he has achieved a spiritual level not disproportionately below her own. After some salutary torture of himself, of Agnes, and of his readers, David realizes his mistake, reaps his reward, and like Mr. Peggotty acknowledges the providential pattern in his life: "The early stars began to shine while we were lingering on, and looking up to them, we thanked our God for having guided us to this tranquility" (p. 739; ch. 62). He can locate the decorum for us; he has become a good man.[32]

These last seven chapters of *David Copperfield*—while they place the hero in the pattern of illusion, imposition, awareness, moral action, and acceptance—seem to me to possess a curiously flat, forced quality, as of the finishing off of a structure no longer fully congenial to the author's vision. However accurate this impression might be, *David Copperfield* is Dickens's last attempt at a straightforward providential fiction, one

---

[32]Stanley Friedman puts it this way: "By emphasizing not any exceptional abilities he might have, but instead merely his effort and perseverance, traits that he suggests all might develop, David Copperfield establishes himself as Everyman, and his autobiography, by justifying the ways of God as seen in David's own life, becomes a theodicy asserting eternal providence and counseling us to be guided by faith, virtue, patience, temperance, and love" ("Dickens' Mid-Victorian Theodicy: *David Copperfield*," *Dickens Studies Annual*, 7 [1978], 150).

which ends with poetic justice for almost everybody and in which most of the suffering is, if not poetically just throughout, of the salutary or spiritually uplifting kind. This is Dickens's last novel where simple love and truth seem to win out decisively over the world's wickedness, where simple Mr. Dick can save the Strong marriage, where a prostitute devotes herself to saving a fallen woman, where a chronic failure like Micawber can outmaneuver and explode the chief embodiment of evil, where even the Byronic Steerforth believes in goodness and wishes he had it.

"The universe," says John Jarndyce in Dickens's next novel, "makes rather an indifferent parent" (p. 68; ch. 6). It is difficult to imagine anybody in *David Copperfield* saying this. As we have seen, the drama of circumstances in *Bleak House* lies between the evidences for a benevolent unifying connectedness in human affairs, a vision of humanity as a great family, and the natural forces of decomposition and their allies in certain social institutions of which Chancery is the primary embodiment. John Jarndyce as the organizing figure "the picture of a good man" (p. 762; ch. 65), has had to develop quite a different sense of decorum from that of Mr. Peggotty or Dr. Strong—more isolated, reserved, defensive. He comes before the reader with his own experience of the dangers of the world; he has learned from the experience of others, from the suicide of his great-uncle Tom Jarndyce; and he knows that no trust can be placed in chance, that once a *will* is resigned to *Chancery* (to take up the novel's dominating pun), ruin follows. "Trust in nothing but in Providence and your own efforts," he tells Richard Carstone, "Never separate the two" (p. 162; ch. 13). He retains his faith in the efficacy of the individual will and in human benevolence (which is why he can be imposed upon by Skimpole),[33] but he also acknowledges the dark circumstances of life. In his world leaving things to Chancery, like

---

[33]See George Ford's "Self-Help and the Helpless in *Bleak House*," *From Jane Austen to Joseph Conrad*, ed. Robert C. Rathburn and Martin Steinmann Jr. (Minneapolis: Univ. of Minnesota Press, 1958), pp. 93, 103-4.

gambling, means abdicating responsibility for moral action, an abdication that produces infectious pockets of social and spiritual decay like Tom-all-Alone's, itself a property in the suit. He sees that the best one can make of life in the world is to reconstruct Bleak House as a home in opposition to the alienation of Tom-all-Alone's, to lay down a kind of moral fortification from which charitable excursions into the world may be made and to which one can retreat like Allen Woodcourt and Esther at the end of the day.

Most critical approaches to *Bleak House* lead (like the names of Miss Flite's birds) toward a hectic reduction of their own subject matter to social and metaphysical ultimata. We have seen that the third-person narration constantly poses the threat that there may be no true order of things, that life is a matter of chance and Chancery, that temporal existence at best is a bleak house, that there is no meaningful sequence, casuality, connection, and that everything is in process of spontaneous combustion. In opposing this threat, the character of John Jarndyce locates the decorum for us not just in his language and moral action but, like Esther and the other virtuous heroines, ontologically. He becomes an embodiment as well as an agent of the providential forces.[34] In Esther's reverential phrasing, "I felt as if the brightness on him must be like the brightness of the angels" (p. 752; ch. 64). Jarndyce's goodness provides a peculiar luminousness, a hearthfire in a fictional edifice that Dickens's readers after *David Copperfield* must have found suddenly and dramatically darker.

Jarndyce has learned that poetic justice cannot be counted on and that the intimations of that "higher justice" which Tom Pinch spoke of in *Martin Chuzzlewit* are primarily intimations that offer no guarantees concerning the circumstances of his world. Tom Pinch, even after his disillusionment, has assured

---

[34]Hillis Miller's qualification may be in order here: "And there is a true Providence in *Bleak House*. It does not, however, work within things, nor does it work within all men, nor in any man all of the time. It appears to be intermittent, even though it may secretly be continuous" (*Charles Dickens: The World of His Novels* [Cambridge: Harvard Univ. Press, 1959], p. 218).

Mrs. Lupin that "all is certain to come right at last" (p. 632; ch. 36).[35] In *Martin Chuzzlewit* and the other novels before *Bleak House*, this works out to be generally true, allowing for an important casualty here or there. In the later novels, however, the failure of poetic justice is not just a matter of never marrying the person one deserves. It is a matter of being driven mad (Ridley, Miss Flite), of acknowledging that your life has been wasted (Magwitch, Miss Havisham), and of willed personal sacrifice (Sydney Carton).

Dr. Manette in *A Tale of Two Cities* has most of the characteristics of the good men in Dickens's earlier novels. Unfortunately, he also cherishes an anachronistic view of the order of things, a view designed to give his years of imprisonment significance, to render them less useless, less absurd. In Paris during the revolution he seeks to use his influence with the populace—influence derived from his status as an innocent victim of the old regime—to free his son-in-law Charles Darnay:

> For the first time the Doctor felt, now, that his suffering was strength and power. For the first time he felt that in that sharp fire, he had slowly forged the iron which could break the prison door of his daughter's husband, and deliver him. "It all tended to a good end, my friend; it was not mere waste and ruin. As my beloved child was helpful in restoring me to myself, I will be helpful now in restoring the dearest part of herself to her; by the aid of Heaven, I will do it!" (p. 300; bk. III, ch. 4)

Dr. Manette reveals here the balance-sheet mentality characteristic of adherents to poetic justice. He wants to believe that his innocent suffering will yield a proportionate amount of power and happiness, that just as others help us so we are

---

[35]In 1846 Dickens is still intent on reassuring his readers that poetic justice will in the main be done. At the end of the preceding chapter Mark Tapley has said to Martin, "It'll all come right in the end, sir; it'll all come right" (p. 628).

empowered to help them, that wrongs done in past generations must be set right in this.

By recognizing his delusion, we can see that the balance sheet of poetic justice bears a disturbing affinity to the retributive justice of the revolutionaries, who refer their actions to an ethic of revenge. They hold that just as they have been persecuted collectively so they have the right to persecute. *A Tale of Two Cities* suggests that one danger of linking the providential intention with poetic justice lies in strong ethical parallels between this linkage and doctrines of retributive justice. Both rely on essentially quantative measures, and such measures constitute a false decorum. Dr. Manette does not see this because he has not healed completely, as his tendency to regress into his prison-self as shoemaker indicates. When he gains apparent mental and physical strength in revolutionary Paris, he develops an illusion of power: "Little Lucie sat by her grandfather with her hands clasped through his arm: and he, in a tone not rising much above a whisper, began to tell her a story of a great and powerful Fairy who had opened a prison-wall and let out a captive who had once done the Fairy a service" (p. 319, bk. III, ch.7). But even before he finishes his fairy tale there comes the knock on the door and Darnay is retaken. This time he is convicted by Manette's own retributive indictment, written in the tenth year of his imprisonment and denouncing his enemies as abandoned by God "to the last of their race" (p. 361; bk. III, ch. 10).

Dr. Manette fails to locate the true decorum in part because his vision of things, his fairy tale of poetic justice, places him presumptuously (though pathetically) at the center of the providential intention. In this he differs from such figures as John Jarndyce and Arthur Clennam, who remain true to the past without enlisting it in the service of their own vanity, without devising a circumstantial design which promotes their centrality in the order of things. The providential aesthetic of *A Tale of Two Cities* rejects poetic justice in favor of sacrifice. This novel, which has sometimes been put aside as a sentimental excursion from the Dickensian mainstream (it falls between *Little Dorrit* and *Great Expectations*), makes a tough ethical and spiritual point. Retributive justice can only be countered by sacrifice; the one action that totally confounds the balance sheet lies in the sacrifice of the innocent for the innocent; and the power to execute this action derives not from some schematic calculation drawn from past experience but from the ability and willingness to transcend it. Or, to relate the movement to the terminology I have been employing, poetic justice—the meting out of merited punishments and rewards—is indicted as morally and aesthetically bankrupt in a circumstantial world dominated by retribution, and the good man—he who locates the decorum—is not simply someone who discovers a pattern in the text of his own experience but someone who in the ultimate moment wipes the slate clean, who wills the sacrifice, effects the substitution. Sydney Carton manages this at the end; and those final words of his which now sound so hackneyed to us stress the newness of his experience, its "betterness," and locate the decorum of a novel whose central motif is resurrection rather than repetition.[36]

So far in this chapter I have approached Dickens's development of a providential aesthetic in his novels through various of its aspects, including certain techniques of narration (person, tense), certain thematic preoccupations (chance, immanence, the bifurcation of providential design from poetic justice), and the sophistication of certain character types (nihilists, virtuous heroines, good men). This approach is practical for the examination of discrete characteristics throughout the range of Dickens's fiction, and I have tried to make it clear that these

[36]Joseph Gold analyzes the resurrection motif in *Charles Dickens: Radical Moralist* (Minneapolis: Univ. of Minnesota Press, 1972), pp. 231–40. The good men of Dickens's last two novels, Joe Gargery in *Great Expectations* and Noddy Boffin in *Our Mutual Friend*, combine the important ways the qualities of their forerunners in the type. Their virtue derives from the use they have made of past suffering. They know that the circumstances of their world offer no assurance that vice is consistently punished and virtue regularly rewarded. They both dispense mercy and kindness without counting. They are capable of sacrifice. And they both advance the function of the good man in Dickens's fiction by locating the decorum for the reader in different ways. Their roles are discussed in the readings which follow.

all in one way or another affect the structure of the novels in question. But the integrity and centrality of the providential aesthetic as it governs individual texts requires some demonstration of its own if its complex allegiance to the novel as a genre is to be appreciated. In the remainder of this chapter I offer brief readings of five novels—*Oliver Twist, Dombey and Son, Little Dorrit, Great Expectations,* and *Our Mutual Friend*— in order to show the various aspects of Dickens's providential aesthetic as they work together in the service of unity and form.

Oliver Twist

Oliver Twist is Dickens's first fully plotted novel, and one that makes almost entirely traditional use of a providential design. The plot itself premises and reveals a providence (closely allied with the narrator) that has set out (like him) to test Oliver, to show him "surviving every adverse circumstance and triumphant at last." As Rose Maylie tells Mr. Grimwig, "He is a child of a noble nature and a warm heart . . . and that Power which has thought fit to try him beyond his years, has planted in his breast affections and feelings which would do honor to many who have numbered his days six times over."[37] Against Oliver's preternatural virtue the evil forces in the world can make no headway, and even the refreshingly intelligent Fagin presents little threat to this inner strength.

Providence not only secures Oliver from within; it directs external circumstances and events. What Edgar Johnson characterizes as a "complex rigmarole" is demonstrably a rigmarole arranged from above.[38] The coincidences in the plot point to a causality beyond the naturalistic. Nancy overhears the villain Monks complain that "it seemed contrived by Heaven, or the devil, against him" that Oliver should fall into the hands of the Maylies (p. 363; ch. 40). "There was some cursed spell, I

---

[37]Preface to the 3d ed., quoted by Edgar Johnson, *Dickens,* I, 281; *Oliver Twist,* ed. Peter Fairclough (Harmondsworth: Penguin, 1966), p. 370; ch. 41.

[38]Edgar Johnson, *Dickens,* I, 280.

think, against us," he admits (p. 463; ch. 51), thus supporting the position articulated by Mr. Brownlow that Oliver has been placed under his protection "by a stronger hand than chance" (p. 438; ch. 49). The narrator himself points the *sentence* for the evildoers; "Let not man talk of murderers escaping justice, and hint that Providence must sleep" (p. 428, ch. 48). Or in Monks's pithy summary, "Blood! How things come about!" (p. 340; ch. 38).

Monks's astonishment stamps him as a character who has failed to see that he participates in a providential decorum. This is true of Fagin as well with his philosophy of "number one." Unfortunately for them the forces of virtue and the power of benevolent human will are socially stronger and more established in *Oliver Twist* than in any succeeding Dickens novel. Evil here lurks in enclaves and corners, waits for nightfall, calls itself by pseudonyms, speaks in dialect, and in the end is hunted out by the enraged mob or falls to brutal official punishment. Even socially sanctioned abuses, like the orphanages and workhouses, are, by comparison with the pervasive social degeneracy of the later novels, contained and isolated. Murderer and master thief, whoremaster and minion, cowardly beadles with their Good Samaritan buttons and corrupt matrons who cheat the paupers, all come to poetic justice. And although this is not done with mathematical scrupulousness—Noah Claypole escapes while Nancy falls victim to Sikes's brutality— the forces of good in the world of *Oliver Twist* seem teased rather than threatened. The "little society" of good people formed at the novel's end nestles in a world which shows no sign of imposing upon it.[39]

But as is usual in providential fiction *Oliver Twist* contains events and circumstances that seem to threaten the premise that God's will controls its world, and characters and readers must learn to interpret them correctly. The most challenging of these threats lurks in the elaborately posed juxtaposition of

---

[39]Bert Hornback observes that "what the mythology of *Oliver Twist* does is pretend to prove the Christian faith in heaven, by means of its local institution, finally, here on earth" (*"Noah's Arkitecture": A Study of Dickens' Mythology* [Athens, Ohio: Ohio Univ. Press, 1972], p. 18).

the prostitute Nancy with Rose Maylie. In childhood Nancy was left bereft of friends, cold and hungry, and Fagin found her and put her to his own uses. Rose was abandoned to poor cottagers who had just begun to tire of their charge when Mrs. Maylie found and adopted her. Why should one be lost and the other saved? We are faced with an explicit inequity. "Thank heaven on your knees, dear lady," says Nancy in their memorable confrontation, "that you had friends to care for and keep you in your childhood, and that you were never in the midst of cold and hunger, and riot and drunkenness, and—and—something worse than all—as I have been from my cradle" (p. 362; ch. 40). She leads us to the elemental questions: Where is the even hand of providence in all this? Where is justice? How can we respect a dispensation in which love brings one woman lasting happiness while it leads another to violent death?

Dickens anticipates these difficulties by planting in the novel a discussion of their traditional solution, the doctrine of immortality and reward after death. Rose Maylie's sudden and unexplained illness can have little other pertinence to the thematic structure of the novel than this.[40] It stimulates discussion of the disparity between what human beings can perceive as just and what may be allotted them by providence. Rose, we are told, "was in the lovely bloom and spring-time of womanhood; at that age, when, if ever angels be for God's purposes enthroned in mortal forms, they may be, without impiety, supposed to abide in such as hers" (p. 264; ch. 29). In other words she is a comparatively faceless prototype of the virtuous heroine and serves briefly as an emblem of immanent goodness. Oliver, who shares the latter function with her, opines that because of this goodness "Heaven will never let her die so young." This infantile providentialism reminds Mrs. Maylie of her "duty" to tell Oliver that "it is not always the youngest and best who are spared to those that love them; but this should give us comfort in our sorrow; for Heaven is just; and such things teach us, impressively, that there is a brighter world

---

[40]Though, no doubt, Dickens based it on Mary Hogarth's sudden fatal illness.

than this; and that the passage to it is speedy" (p. 295; ch. 33).[41] But Rose makes a recovery "little short of a miracle" (p. 298; ch. 33), and it is left for Nancy to embark on the speedy passage, to suffer the fate which makes the point that love and courage do not always meet with a just reward in the here and now.

The dramatization in Nancy's murder of the explanation that is developed during Rose's illness may not be artistically or socially courageous. Nancy after all brings it on herself by returning to the ruthless Sikes,[42] and anyway prostitutes are morally liable to violence. These no doubt are easy moves meant to satisfy an audience expecting poetic justice. But the providential structure of the novel is not impaired by them. Nancy dies with a prayer on her lips lifting Rose Maylie's white handkerchief in her folded hands "as high towards Heaven as her feeble strength would allow" (p. 423; ch. 47). This, we cannot doubt, is acceptable repentance. It looks forward to the last paragraph of the novel where the narrator imagines the spirit of Oliver's deceived and ruined mother benignly haunting a tablet which bears her name: "I believe," says the narrator, "that the shade of Agnes sometimes hovers round that solemn nook. I believe it none the less because that nook is in a Church, and she was weak and erring" (p. 480; ch. 53). Nancy too was weak and erring. There is a place in the Christian scheme for her spirit as well. In the straightforward providentialism of *Oliver Twist* almost everything fits.

Dombey and Son

Almost everything fits in *Dombey and Son* too, but the design is more complicated and less intrusive. In an age when a providential habit of mind does not form a part of our intellectual

[41]Henry Maylie repeats this view of things to Rose herself two chapters later (pp. 214–15).

[42]Dickens defended Nancy's devotion in a famous preface to *Oliver Twist* written in 1841: "the last fair drop of water at the bottom of the weed-choked well" (p. 37).

bias, the novel has seemed to lack clarity of structure. In *Dombey and Son* the providential vision is pervasive and organic throughout; it shapes the novel and holds it together; it serves as a highly controlled unifying aesthetic.

Dombey's character is the *axis mundi* of the work. He begins the novel and as its title character speaks the title line: " 'The house will once again, Mrs. Dombey,' said Mr. Dombey, 'be not only in name but in fact Dombey and Son; Dom-bey and Son!' " (p. 1; ch. 1). Much attention is called to the name as it is reiterated to form the keynote of the opening pages. It is suggestive of Bombay, redolent of a prosperous Eastern trade, but more important it makes us think of dominion, domination, lordship, and mastery. It echoes the Latin word for lord, *dominus,* and for house, *domus.* Dombey's lordly idea of his "house" tells us immediately that there is something wrong:

> Those three words conveyed the one idea of Mr. Dombey's life. The earth was made for Dombey and Son to trade in, and the sun and the moon were made to give them light. Rivers and seas were formed to float their ships; rainbows gave them promise of fair weather; winds blew for or against their enterprises; stars and planets circled in their orbits, to preserve inviolate a system of which they were the centre. Common abbreviations took new meanings in his eyes, and had sole reference to them. A.D. had no concern with anno Domini, but stood for anno Dombei—and Son. (p. 2; ch. 1)

In other words Dombey has a false conception of the proper decorum of his world and his place in it. He sees himself as its providence. "Dombey and Son know neither time, nor place, nor season," says Mr. Carker in his parodic flattery, "but bear them all down" (p. 506; ch. 37).

It is characteristic of Dombey—as of other self-appointed providence figures in Dickens—to be impatient with the ordinary course of events. He chafes during little Paul's childhood, wishing him already grown and dependent only upon himself: "I am enough for him, perhaps, and all in all" (p. 49; ch. 5).

He shows contempt for the christening service, and the narrator tells us that "his arrogance contrasted strangely with its history" (p. 60; ch. 5). For Dombey the father and the son are one: "Mr. Dombey's young child was, from the beginning, so distinctly important to him as a part of his own greatness, or (which is the same thing) of the greatness of Dombey and Son" (p. 92; ch. 8). Thus, to worship the son is to worship the father, as Mrs. Chick and Miss Tox energetically apprehend.

This hectic perversion of Christian devotional practice is carried still farther. Because Dombey and Son as the "house" is bound up with Dombey's own greatness, then in venerating the house, as Mrs. Chick and Miss Tox also undertake to do, characters venerate its lord: " 'My dear Paul,' returned his sister, 'you do Miss Tox but justice, as a man of your penetration was sure, I knew, to do. I believe if there are three words in the English language for which she has a respect amounting almost to veneration, those words are Dombey and Son' " (p. 47; ch. 5). Perch, the confidential messenger of the firm, feels rather than sees Mr. Dombey's presence for "he had usually an instinctive sense of his approach." Perch does not dare to proclaim his devotion in words but "in his manner, You are the Light of my Eyes. You are the Breath of my Soul. You are the Commander of the Faithful Perch" (p. 171; ch. 13). Carker is master of the devotional mode, in part because his hypocrisy and his knowledge of his master's weakness permit him to press it well beyond the limits of the satirical and into the realm of the burlesque: " 'Oh! *I* degraded!' exclaimed Carker. 'In *your* service! . . . a wish from you is, of course, paramount to every other consideration on earth' " (p. 575; ch. 42).[43]

In Edith, Dombey confronts a pride almost as rigid and destructive as his own, but one that draws its strength from consciousness of having been touched too much rather than that of being out of reach. Contact with her has for Dombey

---

[43]Of Dombey's servants only Susan Nipper rebels: "Ordering one's self lowly and reverently towards one's betters, is not to be a worshipper of graven images, and I will and must speak!" (p. 589; ch. 44).

as dangerous an effect as the devotions of the toadies. This again is because Dombey thinks of himself as a god. The narrator explains that "it is the curse of such a nature . . . that while deference and concession swell its evil qualities, and are the food it grows upon, resistance, and a questioning of its exacting claims, foster it too, no less" (p. 538; ch. 40). Edith fails to perceive what for Dombey seems the obvious fact of his primacy in the order of things: "I think you scarcely understand who and what I am, Mrs. Dombey" (p. 540; ch. 40). And of his omnipotence: "I am not to be trifled with. Mrs. Dombey must understand that my will is law, and that I cannot allow of one exception to the whole rule of my life." And of his centrality to the decorum: "Mrs. Dombey does not appear to understand . . . that the idea of opposition to Me is monstrous and absurd" (p. 570; ch. 42).

In thus characterizing Dombey's pride, Dickens was of course satirizing the purse-proud merchantilism of British middle-class society, that view of the world, that false decorum, in which buying and selling, possession and exploitation extend to all relations of life and especially to family life. In presenting Dombey's view of things in the language of Christian devotional practice—father, son, house of worship—he was able to generalize a social evil with a power he had not found before. Dombey's view of his world is a providential view—false because it places him at the center—and this gives it a new resonance. Unlike the wickedness in *Oliver Twist*, the evil in *Dombey and Son* is respectable. The dominant principle of social organization is money, and the structure of Dombey's society is a hierarchy based on wealth. All this corresponds to his notion of the proper order of things. In reaction to it readers accustomed to providential fiction seek as the novel develops some kind of counterorder, a true order of things that can discredit the loveless aridities of Dombey's "house."

Ironically appropriate to a novel in which the social nexus is mercantile, the dominant symbolic motif for the true order of things is the sea. From the opening chapter the sea stands for the eternal, the timeless, the immortal in opposition to the vain and transient. The first Mrs. Dombey "drifted out upon the dark and unknown sea that rolls round all the world" (p 11; ch. 1). Little Paul looks out to sea, wonders what the waves are saying, and goes out down the river of time to the eternal sea (p. 225; ch. 16). Captain Cuttle, drawing on Psalm 107, tells Florence, "It's a almighty element. There's wonders in the deep, my pretty" (p. 657; ch. 49), and a few days after her marriage the sight of the sea makes Florence think of her dead brother and of her living husband: "And the voices in the waves are always whispering to Florence, in their ceaseless murmuring, of love—of love, eternal and illimitable, not bounded by the confines of this world, or by the end of time, but ranging still, beyond the sea, beyond the sky, to the invisible country far away!" (p. 773; ch. 57).

But in the spacious providential design of *Dombey and Son* the symbolic function of this motif is transformed into a literal one. The sea takes away and the sea gives back. Little Paul dies and Walter Gay returns from shipwreck. Walter represents the redeemed promise, "a lad of promise—a lad over-flowing," in the parabolic misquotation of Captain Cuttle, "with milk and honey" (p. 133; ch. 10). Carker sends Walter off in the *Son and Heir*, and he returns to marry Florence and become the son of the ruined house. Like the god with whom he confuses himself, Dombey loses a son; he does not perceive the redeemed pledge in Walter Gay until he has associated Florence with her brother in his mind and heart (p. 798; ch. 59). Walter inherits Florence's love, first as a brother and then, after his sea-change, as a husband. He becomes the instrument of the resurrection of the house. " 'Thus,' " explains Mr. Toots, trying to quote his wife Susan, " 'from his daughter, after all, another Dombey and Son will ascend'—no 'rise'; that was Mrs. Toot's word—'triumphant' " (p. 832; ch. 62).

It is a consummation that Captain Cuttle had anticipated all along in his aspirations for the lovers: "There's a son gone: pretty little creetur. . . . Pass the word, and there's another ready for you . . . who—comes from Sol Gills's daily, *to* your business, and your buzzums" (p. 232; ch. 17). This design of loss and restoration forms the pattern of the work, and the

key to the design lies in a proper understanding of the significance of Walter Gay's return.[44] Captain Cuttle, whose mis-
quotations enrich the original texts, identifies his young friend:
"Wal'r . . . is what you may call a out'ard and visible sign of
a in'ard and spirited grasp, and when found make a note of"
(p. 322; ch. 23). Cuttle's note would refer us to the Book of
Common Prayer and its definition of a sacrament: "an outward
and spiritual sign of an inward and spiritual grace given unto
us, ordained by Christ himself, as a means whereby we receive
the same and a pledge to assure us thereof."[45]

"There's a moral in everything, if we would only avail ourselves of it," observes the portentous Mrs. Chick (p. 11; ch. 2).
Or, as she asserts later, "there's a providence in everything;
everything works for the best" (p. 406; ch. 29).[46] This is more
than a little simplistic, passing over as it does the ruined lives
of such characters as Alice Brown and her more prominent
analogue Edith Dombey. But once the basic providential structure is apprehended, the actions of the characters peripheral
to it become significant. Edith, for example, blocks the schemes

[44]Dickens's early indecision as to what to make of Walter, perhaps to show
him sinking into dishonesty and ruin (Forster, *Life*, II, 25–26), need not
qualify this. As the two endings of *Great Expectations* show, he could make
significant alternations as he developed his themes. Kathleen Tillotson defends
Dombey and Son's planning convincingly. She sees that "in all its recurrences
the sea is charged with its inevitable associations of separation and reunion,
death and eternal life" (*Novels of the Eighteen-Forties*, p. 189).

[45]The words are casually echoed a second time in *Dombey and Son*, p. 814;
ch. 60. Dickens's readers would of course be apt to recognize these allusions,
and they seem to me essential to an understanding of the novel's structure.
Of course this does not invalidate persuasive psychological analyses of its
resolutions, as for example Arlene M. Jackson's "Reward, Punishment, and
the Conclusion of *Dombey and Son*," *Dickens Studies Annual*, 7 (1978), 103–
27.

[46]At one point Edith's "Cousin Feenix" (parodic pun on the resurrection
motif) agrees: "Events do occur in quite a Providential manner" (p. 685;
ch. 51). Some time after this we find him in ashes again "because, in point
of fact, one does see, in this world—which is remarkable for devilish strange
arrangements, and for being decidedly the most unintelligible thing within
a man's experience—very odd conjunctions" (p. 825; ch. 61).

Carker has for Florence by becoming herself the object of his lust and ambition. Her social disgrace is at once a punishment for having sold herself in a loveless marriage and a kind of sacrifice that redeems her. Thus in her marriage to Dombey we see the providential intention at work bringing good out of evil—though of course without justifying the willful perversion of natural gifts implicit in Edith's moral prostitution. And perhaps it should be acknowledged that Carker's poetically just fate does not seem to set right the lifetime of suffering Alice Brown endures, leaving her at the end a Magdalene figure subject to the charity and religious instruction of the noble Harriet Carker. Alice dies virtuous, more repentant than Edith, but both of them may be seen as casualties to their own pride and to a world that encourages the sale of women and children.

Florence Dombey's function as a virtuous heroine and harbinger of divine mercy has been treated in an earlier section of this chapter. A host of more ordinary Christians moves through *Dombey and Son*: Sol Gills, whose name reminds us at once of sun and sea and who has "to wait the fulness of the time and the design" (p. 830; ch. 62); Mr. Toots, whose kindness cannot be expressed in language; Harriet Carker, who mends the broken feet of the Magdalene; the upright Toodles; Miss Tox, who finds her proper sphere. But the most remarkable for my purpose is Captain Cuttle, really Florence's spiritual father, the comic antithesis of Mr. Carker, and the scrupulous reader of the scriptures and prayerbook. He accepts the acts of God, never doubting that "if Providence had doomed [Walter] to be lost and shipwrecked, it was over, long ago" (p. 455; ch. 32), but he recognizes a sacrament when he sees it in the street and knows that the sea is an "almighty element" and no mere avenue for trade. "Faith, hope, and charity, shared his whole nature among them. An odd sort of romance, perfectly unimaginative, yet perfectly unreal, and subject to no considerations of worldly prudence or practicability, was the only partner they had in his character" (pp. 652–53; ch. 49). Dickens is stressing here a spiritual affinity between Captain Cuttle and Florence. The glazed hat, an important signature, leaves a red rim around the captain's head; and, if we had not guessed it before, the narrator tells us in the final chapter that "there is a very halo of delight round his glowing forehead" (p. 829; ch. 62). It is he who embodies the comic affirmation of a providential universe and who pipes the keynote of the early novels: " 'Cap'en Cuttle is my name, and England is my nation, this here is my dwelling-place, and blessed be creation—Job,' said the Captain, as an index to his authority" (p. 442; ch. 32).

Little Dorrit

We have seen that in Dickens's fiction a tension develops between the conventions of poetic justice and his representation of the "ways of providence." After *David Copperfield* this tension becomes a conflict or disjunction as the providential intention appears less frequently in generalized social reflections of cosmic order and relies more heavily on discrete manifestations of divine immanence. The providential aesthetic becomes radical, at once more brilliantly specific and more disturbingly abstract. The dominant cosmic harmonics of the early works sharpen off and are replaced by sudden disconsonant epiphanies.

In *Little Dorrit* the central providential pattern is traced by means of a dramatic shifting of perspective, a transformation of the way circumstances are perceived. This shift results in part from the education and development of certain characters and in part from a change in the allusive parabolic emphases of the narration itself. Near the novel's end Amy Dorrit counters Mrs. Clennam's Old Testament retributive justice with a short sermon on the New Testament doctrine of forgiveness and love; then, as she accompanies the old woman to her home on an errand of mercy, nature cooperates in illuminating her message, and the ruthless sun, a "great flaming jewel of fire" in the first chapter, a blinding "universal stare" (p. 1), gently lights the human world with a sign from the true order of things:

As they crossed the bridge, the clear steeples of the many churches looked as if they had advanced out of the murk that usually enshrouded them and come much nearer. The smoke that rose into the sky had lost its dingy hue and taken a brightness upon it. The beauties of the sunset had not faded from the long light films of cloud that lay at peace in the horizon. From a radiant centre, over the whole length and breadth of the tranquil firmament, great shoots of light streamed among the early stars, like signs of the blessed later covenant of peace and hope that changed the crown of thorns into a glory. (p. 771; bk. II, ch. 31)

Just as they are about to enter Mrs. Clennam's house it collapses, burying the satanic Rigaud and symbolizing the fall of the old order. Amy Dorrit (A.D.) completes the transformation with a little sacrament of forgiveness by burning the codicil which Arthur's mother had withheld and which is the remaining stain on the now nearly purified name of Clennam. " 'Does the charm want any words to be said?' asked Arthur, as he held the paper over the flame. 'You can say (if you don't mind) "I love you!" ' answered Little Dorrit." Under the new dispensation, the true decorum, love is the fulfilling of the law. They are married "with the sun shining on them through the painted figure of Our Saviour on the window" (pp. 800–801, bk. II, ch. 34).[47]

The resolution of *Little Dorrit* in terms of Christian parable seems very clear at this point, and of course such resolution is an expression of providential intention. But for this transformation from retribution to mercy to make structural sense in the novel's larger providential aesthetic, it must be connected in some way with the dominant themes and techniques of the

---

[47]Such patterns as these provide an ultimate refutation to recent arguments that present a fundamentally skeptical Dickens. Barry Qualls, for example, asserts incredibly that Dickens "never finds anything beyond the human except the bestial: no order, no nature, nothing conquers his doubt" (*The Secular Pilgrims*, p. 110).

whole text. What does this shift of perspective from the world according to Merdle to the world interpreted by Amy Dorrit have to do with the central motif of prisons and imprisonment or with the preoccupation shared by most of the characters with the determinations of the past? *Little Dorrit* is concerned not only with social prisons and with their internalization as disorders of the individual will[48] but with the still more ambitious enterprise of imagining and locating opportunities for freedom and fulfillment in space and time.

In my first chapter I observed that what distinguishes the treatment of time in the providential aesthetic from its application in the more formally or naturalistically based aesthetics that followed is its premise that temporal sequence, linear time, reveals and participates in an order of reality that is transcendent and timeless. History continuously acknowledges eternity. In *Little Dorrit*, where most characters find themselves in prisons of one kind or another, this acknowledgment must overcome the threats of blind repetition, circumlocution, incarceration, stasis. Nevertheless, time—linear, providential time—again provides the liberating element.[49] Its antithetical relation to the threats of enclosure, of spatial confinement, advances Dickens's great exploration of the theme beyond the relatively hopeless circularities of *Bleak House* and represents an impressive enrichment of the providential aesthetic.

[48]As Lionel Trilling identified them in his introduction to the Oxford Illustrated edition.

[49]The theme of time in this novel has stimulated some interesting criticism. Jerome Beaty has argued that *"Little Dorrit* explores more insistently than [the other novels] one arc of the circle of [Dickens's] cosmology: the moral necessity of seeing the temporality of this world as organically cyclical and benevolent" ("The 'Soothing Songs' of Little Dorrit: A New Light on Dickens' Darkness," *Nineteenth Century Literary Perspectives*, ed. Clyde de L. Ryals et al. [Durham, N.C.: Duke Univ. Press, 1974], p. 235). Mike Hollington is correct, however, in identifying the "confusing cyclical *perpetuum mobile*" as a threat to human freedom and well-being: "If the static present of *Little Dorrit* appears hopelessly unalterable, it is nonetheless only through the medium of time that it will be cast away" ("Time in *Little Dorrit*," in *The English Novel in the Nineteenth Century*, ed. George Goodin [Urbana: Univ. of Illinois Press, 1972], pp. 114, 124).

At the beginning of the second part of the novel, William Dorrit remarks upon the "confinement" of the monastery of the Great St. Bernard.[50] He focuses on the fact that "the space was so—ha—hum—so very contracted. More than that. It was always the same, always the same." The host, a monastic far too polite and urbane to enter into metaphysical argument at table, merely observes "that almost all objects had their various points of view. Monsieur and he did not see this poor life of his from the same point of view. Monsieur was not used to confinement" (p. 430; bk. II, ch. 1). The point seems to be that freedom depends upon individual perspective. Mr. Dorrit sees freedom spatially, as luxurious travel and large rooms, and temporally in terms of variety of amusement and advancing social prestige. The host presumably has what may be called a "vertical" sense of space in which the mind ascends to God, and his apprehension of the temporal would be in its relation to the timeless. Or, to adopt this "point of view" to a domestic context, it is what makes Little Dorrit less of a prisoner in the Marshalsea when she is there with her father and Clennam than when she is confined in what for her are the great social prisons of Rome and Venice.

"Do you mean," asks Miss Wade of Mr. Meagles early in the novel, "that a prisoner forgives his prison?" (p. 22; bk. I, ch. 2). She doubts the possibility, but the answer of the novel is that a prisoner must forgive his prison because human beings must live somewhere, and all earthly spaces are prisons and all mortal time is imprisonment. The novel presents this view of temporality in many ways. We hear early on of an old turnkey who "went off the lock of this world" (p. 65; bk. I, ch. 6), and near the end the slanting sunlight through the bars of the Marshalsea gate forms "long bright rays, bars of the prison of this lower world" (p. 741; bk. II, ch. 30). Not to forgive the

[50]Elaine Showalter points out that the monastery is the symbolic and structural parallel to Marseilles, where the novel begins ("Guilt, Authority, and the Shadows of *Little Dorrit*," *Nineteenth-Century Fiction*, 34 [1979], 27). This essay is another example of acute psychological analysis perfectly compatible with, though independent of, a providential reading.

prison would be to reject the universal human condition, the common lot. It is a negation variously attempted, but only by the wicked or the mad—by Miss Wade, Rigaud, William Dorrit, Mrs. Clennam, and the novel's other willful fugitives from life.

What saves the good characters in *Little Dorrit*, saves them more fully than anyone in *Bleak House* can be saved, is their acceptance of the imprisonment as significant, a trust in time itself and in their own efforts through time to find freedom within the bars. *Bleak House* stresses the imprisonment of enclosed space, the meaningless round of Chancery, and the only solution there seems to be the establishment of fortified enclaves, like Bleak House itself, into which to retreat. In *Little Dorrit* the Circumlocution Office, however frustrating, poses a lesser threat because here our perception of circumstances changes in time: "Time shall show us. The post of honor and the post of shame, the general's station and the drummer's, a peer's statue in Westminister Abbey and a seaman's hammock in the bosom of the deep, the mitre and the workhouse, the woolsack and the gallows, the throne and the guillotine—the travellers to all are on the great high road; but it has wonderful divergences, and only Time shall show us whither each traveller is bound" (p. 173; bk. I, ch. 15).

Time reveals the true order of things to us. Like Sol Gills in *Dombey and Son*, characters in *Little Dorrit* must "wait the fulness of time and the design."[51] Because the design provides the way out of negation and meaninglessness, it becomes essential to be true to the past, to cherish it. The pattern can be traced in no other way. "Do Not Forget" says Clennam's father's watch in a message from the past, and from eternity. To remember, not selectively as Mrs. Clennam chooses to do, but fully and truly, is to accept what has become of us, to be what we are. Mrs. Clennam's system is static, paralyzed, because she rejects the continuing narrative, the movement of time in which forgiveness and salvation become possible. Figuratively

---

[51]*Dombey and Son*, p. 830; ch. 62.

and literally she reads the same dark texts over and over (p. 36; bk. I, ch. 3). She tells Amy that she has been commissioned to punish sin as others have been chosen to punish it "in all time." " 'In all time?' repeated Little Dorrit" (p. 770; bk. II, ch.31).

The phrase means nothing to her. The providential design is not fixed, circular, retributive. To be true to the past, to remember fully, acts in this novel to validate narrative itself, to accept the sequential, moving, changing event as it passes into that inalterable realm upon which in this decorum all significant freedom is founded. The narrative structure of *Little Dorrit* thus intimately collaborates or perhaps even becomes one with its thematic significance—and not to forget one's own story, to remember one's prison, is to forgive it.[52] And this collaboration, this junction, negotiates the deepest possible alliance between Dickens's providential aesthetic and the narrative form it governs.

Great Expectations

Like Mrs. Clennam in *Little Dorrit*, Miss Havisham in *Great Expectations* tries to arrest the linear movement of time and to substitute a stasis or repetitive cycle that justifies her suffering by making it central to her universe. We know that in Dickens's providential aesthetic such an action opposes the true order of things, the providential decorum.[53] Any attempt to stop the

[52]At the end of *Little Dorrit* Dickens permitted himself an endearing reference to the text of the novel, one that reflects on the discovery of freedom in narrative time. Amy Dorrit's old friend the verger, who takes her into the church with Maggie, remarks: "This young lady is one of our curiosities, and has come now to the third volume of our Registers. Her birth is in what I call the first volume; she lay asleep on this very floor, with her pretty head on what I call the second volume; and she's now a-writing her little name as a bride, in what I call the third volume" (p. 801; bk. II, ch. 34).

[53]From the preceding discussion of *Little Dorrit*. In reference to *Great Expectations* S. L. Franklin points out that the stopped clocks at Satis House "point to Dickens' Christian moral that temporal flow continues regardless

forward movement of time imprisons the character in a dead past by cutting off the flow of sequence and causation that brings the saving knowledge. To stop time means to arrest the narrative flow of events and therefore the changing text of experience.[54] Miss Havisham, like Mrs. Clennam, reads the text of her betrayal over and over. Her interpretation of it cannot change until she accepts the inevitable changes of linear time with their necessary alteration of circumstances and individuals.

In a static universe forgiveness is impossible. That, of course, suits the retributive ethics of these two crippled women. But Miss Havisham goes beyond this by devising an active scheme for revenge. This revenge is not designed to free her from her prison or to enable her to enter the moving stream of life outside it. On the contrary, she plans to use a surrogate, Estella, to project a reinforcing vision of her own redundant obsession— with the simple reversal that now *men* will have their hearts broken. In her manipulation of Estella and Pip, Miss Havisham thus elects herself the providence of her cyclical cosmos. She wants to be central and unmoving, an entirely self-referential power that acts through agents it has designed to serve its destructive will.

The motive of revenge, as I have suggested elsewhere, has a peculiar psychological relation to the flow of time.[55] Its impulse is regressive, repetitive. The obsession leads not to creation but to re-creation, and for this reason it provides a

---

of individual attempts at stasis." He goes on to deduce a providential intention from the novel's treatment of time: "And if, as Dickens' many symbolic clocks suggest, duration is the mode of time in the exterior universe as well as in the human mind, then that duration—to which man is free to conform and which he must confront to function for the good—must be an expression of the consciousness of a greater mind, the mind of God" ("Dickens and Time: The Clock without Hands," *Dickens Studies Annual*, 4 [1975], pp. 28, 35).

[54] See George Ford's eloquent "Dickens and the Voices of Time," *Dickens Centenial Essays*, ed. Ada Nisbet and Blake Nevius (Berkeley: Univ. of California Press, 1971), pp. 57–58.

[55] "Revenge and *Wuthering Heights*," *Studies in the Novel*, 3 (1971), 13–15.

classic aesthetic device for the development of patterns in drama and narrative. In *Great Expectations*, as in revenge tragedies like *Hamlet*, the retributive ethic justifies precisely the action that the avenger seems to need. Revenge suggests a source of purpose and meaning (break their hearts) when all other purpose and meaning has been lost (because my heart is broken). It temporarily provides a margin of reference that sustains at least the illusion of identity. Its destructive aims for a time become sources of order for the character and the narrative. It offers an interval of direction and form when all other impulses toward direction and form have been blocked by the loss of a supreme value. But in Dickens's providential aesthetic it shows itself to be cyclical rather than progressive, reflexive rather than liberating, and thus in final and hopeless conflict with the coordinates of the providential decorum.

Miss Havisham's attempt to cheat the past leads her to "reverse the appointed order of [her] Maker" (p. 385; ch. 49), to recapture time by revenging her life through Estella's. In a parallel action her socially degraded analogue Magwitch tries to retrieve time lost in his wretched lifelong career as jailbird and "warmint" (p. 311; ch. 40) by living through a surrogate "gentleman" in Pip.[56] Magwitch wants to be Pip's providence, his provider, as his alias "Provis" suggests. This is only partly in gratitude for Pip's childhood provision for him on the marshes. Magwitch really intends Pip to become the "gentleman" society exempts from the persecution it deals the "warmint." "If I ain't a gentleman, nor yet ain't got no learning, I'm the owner of such. All on you owns stock and land; which on you owns a brought-up London gentleman?" (p. 310; ch. 39). Pip is to *justify* (revenge, correct, compensate for, rewrite) Magwitch's deprivation. Both Magwitch and Miss Havisham are in the business of cosmic accounting, bookkeeping for providence, and in making up what they see as the deficit due them they commit the sin of appropriating and twisting other lives.

Miss Havisham, no doubt, is the most clearly culpable. She was brought up a lady with a lady's advantages. The wrong

[56]Moynahan develops this point throughout "The Hero's Guilt."

done to her, though grievous, is not to be compared to the blind pain of Magwitch's childhood and youth. And her twisting of Estella's nature seems more consciously malevolent than his plans for Pip. Indeed, perhaps her willfulness earns her the severe punishment she receives at the end. Perhaps in addition to a providential admonition an austere poetic justice is at work in her case. But what about Magwitch? In what sense can the bitterness and brutality of his experience be seen as just?

As he lies dying in prison, Magwitch looks back over the waste of his life: "The kind of submission or resignation that he showed, was that of a man who was tired out. I sometimes derived an impression, from his manner or from a whispered word or two which escaped him, that he pondered over the question whether he might have been a better man under better circumstances. But he never justified himself by a hint tending that way, or tried to bend the past out of its eternal shape" (p. 441; ch. 56). Magwitch does ponder the justice of his lot, the effect that "circumstances" have had on his life, but he also accepts it. The shape of the past is eternal. There is nothing to be done about it. It cannot (to employ the operative metaphor) be reforged. To possess that mysterious and heartbreaking knowledge as Magwitch and Pip possess it at the end, and to accept it, is to be as free and as powerful as one can be in this melancholy book. To participate in the true order of things in *Great Expectations* is to achieve this resignation.

This is a somewhat different perspective on the importance of being true to the past from that which emerges from the affirmations of *Little Dorrit*. But this one too is liberating. There is a curiously moving exchange between Pip and Magwitch as they begin their solemn escape attempt. Pip asks Magwitch if he really believes that he will be free and safe:

> "Ay, I s'pose I think so, dear boy. We'd be puzzled to be more quiet and easy-going than we are at present. But—it's a flowing so soft and pleasant through the water, p'raps, as makes me think it—I was a-thinking through my smoke just then, that we can no more see to the bottom of the next few hours, than we can see to the

bottom of this river what I catches hold of. Nor yet we can't no more hold their tide than I can hold this. And its run through my fingers and gone, you see!"

"But for your face, I should think you were a little despondent," said I.

"Not a bit on it, dear boy! It comes of flowing on so quiet, and of that there rippling at the boat's head making a sort of a Sunday tune. Maybe I'm growing a trifle old besides." (p. 423; ch. 54)

At this point Pip is still trying to manipulate the flow of events. Magwitch, having received at last a little trust and love, has passed him by. The indignation that led Magwitch to struggle against the temporal current is gone, and the acceptance of things as they were, and are, and will be, has replaced it. In this acquiescence time no longer wastes Magwitch. He is no longer trying to be "Provis." He has already made his escape.

It is Pip's devotion and sacrifice that frees Magwitch. In trying to help Magwitch escape, Pip finds in himself the strength to deny his corrupt personal ambition, a strength he could have learned only from Joe. Pip goes on to learn that in being faithful to Magwitch he has atoned for his lack of faith to Joe. He has rendered compensation to Joe as fully as compensation can be rendered in this world.[57] That such indirect compensation can function suggests the presence of a providential

---

[57]Pip tells Joe and Biddy on their wedding day that he would not cancel his moral debt to them even if he could (p. 464; ch. 68). The expectation of *compensation* to oneself is evil and dangerous. I take this to be the pun on "Compeyson," the wicked link between Miss Havisham and Magwitch. Though he doesn't say so, Robert Caserio's important observations on the "literalizing of coincidental identity in Dickens" advance our understanding of these providential connections: "For Dickens sees his characters as an arbitrary metonymic chain, whose links come to accept—without any Eliotic contradiction or qualification—their purely nominal differences (differences that make no difference) in exchange for the sake of making a clear and definite difference for each other on the level of action. Dickens's responsibility to the real is manifested in his belief that reality is preeminently an urgent and practicable desire for a liberation from arbitrariness and indefiniteness of action" (*Plot, Story and the Novel: From Dickens and Poe to the Modern Period* [Princeton: Princeton Univ. Press, 1979], pp. 115, 116).

decorum: from among the many dreadful concatenations in *Great Expectations* emerges the divine chain of sacrifice and selfless love. It is an advanced form of what I have called inconsequent actualization. The link forged by Joe holds the one Pip hammers out in his service to Magwitch. The inalterable past, mysterious in its unchanging inequities, also preserves these links inviolate and accessible.

Readers of *Great Expectations* often ask whether it would have been better for Pip if he had never left the forge. *He* thinks so off and on and even contemplates a feeble attempt to rejoin his old life by means of a self-abasing proposal to Biddy. He arrives on the day of her marriage to Joe and thus learns again that he cannot ignore what time has changed. He cannot go home. He gave it up. The question that begins "What would have happened if" has no answer in this novel. The conditional here has no meaning in the past. What might have been must always meet what was; fairy tales must always meet history; our speculation as readers must always meet the text as it stands. If we ask, like Pip in the throes of his disillusionment, whether it would have been better had he never left the forge, the answer has to be another question: Better for what? There can be no *better* way in things past. There is only the past—one past, personal and providential.

As Joe puts it, "What have been betwixt us—have been" (p. 456; ch. 57). And yet he is the reverse of fatalistic. Joe sees what Sydney Carton sees in the novel that preceded *Great Expectations*, that there will never be a "rational" balancing of accounts, that nobody ever directly pays off a debt of kindness, that personal compensation and retribution have no place in the decorum. All we can do is to wipe the slate clean and start again—with Estella or without her.[58] There can be no permanent, fixed poetic justice. To establish poetic justice we

---

[58]Lee T. Lemon notes that "Pip's maturation by the end of the novel is due not to the fact that he is rewarded with everything due him—in the manner of a typical Fielding or Austen ending—but, rather, that he is deprived of those things that are not due him" ("The Hostile Universe: A Developing Pattern in Nineteenth-Century Fiction," *The English Novel in the Nineteenth Century*, p. 11).

would have to stop the narrative, the flow of the river. If Pip marries Estella at the end, if that is what he sees through the rising mists, that chiefly means that for us the text has stopped at a moment of gratification. Sometimes that still happens and such moments may be signs of grace. But the moral substance of narrative, its liberating quality in the providential decorum, here as in *Little Dorrit*, lies in its mysterious flow. And to participate in that flow means to give up the solipsistic evasions of revenge, fairy tale, poetic justice—to stop being an accountant in the service of delusion, to forgive and go on. This is the rhythm Joe suggests when he tells Pip that "life is made of ever so many partings welded together" (p. 215; ch. 27). The longer we dwell on this remark the more piercing it seems, but surely one of its meanings may be that those agonizing disjunctions from our cherished illusory past form the concatenation that makes movement into the unseen future possible. Or, as Estella applies it in the ending Dickens chose to publish, the one which most fully affirms the premise of a true providential intention, "I have been bent and broken, but—I hope—into a better shape" (p. 469; ch. 69).

Our Mutual Friend

Eugene Wrayburn in *Our Mutual Friend* is also bent and broken. He begins as a typical bored gentleman, persuaded that "everything is ridiculous" (p. 213; bk. I, ch. 13). His nihilism, really a form of well-bred despair, leads him to the verge of attempting to seduce Lizzie Hexam: "Out of the question to marry her," he says to himself, "and out of the question to leave her. The crisis!" His moral disorder requires a strong remedy, and precisely at this point Bradley Headstone administers it with an oar:

> In an instant, with a dreadful crash, the reflected night turned crooked, flames shot jaggedly across the air, and the moon and stars came bursting from the sky.
> Was he struck by lighting? (pp. 766–67; bk. IV, ch. 6)

The question activates the pun latent in Wrayburn's name. The lighting, working through the naturalistic medium of his rival's jealousy, is a message from the true order of things, the decorum which asserts that everything does not become ragged and ridiculous.[59] When Eugene awakens he is transformed. Having wronged Lizzie in his heart, he attempts to make reparation through marriage, and this attempted reparation, like Pip's, effects the salvation of the penitent. Eugene saves not Lizzie but himself.

Eugene's moral rebirth follows his baptism in the river Thames, here imbued with biblical associations involving especially the river Jordan. The baptism motif is central to *Our Mutual Friend*: it functions both as a parabolic revelation of the providential intention and more importantly as a coordinate of the providential decorum. It develops a flexibility unusual even for Dickens's later novels. The various baptisms suggest a range of applications rather than a clear dogmatic. One can be baptized into a new life like Wrayburn and Harmon, "baptized unto Death" (p. 222; bk. I, ch. 14) like Gaffer Hexam, or simply soaked in the Thames with no spiritual improvement whatever like Rogue Riderhood in his first dunking. In all its variety the baptism motif lies open on the surface of the novel, and, as most of Dickens's original readers must have recognized without effort, refers to the Book of Common

[59]The providential element in Eugene's punishment and Lizzie's subsequent rescue was noticed by Charles H. McKensie in 1884: "There is a realization here of something more than mere prayerful reliance; there is an acknowledgment of God's overruling Providence, of his moving in mysterious ways, His wonderous works to do, and a recognition of the great assurance that 'all things work together for good to those who love God' " (*The Religious Sentiments of Charles Dickens, Collected from His Writings* [London: Walter Scott, 1884], p. 112). James R. Kincaid says of Eugene that "very simply, his comic detachment must be eliminated, and he must be made one with the river's redemptive slime before he can marry the corpse-catcher's daughter. Their marriage ceremony, conducted on the edge of death, is the perfect symbol of his comic rebirth, a rebirth which assaults the old society by the creation of a new and competing one" (*Dickens and the Rhetoric of Laughter* [Oxford: Clarendon Press, 1971], p. 244). Bill Sikes in *Oliver Twist* is also punished "as if struck by lightning" (p. 453; ch. 50).

Prayer and the baptism service: "Almighty and everlasting God, who of thy great mercy didst save Noah and his family in the ark from perishing by water; and also didst safely lead the children of Israel thy people through the Red Sea, figuring thereby thy holy Baptism; and by the Baptism of thy well-beloved Son Jesus Christ, in the river Jordan, didst sanctify Water to the mystical washing away of sin." Although the water of the Thames cannot save everybody—Riderhood and Headstone drown in the end—it does possess the sacramental purifying power for those who have not put themselves beyond recall, the resurrecting power associated with baptism.

The other great figuring of renewal in *Our Mutual Friend* is the raising of Lazarus, a parable that enforces the idea of rebirth. Charlie Hexam even manages to link the Lazarus story with the passage from the baptism service when he announces to Mortimer Lightwood that the supposed Harmon body has been found drowned: "Were there any means taken, do you know, boy," asks Mortimer, "to ascertain if it was possible to restore life?" "You wouldn't ask, sir, if you knew his state. Pharoah's multitude that were drowned in the Red Sea, ain't more beyond restoring to life. If Lazarus was only half as far gone, that was the greatest of all the miracles" (p. 61; bk. I, ch. 3). And the Lazarus motif too is repeated with varying degrees of affirmation. Eugene returns from death's door; Harmon decides to return to life in his proper name; Riah comes up onto Fledgby's roof like a pilgrim ascending a prophet's tomb; Riderhood comes back to consciousness in very bad humor.

In fact the diversity of these symbolic or parabolic associations gives them a curious ambiguity. Although the Thames can seem to be a source of renewal it is also a filthy, lethal sewer. Although Lazarus can sometimes be brought back from the dead, it isn't always clear that he wants to be brought back. John Harmon decides for a long period that he does better to stay officially dead and not resurrect his old identity. Eugene almost yields "to the attraction of the loadstone rock of Eternity," recalled to life periodically by the voice of his new wife but with "a sharp misgiving in my conscience . . . that I ought to die" (pp. 822, 825; bk. IV, ch. 11). The ambiguity associated with these religious motifs expresses a fundamental ambivalence about the value of being alive. *Our Mutual Friend*, as many readers have observed, seems to be about death. The question the novel poses in the spiritual pilgrimages of Wrayburn and Harmon (with parodic reinforcement from Mr. Venus) is radical to the providential decorum: Is life worth living?

The answer is not an easy affirmative. As Rogue Riderhood struggles back to consciousness after being pulled out of the Thames, the narrator suggests that a fundamental ambivalence toward living is universal: "Now he is struggling harder to get back. And yet—like us all, when we swoon—like us all, every day of our lives when we wake—he is instinctively unwilling to be restored to the consciousness of this existence, and would be left dormant, if he could (p. 505; bk. III, ch. 3). This ambivalence appears in Jenny Wren, who dreams of angel children and who calls to Riah, "Come back and be dead!" (p. 334; bk. II, ch. 5). It appears in Twemlow, who knows his life to have been "a waste" (p. 164; bk. I, ch. 10). It appears in Bradley Headstone, who decides the question in the negative.

" 'We give thee hearty thanks for that it hath pleased thee to deliver this our sister out of the miseries of this sinful world.' So read the Reverend Frank Milvey in a not untroubled voice" (p. 577; bk. III, ch. 9). He is reading from the burial service of the Book of Common Prayer. Betty Higden has chosen death from exhaustion and exposure in preference to life as a dependent. Her sought-after death could have been the darkest moment in the novel, pessimistically identifying—as the book so often seems on the point of identifying—death itself as our mutual friend. But Betty Higden's death lets the light in. She dies in Lizzie Hexam's arms, lifted "as high as Heaven," thinking of herself as at the foot of the cross, "thankful for all" (pp. 577, 575; bk. III, ch. 8). Given her hard life, marked by the deaths of those children she has loved, she has some right to bitterness, and the social indignation attached to her is bitter. But there is another message, a message which again bypasses the question of justice and due reward and which

Our Mutual Friend asserts more gleefully than any other Dickens novel. Where Magwitch in *Great Expectations* resigns himself and passively accepts his life, Betty Higden somehow steadily affirms hers.

Our Mutual Friend takes on the human problem of locating the fact of death in relation to the providential decorum, the true order of things. The answer it provides is in part that of immortality, as in the symbolism of resurrection surrounding Betty Higden's death and Jenny Wren's vision of the angel children. But it also attempts to bring that solution down into linear time and into the sequence of temporal narration. In a somber moment Jenny Wren points out to Riah the obvious inequity of her lot and then, in longing for her absent friend Lizzie, asks, "Is it better to have had a good thing and lost it, or never to have had it?" It is the question to be asked of all temporal properties. Riah answers, "Some beloved companionship fades out of most lives, my dear . . . that of a wife, and a fair daughter, and a son of promise, has faded out of my life—but the happiness was" (p. 494; bk. III, ch. 2). His meaning seems to be that what was can never be taken away and that the immutability of the past—that major theme in Dickens's late novels which we have been tracing—insures its service to the present.

Riah, I think, takes the question about as far as it can go in *Our Mutual Friend*. Although clear providential patterns for certain sets of characters help to establish the novel's structure, its deeper affirmations do not ultimately depend on them any more than they depend on articulate metaphysical speculation (of which Silas Wegg is perhaps the most vigorous exponent). If, as I believe, a providential aesthetic is organic to *Our Mutual Friend* but not solely contingent on echoes from the prayer book and the Wrayburn-Hexam and Harmon-Wilfer actions, then it lies pervasive in the opaque comic assertiveness of the book's texture and tone. It lies in those various and diffuse comic elements that ineffably but continuously serve to involve the sacred in the profane. It is, as the narrator observes in a description of an evening landscape, "as if there

were no immensity of space between mankind and Heaven"
(p. 757; bk. IV, ch. 6). ·

I am not sure that so fundamental an integration can be
demonstrated critically, at least not with a brevity that would
make the demonstration endurable. But I can point to an
emblem of it. The character of Mr. Boffin, the last complete
"good man" in Dickens, will serve for this. Like his predecessors in virtue Mr. Boffin locates the providential decorum. He
remains true to the realities around him, to his own principles,
and to the events of the past. John Harmon and Bella owe
their happiness to the Boffins' unfailing memory of their dead
master's lonely child. They bring John Harmon back from the
dead.

But unlike most of his predecessors in the type—David Copperfield, John Jarndyce, Arthur Clennam—Mr. Boffin is not
wet. Instead he is "dusty," as Silas Wegg calls him. We have
chapter titles in which "The Golden Dustman Rises a Little"
and in which "The Golden Dustman Sinks Again." He brings
echoes of that enigmatic song from *Cymbeline* in which the
familiarity, the kindliness of death is whimsically figured:
"Golden lads and girls all must/ As chimney-sweepers, come
to dust."[60] Mr. Boffin knows about death. He knows all about
money and wills and other forms of refuse. He also knows
about "some things that I never found among the dust" (p. 136;
bk. I, ch. 8). But his knowledge does not prevent him from
enjoying himself, from affirming life. He finds it persistently
worthwhile.

Mr. Boffin is the only fully developed "good man" in Dickens's fiction to disguise his moral identity. At one point in his
role as miser he makes a profound and dusty comment on the
vanity of human sentiment. He remembers this comment and

---

[60]IV.ii.62–63. For other parallels between Dickens and Shakespeare see
Harbage, *A Kind of Power*, especially p. 27: "Providence is an unseen character who moves on the stages of both, without offense, because most of
us, in spite of our rational orthodoxy, still believe in Good Luck, meaning
luck for the good."

repeats it with delight during the denouement. It is a ridiculing of John Harmon's pledge of devotion to Bella: "Win her affections and possess her heart! Mew says the cat, Quack-quack says the duck, and Bow-wow-wow says the dog . . . A pretty and a hopeful picter? Mew, Quack-quack, Bow-wow!" (pp. 848–49; bk. IV, ch. 13). Like an earth-clown from Shakespearean comedy he thus mockingly ties high romantic aspiration to mortal bestiality and cheerfully refers the lovers to their common element in the dust. Silas Wegg had said that Boffin came to the dust mounds to dig "like a thief in the dark" (p. 645; bk. III, ch. 14),[61] suggesting with ignorant precision the Golden Dustman's consonance with the convivial eschatology of *Our Mutual Friend*.

When Mr. Boffin discards his disguise, he returns to domestic harmony and love. At the end most of the other good characters come to see life as worth living, worth the personal pain and social injustice. The great cosmic influences are benevolent, comic. "Evil," the narrator tells us, "often stops short at itself and dies with the doer of it; but Good, never" (p. 146; bk. I, ch. 9). "God is good, and hearts may count in Heaven as high as heads" (p. 246; bk. I, ch. 16). The universe is so constituted that in order to become wicked human beings must struggle toward crime, not away from it (p. 609; bk. III, ch. 11). Such assertions are rare in the later novels. Their explicit intrusion supports the suggestion that although here Dickens's providential aesthetic bases itself on the harshest realities, on dust and death, it imbues them in the end with comic affability. If we are dust and return to dust, then that is what we have in common, that is our mutuality, our mortality, and the fact is alienating only if we fail to value it.

---

[61]"The day of the Lord will come as a thief in the night" (2 Peter 3:10).

4

GEORGE ELIOT
Providence as
Metaphor

GEORGE ELIOT'S FICTION, like that of Brontë and Dickens, makes extensive use of the providential aesthetic. For her, however, it has no basis in a conviction about the ultimate order of things but serves instead as a pool of literary conventions and techniques accessible to calculated artistic manipulation. We have seen that when Charlotte Brontë left her childhood fantasy, the world of Angria, it was to engage in representing reality, a reality ordered by an active providence; and that Dickens's wonderfully ingenious development of devices traditional to providential fiction drew support from his conviction that "all art is but a little imitation" of "the ways of Providence." The worlds of their novels are informed throughout by their consciousness of divine presence, a providential intention that can be apprehended (though often not fully understood) by the protagonists. The worlds of George Eliot's novels are populated with characters, shaded good and bad, who believe in such presence and such intention and who seek and sometimes find corroboration of their beliefs in circumstances. But the circumstances represented never themselves offer the reader the providential proofs of a divinely informed universe central to the novels of Brontë and Dickens and to most earlier English fiction. And yet George Eliot did not abandon the narrative techniques that advance the novelistic representation of providential intention. Instead, the familiar elements of the providential aesthetic—coincidence, a sense of fatality or destiny, the unplanned or inconsequent actualization of individual desires, the perception of plan or pattern in individual or social history—are exploited, and sometimes subverted, in the interests of structural unity. They undergo an ironic transformation in the development of her fiction—different in each of her novels—from their former status as external evidence to consideration as psychological correlative, from type to metaphor.

Most of her contemporaries only gradually recognized the extent of George Eliot's transformation of the providential tradition,[1] but they did recognize it. As early as 1863 Richard Simpson identified the influence of Goethe, Comte, Strauss, and Feuerbach in what he described as a "Christian anthropology, without the basis of Christian theology." He found an antidogmatic principle evident in her work from *Scenes of Clerical Life* through *Romola* (the occasion of his review) that was "inconsistent with a religion founded on miracle, with the belief in a personal Providence, or in any other God than the system of the Universe." Ten years later R. R. Bowker observed with approval "the rationalistic mind of George Eliot" assimilating and reducing the eternal religious struggles of humanity to "the conflict between character and circumstance." W. H. Mallock, in an unsigned review of *Impressions of Theophrastus Such,* declared that although most of her characters were Christian her books really were not: "She is the first great *godless* writer of fiction that has appeared in England."[2]

One of the reasons this awareness grew slowly is the obvious one that George Eliot herself only gradually broke away from the religious and moral narrative conventions of the serious fiction that preceded hers.[3] The narrator of *Scenes of Clerical Life* maintains throughout an earnest and generally conventional moral tone, even at points calling on God to save us all

---

[1] See David Carroll's comprehensive introduction to *George Eliot: The Critical Heritage* (New York: Barnes and Noble 1971), pp. 1–48.

[2] Ibid., pp. 247, 248–49, 434, 453.

[3] Another, as W. J. Harvey points out, is that "George Eliot would not have achieved general and immediate popularity had she stated her philosophic position directly in her novels" (*The Art of George Eliot* [London: Chatto and Windus, 1961], p. 36).

from the worst. *Adam Bede* preserves at least an ostensible neutrality on the questions of providential order and divine justice it raises. From our present perspective the catastrophe at the end of *The Mill on the Floss* may seem calculatedly anti-providential, but at the time of its publication readers were more apt to see it simply as false or inappropriate. The apparent providentialism of *Silas Marner* appears to have satisfied ortho-dox readers for generations. Not until the open secularism of *Middlemarch,* where the lack of satisfying religious practice in the lives of the characters struck readers as telling, did the absence of providential premises become widely acknowl-edged. And then *Daniel Deronda* seemed strangely to reinsti-tute the conventional assumptions.

Nevertheless, George Eliot's increasingly radical transmu-tation of the elements of the providential aesthetic to subserve a fundamentally secular fiction contains, novel by novel, a clear and steady development. This development seems to me to be one of the achievements of our literature, and one that has passed largely without understanding or acclaim. George Eliot took the chief thematic and structural convention of the Eng-lish novel and adapted it to the representation of a reality uninformed by the premises upon which that convention was founded. In her work we can see the late tendency of Christian providentialism to diffuse and disguise itself in other moral and philosophical paradigms or systems. We can see these systems begin to do the work of a providential intention in the structuring of her novels and in the human worlds they present to us.

Adam Bede

The general structure of George Eliot's first novel—its order-ing of events and the final resolution of circumstances for its protagonists—conforms in broad outline to the traditional providential pattern of English fiction, the pattern of *Jane Eyre,* a pattern that subsists in varying configurations and degrees of prominence through all of Dickens. The text of *Adam Bede* in fact points repeatedly to its own structural conformity to the providential tradition: "I should never ha' come to know that her love 'ud be the greatest o' blessings to me," thinks Adam of Dinah, "if what I counted a blessing hadn't been wrenched and torn away from me, and left me with a greater need, so as I could crave and hunger for a greater and a better comfort."[4] So in the traditional application of the providential aesthetic does fictional structure show good coming out of evil. But throughout *Adam Bede*—as in *Villette* and in the later Dickens—the facile solipsistic comforts of this primitive form of interpretation are rejected: "Adam could never cease to mourn over that mystery of human sorrow which had been brought so close to him: he could never thank God for another's misery. . . . 'Evil's evil, and sorrow's sorrow, and you can't alter its nature by wrapping it up in other words. Other folks were not created for my sake, that I should think all square when things turn out well for me' " (p. 442; ch. 54).

For Adam Bede human sorrow is a "mystery." That, indeed, was what Lucy Snowe called it and what the good characters in Dickens's later novels think of it. They all believe in a providential universe that human beings cannot fully comprehend, a universe obscurely but divinely ordered. Charlotte Brontë and Charles Dickens believed in such a universe too. But George Eliot did not, and in various quiet but decisive ways this denial informs her first novel.[5] *Adam Bede* goes beyond an attack on

[4]*Adam Bede,* ed. John Paterson (Boston: Houghton Mifflin, 1968), p. 430; ch. 53.

[5]See Paterson's excellent introduction, ibid., pp. vii–xii, xvi, xxvi; Basil Willey, *Nineteenth Century Studies: Coleridge to Matthew Arnold* (New York: Harper and Row, 1966), pp. 218, 229–30, 237; and for more thorough discussions of her whole religious and philosophical position, Bernard J. Paris, *Experiments in Life: George Eliot's Quest for Values* (Detroit: Wayne State Univ. Press, 1965), pp. 1–148; U. C. Knoepflmacher, *Religious Humanism and the Victorian Novel* (Princeton: Princeton Univ. Press, 1965), pp. 24–71; Martin Svaglic "Religion in the Novels of George Eliot," *Journal of English and Germanu Philology,* 53 (1954), 145–59; Neil Robertson, *George Eliot: Her Beliefs and Her Art* (Pittsburgh: Univ. of Pittsburgh Press, 1975), pp. 19–52; and of course Gordon Haight, *George Eliot: A Biography* (New York: Oxford Univ. Press, 1968), pp. 32–147 passim.

that Pecksniffian view of things in which circumstances seem concentric to the perceiver's desires. It raises questions about the very methodology of providential interpretation, that retrospective view of events, that reading of the text of experience which reveals a providential design—good coming out of evil, suffering as the rod of a divine pedagogue, circumstances as in some way divinely ordered, consequences as divinely foreseen. The intellectual excitement of *Adam Bede*—and its contribution to the providential aesthetic—emerges from the tension between its superficially providential structure and its complex qualification of the modes of perception and interpretation upon which the validity of such a structure depends. It is this tension and its implications that I want to explore in what follows.

The characters in *Adam Bede* believe in God and in God's provision for them, his providence. The protagonist himself believes in a form of it. In Adam's case, however, belief in divine order is qualified by personal pride in his own farsightedness and objectivity. His inner enemy is clarity, or that assumption of it which blinds him to the lack of order within himself. He criticizes for example the tendency of evangelical ministers to discourse on the right state of the heart, the inner spirit: "You'd think as a man must be doing nothing all's life but shutting's eyes and looking what's a-going on inside him." Adam prefers to find his religion in external works of nature and of man: "And this is my way o' looking at it: there's the sperrit o' God in all things and all times—weekday as well as Sunday—and i' the great works and inventions, and i' the figuring and mechanics" (p. 9; ch. 1). Adam believes in the existence of an external, objective moral geometry which, like the geometry of carpentry, "is as true when a man's miserable as when he's happy; and the best o' working is, it gives you a grip hold o' things outside your own lot" (p. 99; ch. 11).

Adam's opinions are intelligent; they have dignity; their allegiance to fact or objectivity makes them preferable to the self-serving egocentric providentialism of, for example, Arthur Donnithorne.[6] But they are not the whole story; they are criticized by the narrative just as surely as Arthur's. Arthur must learn that he is not the center of his universe, that what he wants and feels is not coincident with what is. Adam knows that very well from the start. He needs to learn another and in some ways more humiliating truth: that the self necessarily stands at the center of its perceived circumstances, that there is no objective moral geometry, that he is for himself the emotional pivot of his universe, and consequently that his feelings (that inner life the evangelical preachers harp on) do help to shape his reality. What happens to Adam, like what happens to Arthur, forces on him a moral or spiritual development; and this development leads him not to a perception of the true order of things (as it would a protagonist in Dickens) but to a greater tolerance of the multiplicity of individual viewpoints.

George Eliot achieves this by forcing Adam through the ordeal of his disillusionment with Hetty and Arthur—"I seem as if I'd been measuring my work from a false line" (p. 267; ch. 29)—and consequently with the conditions of his moral universe. At the first blow Adam manages to accept the disillusionment and even to find in it what he sees as a personal application of divine mercy: "It 'ud ha' gone near to spoil my work for me, if I'd seen her brought to sorrow and shame, and through the man as I've always been proud to think on. Since I've been spared that, I've no right to grumble" (p. 274; ch. 30). He felicitates himself with Sophoclean precision on escaping the consequences that await him. When he discovers that he has not been "spared that" and Hetty's sorrow and shame exceed anything he could have anticipated, he momentarily gives way, insisting that "It *can't be*! . . . it's too hard to

---

[6]Arthur starts out as a classic combination of the egoist who wants to play at being providence ("I always take care that the load shall fall on my own shoulders," p. 107; ch. 12) and the egoist who believes the cosmos revolves around himself ("There was a sort of implicit confidence in him that he was really such a good fellow at bottom, Providence would not treat him harshly," p. 266; ch. 39).

lay upon me" (pp. 342–43; ch. 39). Nevertheless, he shortly reaches an attitude of charity based on a recognition of the human necessity for compassion: "We hand folks over to God's mercy, and show none ourselves. I used to be hard sometimes: I'll never be hard again" (p. 360; ch. 42). But although he recognizes the value of his education in suffering, Adam nevertheless steadfastly rejects all invitations to comfort himself with the conventional providential explanation of Hetty's fate. He refuses to view the sorrows of others as a "necessary" part of the divine arrangement for his own moral development. He simply and bravely acknowledges that this is the way things are, that it *can be* because it is.

But despite the protagonist's speculative reticence, a reader predisposed to interpret events as providentially ordered is permitted by the progress of Adam's moral education to claim to see farther than he does and trace the outline of a divine hand in the happy resolution. Such a reader would share the view of the Reverend Mr. Irwine, who interprets Adam's marriage to Dinah as to some degree an explanation of Hetty's suffering—as good coming out of evil, love out of sorrow. Dinah had softened Hetty's heart in the prison; Irwine had witnessed Adam's dark night of the soul. His act of joining Adam and Dinah seems fitting to him: "What better harvest from that painful seed-time could there be than this?" (p. 446; ch. 55). But again the interpretation is partial, subject to correction in the continuing dialectic of the novel. Hetty at this point has yet to die so that all the harvest has not come in, and Irwine's gladness does little to explain the harrowing lacerations—the infanticide for example—of the "seed-time."[7] Noticing this, other readers, those not addicted to the simple providential explanations of consequences, can see past Irwine's view without being invited to scorn it. Providential and anti-providential draw support from the same event by emphasizing different aspects or viewpoints.

[7]Jerome Thale discusses the "bankruptcy of Christianity" in Hayslope in *The Novels of George Eliot* (New York: Columbia Univ. Press, 1959), pp. 20–29.

Dinah Morris's way of looking at things usually avoids simple providential explanations of particular events—at least where others are concerned—and she avoids the Donnithorne tendency to see herself as a central object in the universal order. Nevertheless, she sees signs of providential design everywhere. She shares the "old-fashioned" belief in portents (p. 34; ch. 3) and regards herself as a channel for God's spirit (p. 77; ch. 8). She believes not in trying to arrange circumstances to suit herself but in "loving obedience" to the divine will (p. 403; ch. 50), thus showing not only an attractive humility but also an exhilarating consciousness that God has her (along with everybody else) in mind. Most important, Dinah is a providentialist in holding that "all things will turn to good" (p. 28; ch. 2). She movingly poses the key question on this subject in her sermon on the green: "Why does the blight come, and the bad harvests, and the fever, and all sorts of pain and trouble? For our life is full of trouble, and if God sends us good, he seems to send bad too. How is it? how is it?" (p. 23; ch. 2). She can hardly be expected to answer this to the satisfaction of skeptics and unbelievers, and she does not answer it rationally.[8] Instead she *meets* it with narrative, the narrative of Christ's mercy and suffering, and with the assurance—so central to the providential tradition—that suffering can be endured because it is not absurd, because it is God's will, "because we are sure that whatever he wills is holy, just, and good" (p. 28; ch. 2).[9] It is this conviction that enables her to comfort Hetty in prison with the radical assurance that "it makes no difference—whether we live or die, we are in the presence of God" (p. 376; ch. 45).

[8] See John Goode's account of the sermon in *"Adam Bede," Critical Essays on George Eliot,* ed. Barbara Hardy (New York: Barnes and Noble, 1970), pp. 38–39.

[9] In a review of 1859 Anne Mozley criticized the social credibility of Dinah's sermon: "Its plan is the result of reasoning, not impulse; what a person would write who had studied the line taken by St. Paul in his sermon to the Athenians. A woman of Dinah's class and views would have begun at once to assert some leading truth of the gospel, not have led up to it by the gradual process of proving God's providential care and our inborn consciousness of the being of a God" (*George Eliot: The Critical Heritage,* p. 96).

And although to Hetty the spiritual meaning of such an assertion must remain opaque ("Oh, Dinah," she answers, "won't nobody do anything for me?"), the meaning of Dinah herself suffices. Hetty weeps and tells *her* story. When Dinah returns with Adam, the love in her face seems to Hetty "like a visible pledge of the divine mercy" (p. 385; ch. 46).

Dinah has not been able to answer Hetty's dreadful question, "Do you think God will take away that crying and that place in the wood, now I've told everything?" (p. 381; ch. 45), any more than she was able to say why the blight comes. Instead she meets its emotional purport with her own love and faith. She embodies the answer in herself. Her conventional verbal explanations become extensions and descriptions of her own character. She answers Hetty's questions in the same way that her narrative of Christ's life answers questions about the reason for evil in the world.

We have seen that Dickens's virtuous heroines help to explain and embody the providential intention in his fiction. Providence shows itself immanent in them. But Dickens's heroines are supported in this function by other textual evidence—the pattern of events and the narrative commentary on it. These domestic angels provide glimpses into a true order of things that as far as the novel goes (and as Dickens believed) exists outside themselves. Providence in Dickens is no more metaphoric than London is. Human examples of goodness and responsibility imitate those very qualities in the order of things. But in *Adam Bede* neither the pattern of events nor the narrative commentary on it supports Dinah or her beliefs in this way. There is no evidence that her embodiment of charity and compassion proceeds from anything outside the human world. She is therefore at once more spiritually eccentric in her context and more humanly fallible than, say, Agnes Wickfield or Amy Dorrit, and she can be treated with a kind of zephyrous irony which they could not sustain.

This irony touches the reasoning that permits Dinah to accept Adam's proposal of marriage. The novel's sixth book begins with Dinah preparing to leave Loamshire for Snowfield, this time to avoid a "temptation," as she obliquely phrases it to Mrs. Poyser, "lest the love of the creature should become like a mist in my soul shutting out the heavenly light" (p. 398; ch. 49). Before she goes Adam proposes to her. She admits that "my heart is drawn strongly towards you" but insists that "we must submit ourselves entirely to the Divine Will" (p. 426; ch. 52). After a few weeks Adam follows her and they meet on a hill overlooking the village of "Sloman's End" (Adam is about to reach his true happiness at last). He speaks her name before she sees him: "She started without looking round, as if she connected the sound with no place. 'Dinah!' Adam said again. He knew quite well what was in her mind. She was so accustomed to think of impressions as purely spiritual manifestations, that she looked for no material visible accompaniment of the voice." In other words, she takes it to be an inner voice reaching her from God. "It was Dinah who spoke first. 'Adam,' she said, 'it is the Divine Will' " (p. 444; ch. 54).

The ironic commentary is winsome and gentle here. It has that affectionate and supportive warmth which George Eliot reserves for her noblest heroines, for Maggie Tulliver and Dorothea Brooke. That a deeply religious woman deeply in love would take her lover's words for a divine call and her marriage to him as acquiesence in the divine order is not necessarily an attack on her nobility of spirit or on the providential explanation of consequences. Jane Eyre does just that, and the configurations of events in Brontë's novel support Jane's interpretation—insist upon it in fact. But this is not Jane Eyre's world. Although nothing in *Adam Bede* denies Dinah's interpretation of the event—providence *may* be speaking in Adam's call to her—this novel permits another explanation. This of course is that Dinah wants to reconcile her spirituality with her human need for human love and that she finds this way to do it. Her decision to accept Adam is a decision to unify her life ("It is but a divided life I live without you"), so that she will have "a fullness of strength to bear and do our heavenly Father's Will, that I had lost before" (p. 444; ch. 54). Technically the ambiguity or tension (as I have called it) between the providential and naturalistic modes of interpretation is preserved. A "providential" reader could stay with Dinah's providential explanation. A "naturalistic" reader could see the force of romantic love at work in Dinah's character and interpret her solution as a successful attempt to accommodate her love for Adam to her love for God.

Technically the ambiguity is preserved. But providential explanations of events do not tolerate competition very well. To maintain an independent status in any fiction, the providential interpretation must be the ultimate interpretation, just as God's will must be perceived as a first cause if it is perceived at all. To offer a naturalistic or psychological explanation as of equal significance has a withering effect upon our confidence in a providential intention. Traditionally, providence may work through nature and the human mind, but not in equal partnership with them or as an *alternative* causal explanation. In Brontë and in Dickens the providential view of things is often threatened, but (as we have seen) these threats are repulsed— even in such dark narratives as *Villette* and *Bleak House*—by uncompromising assertions from the narrators and by clearly specified deductions explicitly drawn from the patterns of events. When providential explanations go unsupported in such ways, naturalistic explanations have a usurping tendency.[10] In order to counteract such usurpation and to maintain a real intellectual tension between providential and naturalistic explanations, George Eliot took pains in *Adam Bede* to emphasize what for want of more precise terms I will call the "mystery of things." Under this heading I include such metaphysical mysteries as the ultimate reasons for suffering as raised by Dinah in her sermon and by Adam in his ruminations, but also such basic and persistently opaque mysteries as the causes of simple events and even the legitimate status of causality as a mode of perceiving immediate circumstances as consequential.

The mystery of things in their causes is raised almost formally in the fourth chapter of *Adam Bede* with the famous rap on the door of Adam's house the night his father drowns. The

---

[10]What John Henry Newman called the "usurpations of reason" in a University Sermon of 1831. See Vargish, *Newman* pp. 33–43.

sound is made "as if with a willow wand" and "was so peculiar that the moment he heard it, it called up the image of the willow wand striking the door." Seth glimpses their drowned father "sticking against the willows." Both times the rap comes "Gyp, instead of barking, as might be expected, gave a loud howl." Adam, we are told, is "at once penetrating and credulous." "He had that mental combination which is at once humble in the region of mystery, and keen in the region of knowledge." When he finds his father dead, he concludes that "this was what the omen meant, then! And the grey-haired father, of whom he had thought with a sort of hardness a few hours ago, as certain to live to be a thorn in his side, was perhaps even then struggling with that watery death!" (pp. 43–46; ch. 4).

In this event the narrator does not permit us to see past Adam's interpretation: "To his dying day he bated his breath a little when he told the story of the stroke with the willow wand. I tell it as he told it, not attempting to reduce it to its natural elements" (p. 44; ch. 4). The narrator does not say that "natural elements" cannot explain the rap on the door. The narrator simply and opaquely rejects the attempt to explain it naturalistically. As readers we are free to speculate; but on what? The narrator has said that the story is offered us as Adam told it. Adam does not lie anywhere in the text. If, in his unhappiness and shame caused by his father's defection and during the grim task of constructing a coffin Adam is prey to a delusion, then the delusion includes the dog's peculiar howl. And although a *willow* wand has suitable associations with sorrow and death (in addition to suitable natural properties of flexibility and strength) it also happens that the drowned man is found by Seth among the willows in the flood.

The narrator refuses to attempt "to reduce [the event] to its natural elements" because "in our eagerness to explain impressions, we often lose our hold of the sympathy that comprehends them" (p. 44; ch. 4). This is to say that a predisposition to offer naturalistic explanations distracts from a rich or full understanding, a loss of "sympathy" that comprehends not the events themselves but the "impressions." The impressions of the events, not the events in their "natural elements," are what this book looks to. Just as Adam has to learn that the rules of geometry provide a poor model for judging human feeling and action, so the reader is instructed—and sometimes forced—to apprehend the train of events with a sort of epistemological negative capability, a willingness to function among a variety of logical, natural, and psychological uncertainties without becoming irritably judgmental. In this way only can we develop that "sympathy" which "comprehends" the otherwise unintelligible variousness of "impressions."

This novel makes no statement about final causes or about what in the preceding chapter on Dickens I called the true order of things. Instead it permits both readers and characters to hold a variety of predispositions and viewpoints. Logically contradictory positions can be held by the same character, as in Adam's preliminary adherence to a moral geometry on the one hand and his strong sense of mystery on the other. Mrs. Poyser allows herself to be cuttingly critical of Dinah's belief in divine leadings ("When there's a bigger maggot than usial in your head you call it 'direction' " [p. 69; ch. 6]), but all the same she feels "safer" when Dinah is in her house ("Anybody might sin for two as had her at their elbow" [p. 428; ch. 52]). Both Mrs. Poyser and Adam's mother believe that "things always happen so contrairy" (p. 70, ch. 6; pp. 120–21, ch. 14; p. 413, ch. 51), but Mrs. Bede has a strong sense that a divine decorum has designed Dinah for Adam "when she's just cut out for thee; an' nought shall make me believe as God didna make her an' send her there o' purpose for thee" (p. 418; ch. 51).

It would be vain to try to persuade a Mrs. Poyser or a Mrs. Bede that their views of things contain logical contradictions, especially as contradictions of a parallel kind seem to predominate in the natural order itself. The narrator is at some pains to point out that natural beauty contains no corollary of moral goodness. Hetty's beauty signifies no corresponding illumination of spirit: "Hetty's face had a language that transcended her feelings" (p. 240; ch. 26) and "One begins to suspect at length that there is no correlation between eyelashes and morals" (p. 131; ch. 15). Seth walks along singing one of the innumerable hymns celebrating the immanence of God in nature, "More and more thyself display, / Shining to the perfect day" (p. 328; ch. 38), but the narrator tends to stress the apparent inconsistency in the relation of nature to human life: "For if it be true that Nature at certain moments seems charged with a presentiment of one individual lot, must it not also be true that she seems unmindful, unconscious of another? . . . There are so many of us, and our lots are so different: what wonder that Nature's mood is often in harsh contrast with the great crisis of our lives?" (p. 247; ch. 27). The day on which Hetty leaves Loamshire on her fatal journey is extraordinarily lovely—"What a glad world this looks like"—but the narrator remembers seeing on similar days in foreign countries "something by the roadside which has reminded me that I am not in Loamshire: an image of great agony—the agony of the Cross. It has stood perhaps by the clustering apple-blos- soms. . . . Such things are sometimes hidden among the sunny fields and behind the blossoming orchards; and the sound of the gurgling brook, if you came close to one spot behind a small bush, would be mingled for your ear with a despairing human sob. No wonder man's religion has much sorrow in it: no wonder he needs a Suffering God." The image of the suffering God built by human hands as an emblem of human experience would seem "strangely out of place" to "a traveller to this world who knew nothing of the story of man's life upon it" (pp. 305–6; ch. 35).

It may seem that this passage at last lifts the veil from the narrator's own conviction and that this conviction must be antidogmatic and antiprovidential. It seems to say that reli- gious practice and doctrine are the metaphors for humankind's individual and social experience throughout history: "no won- der [humanity] needs a suffering God."[11] In a novel by Hardy this would certainly be so, and the passage looks forward to

---

[11]A similar use of traditional Christian symbolism may be found earlier, in "Janet's Repentance," when Janet's suffering at the hands of her husband is correlated with a picture in her mother's home, "a head bowed beneath a cross, and wearing a crown of thorns" (*Scenes of Clerical Life,* ed. David Lodge [Harmondsworth: Penguin, 1973], p. 285).

Hardy in depicting the conflicts and contradictions that his fiction presents as philosophically decisive. But the narrator of *Adam Bede* is more reticent and, in one respect at least, more philosophically consistent than Hardy's narrators. Humanity may need a suffering God and therefore erect images to him, images that embody human experience of human sorrow. But humanity's need for such images says nothing about their doctrinal or objective status. From the evidence of this text we can be sure only that *need* in itself proves very little one way or the other about the order of things. We do not have to accept Mrs. Bede's view that God made Dinah especially for Adam, but there is nothing in her world that conclusively denies it. And if we allow our own intellectual predispositions to impose naturalistic interpretations upon noncommittal narrative, then our reading has only the same kind of validity that Mrs. Bede's does, or Seth's, or Dinah's.

In stressing the subjective or solipsistic quality of all perspective, the narrator includes that of the narrative itself: "My strongest effort is to give a faithful account of men and things as they have mirrored themselves in my mind. The mirror is doubtless defective." The passage is a deservedly famous one, explicitly altering as it does the status of the narration, perhaps in a new way for English fiction. What has been less often noticed is that this disclaimer to objectivity is linked to a rejection of certain conventions of poetic justice. The narrator goes on to imagine a reader, dissatisfied with the portrait of Mr. Irwine, urging a clearer moral line for the story: "Do improve the facts a little. . . . The world is not just what we like. . . . Let your most faulty characters always be on the wrong side, and your virtuous ones on the right. . . . Then we shall be able to admire, without the slightest disturbance of our prepossessions" (p. 151; ch. 17). But the narrator rejects this hypothetical blandishment in favor not of the representation of reality but of the representation of that individual reflection, reality mirrored "in my mind." Such a narrator makes no final adjudication of punishment and reward, resolves no questions of immanence or providential interposition. What, given the disclaimer, would such a position be worth? And we as readers are not merely encouraged but forced (if we stay within the text) to follow the narrator's example.

What the narrator of *Adam Bede* does come out for is the connectedness, the community, of human experience through suffering and through time: "Let us rather be thankful that our sorrow lives in us as an indestructible force, only changing its form, as forces do, and passing from pain into sympathy—the one poor word which includes all our best insight and our best love. . . . For it is at such periods that the sense of our lives having visible and invisible relations beyond any of which either our present or prospective self is the centre, grows like a muscle that we are obliged to lean on and support" (p. 407; ch. 50). Here the narrator sees that sorrow over a period of time becomes sympathy, the generalized conscious love of our neighbors. Suffering is thus seen as a profoundly socializing force, a universal force binding people together.

In the earlier providential tradition, the tradition of Dickens, suffering is often treated as a divinely prescribed specific to chasten pride, to discipline the heart and open it to charity, to force the admission of the essential kinship of humankind. This is the way it works in *Adam Bede* as well, except that the source of the remedy is left obscure even when the language of religion serves to describe it: "Deep, unspeakable suffering may well be called a baptism, a regeneration, the initiation into a new state." In that phrase "may well be called," which looks like an affirmation of the religious terminology but which works equally well as a qualification, the ambiguity of the narration is preserved. "The yearning memories, the bitter regret, the agonized sympathy, the struggling appeals to the Invisible Right . . ." (p. 357; ch. 42). But what "Invisible Right"? God? Providence? Or some idea of justice that Adam or anyone else might have in mind? The religious language serves an important purpose, the purpose of supplying metaphors and symbols of broadly accessible meaning and appeal and—like the roadside shrines in foreign countries—of providing in itself a kind of poetic evidence that sorrow is the universal unifying element in the human lot. It may be perceived as universal not because we know that God distributes it to all but because we know that all endure it.

The distinction marks a crucial alteration in the providential aesthetic. In fiction where a providential intention can be discerned—all the novels of Dickens and Charlotte Brontë and most of the serious fiction before them—a reader can in a general way count on redress for unmerited pain either in this world or the next. Sometimes, as in *Villette* and *Great Expectations,* this redress is obliquely implied or found in deepening awareness rather than in simple restitution, but it is redress nevertheless. In the providential tradition of English fiction the reader is permitted a prospective consolation that the characters, being in the thick of the action, may share or not depending on the strength of their own fictive providentialism. The reader takes no risks with his own convictions; he need only be persuaded that the novel will fulfill the familiar expectations. But when, as in *Adam Bede,* the existence of a providential intention is left an open question the reader cannot count on things being set right. The consequences of the characters' actions may suddenly seem much more serious. Every action must now be regarded as potentially uncorrectable, irrevocable.[12] There may be no ultimate forgiveness. Every action thus becomes the eternal responsibility of the actor, an irredeemable moral liability, with concatenations of consequences extending outward to infinity.

Mr. Irwine tells unheeding Arthur Donnithorne that "consequences are unpitying. Our deeds carry their terrible consequences, quite apart from any fluctuations that went before—consequences that are hardly ever confined to ourselves"

---

[12]The idea of an irrevocable act is important from the beginning in George Eliot's fiction: "God send," says the narrator piously in "Mr. Gilfil's Love-Story," "the relenting may always come before the worst irrevocable deed!" (*Scenes of Clerical Life*, p. 206). The idea goes right through to Gwendolen Grandcourt's despairing exclamation on her guilty implication in her husband's death, "It can never be altered" (*Daniel Deronda*, ed. Barbara Hardy [Harmondsworth: Penguin, 1967], p. 761).

(p. 147; ch. 16). This observation is well within an orthodox providential tradition. Whatever God may perform in the way of redress or restitution, individuals carry full responsibility for their actions. It is a lesson proclaimed throughout Dickens and Brontë. The significant difference here is for the reader, who can no longer find in the text the assurance that good will come out of evil either here or in the hereafter, cannot be sure as Dinah Morris is sure that "all things will turn to good." Anne Mozely in an early review took as the "prominent moral" of the novel "that the past cannot be blotted out, that evil cannot be undone. This conviction is expressed with a strength and persistency that turns into a sort of inspiration the author's motive for the labor of composition; which, if a delight, is assuredly in this case also a labor."[13] Adam's response to Bartle Massey's attempt at consolation—"Good come out of it! . . . That doesn't alter the evil: *her* ruin can't be undone. I hate that talk o' people, as if there was a way o' making amends for everything" (p. 384; ch. 46)—and to Arthur Donni-thorne—"There's a sort o' dammage, sir, that can't be made up for" (p. 390; ch. 48)—show that he would make an unsym-pathetic reader of providential fiction. And although Adam comes to see that his own suffering has enriched and deepened him he never allows that to justify Hetty's suffering. Almost the last words of the novel are those in which he quotes Arthur Donnithorne quoting him: "You told me the truth when you said to me once, 'There's a sort of wrong that can never be made up for'" (p. 450; Epilogue). To accept this "moral" as a premise of the novel is to relinquish many of the traditional satisfactions of the providential aesthetic in English fiction, even as they are sophisticated in Brontë and Dickens.

Nevertheless, *Adam Bede* remains closely engaged with the earlier tradition, and its readers do enjoy certain consolations developed there. Most important of these is the assurance of narrative continuity itself. In *Great Expectations* Joe Gargery tells Pip that "life is made of ever so many partings welded

[13]*George Eliot: The Critical Heritage*, p. 88.

together" (p. 215; ch. 27), and we saw that the links of separation are what make possible movement into the future, the consoling movement of narration. This metaphor in Dickens carries a profoundly religious message of acceptance and resignation. When Adam Bede's sorrow over Hetty's fate develops into a sympathy which prepares him for Dinah, he realizes that "there's a parting at the root of all our joys" (p. 430; ch. 53).[14] Adam thinks of this in relation to harvesttime and harvest celebration. In both novels the existential disjunction that lies at the core of human experience is transformed into a kind of continuity, a continuity that has the paradoxical but beneficent effect of bringing human beings together. *Adam Bede,* like its predecessors in the providential aesthetic, provides a narrative of separation and connection that is gratifying even though here the causes of these movements have lost their ultimate definition.

The Mill on the Floss

George Eliot's second novel presents in various ways an antithesis to her first, and none of these is more central to her adaptation of the providential aesthetic than the contrasting visions of social organization in the two books. One of the great charms *Adam Bede* had for its earliest readers (and retains in a lesser way for us) was its celebration of the rural community and by extension the idea of community itself. However diverse their personalities and perspectives, Mr. Irwine and Adam, Mrs. Poyser and Bartle Massey, Seth Bede and his mother all find room for themselves and for each other. Dinah Morris may be spiritually eccentric, but that does not prevent her from being perceived as socially central.[15] *Adam Bede* is a

[14]Dickens may have adopted Adam's remark to suit Joe Gargery. He admired *Adam Bede* and wrote an enthusiastic letter about it to George Eliot in July of 1859 (reprinted in *George Eliot: The Critical Heritage,* pp. 84–85).

[15]Hetty and Arthur are both exiles, but partly at least by choice.

social success story in the sense that in it society succeeds, succeeds in accommodating most of its members—a cheering and by 1859 nostalgic affirmation of belonging in a community that is strong enough to tolerate the inevitable diversity, insisted upon throughout the novel, of conduct and conviction among its membership.

The Mill on the Floss is a story of social failure in the sense that in it society fails to make this accommodation. In *Adam Bede* the solidarity of the community is associated (at least metaphorically) with a variety of providential perspectives largely tending toward recognition of common elements in the human condition. In *The Mill on the Floss* the loss of this recognition parallels the disintegration of social ties. Dr. Kenn, advising Maggie on her return to St. Ogg's after her fatal excursion with Stephen Guest, puts it this way:

> "The Church ought to represent the feeling of the community, so that every parish should be a family knit together by Christian brotherhood under a spiritual father. But the ideas of discipline and Christian fraternity are entirely relaxed—they can hardly be said to exist in the public mind: they hardly survive except in the partial, contradictory form they have taken in the narrow communities of schismatics. . . . At present everything seems tending towards the relaxation of ties—towards the substitution of wayward choice for the adherence of obligation, which has its roots in the past." (pp. 432–33; ch. 55)

But even given this awareness, Dr. Kenn underestimates the degree of degeneration in St. Ogg's from his Tractarian ideal of a primitive Christian community.[16] The world and the world's

---

[16]The *Tracts for the Times* were at the high point of their influence about the time (1839) that Maggie returns to St. Ogg's. Dr. Kenn probably owes his name to Thomas Ken (1637–1711), one of whose hymns is quoted on the opening page of *Adam Bede*.

wife eventually force him to dismiss Maggie from her responsibilities as governess in his home.

By this late point in the novel we have had numerous hints that St. Ogg's is spiritually dead. "The days were gone when people could be greatly wrought upon by their faith, still less change it" (p. 106; ch. 12). The Reverend Mr. Stelling rather than Dr. Kenn seems in accord with his times: "He thought religion was a very excellent thing, and Aristotle a great authority, and deaneries and prebends useful institutions, and Great Britain the providential bulwark of Protestantism, and faith in the unseen a great support to afflicted minds: he believed in these things, as a Swiss hotel-keeper believes in the beauty of the scenery around him, and in the pleasure it gives to artistic visitors" (p. 123; ch. 14). Indeed, like most certainties in this preflood, secularized society, Mr. Stelling's convictions are validated for him by a certain evident commercial value; and commerce and a waning vestigial tribal loyalty are what remain to hold society together in *The Mill on the Floss*.

In the famous chapter "A Variation of Protestantism Unknown to Bossuet" the narrator professes to be thrilled by the glorious faith that built the Rhine castles and the cathedrals, that led the crusades, that inspired "the grand historic life of humanity," and in contrast to be oppressed by the ruins of villages along the Rhône. The narrator goes on to suppose that we, the cosmopolitan readers, might be similarly oppressed by life on the banks of the Floss. Looking for high romance we receive instead "sordid" accounts of Dodsons and Tullivers, "worldliness without side-dishes." Nevertheless, according to the narrator, we must experience this "oppressive narrowness . . . if we care to understand how it acted on the lives of Tom and Maggie" and through their lives to apprehend the suffering "which belongs to every historical advance of mankind." Indeed, does not "science" tell us "that its highest striving is after the ascertainment of a unity which shall bind the smallest things with the greatest?" (pp. 237–39; ch. 30).

What appears at first a characteristic affirmation of realism and its causalities becomes curiously ironic in this context. The fact is that this novel does *not* go on to associate suffering with any high or great "historical advance of mankind," and no comprehensive vision of "unity" emerges from its pages. Its resolutions suggest more aptly a morally and aesthetically counterevolutionary statement in which the nobler individuals meet extinction while the lesser forms survive the flood. If this is the case (as I will maintain in what follows) then what is the point of the uneasy transitions and shifty logic of this discussion of "Protestantism"? What does it all have to do with castles, crusades, cathedrals, and the faith that founded them? The rhetorical shifts and moves seem to point to some far-reaching and perhaps sinister association. In fact, what the narrator keeps going back to, and what the chapter really seems to be about, concerns the secularism, the essential faithlessness of St. Ogg's. "Observing these people narrowly, even when the iron hand of misfortune has shaken them from their unquestioning hold on the world, one sees little trace of religion, still less of a distinctively Christian creed. Their belief in the Unseen, as far as it manifests itself at all, seems to be rather of a pagan kind; their moral notions, though held with strong tenacity, seem to have no standard beyond hereditary custom." In other words, the narrator goes on saying to the putatively large-minded reader, "You could not stand to live among such people." Even a "vigorous superstition" (of the kind that built the cathedrals? led the crusades?) would better represent "the mystery of the human lot, than the mental condition of these emmet-like Dodsons and Tullivers" (p. 238; ch. 30).

They were, we are told, "part of the Protestant population of Great Britain," but you could not deduce their "religious and moral ideas" from that. Their "theory of life . . . had the very slightest tincture of theology." They found themselves on their works, not on their faith: "A Dodson would not be taxed with the omission of anything that was becoming, or that belonged to that eternal fitness of things which was plainly indicated in the practice of the most substantial parishioners and in the family traditions." They are proud, but their pride is largely negative "in the frustration of all desire to tax them with a breach of traditional duty or propriety." And "the family badge was to be honest and rich; and not only rich but richer than was supposed" (pp. 239–40; ch. 12). The Dodsons and Tullivers align righteousness with conduct rather than feeling, know nothing of faith and little about love, live almost entirely in the material, commercial world. Their ethos is in many respects as far from that of Dinah Morris as can be imagined, just as the commercial social order they help perpetuate is far from the community that surrounds her. The Dodsons embody a transitional stage on the way toward the spiritual alienation felt by those survivors of predestinarian Protestantism foreseen at the conclusion of Weber's *The Protestant Ethic and the Spirit of Capitalism,* a race cut off from their spiritual source and center for whom the "light cloak" of care for external goods has become "an iron cage."[17]

The richness of George Eliot's analysis, a startling achievement forty-five years before Weber's great essay, is not confined in *The Mill on the Floss* to the somewhat evasive abstraction of the chapter on "A Variation of Protestantism." She shows us from the beginning that the Dodsons' system, their "theory of life" or paradigm or view of the order of things, although exclusively material, contains the exacting specificity of a dogmatic religion that professes to conform to a revealed providential order. We are told that "there were particular ways of doing everything in that family." Like orthodox Jews, they have their own dietary laws and they distrust food prepared in "strange houses" (pp. 39, 40; ch. 6). They have traditional times for different activities and for family meetings. They treat articles of clothing (especially bonnets) with a care reserved for sacred vestments. They lay up linen in drawers as an evangelical Christian might record internal evidence of spiritual progress. Mrs. Glegg believes that to wear a good "front" of

---

[17]Max Weber, *The Protestant Ethic and the Spirit of Capitalism,* trans. Talcott Parsons (New York: Scribners, 1958), p. 181. Jerome Thale observes that *"The Mill on the Floss* suggests many of the sociological insights formulated by such thinkers as Marx, Weber, Sombart, and Tawney" (*The Novels of George Eliot,* p. 40). Martin Svaglic discusses the survival of "the Calvinist tradition" in which "material prosperity has long been interpreted as one of the signs of election" into George Eliot's day and her reaction to it ("Religion in the Novels of George Eliot," pp. 149 f.).

curls on a weekday "would be to introduce a most dreamlike and unpleasant confusion between the sacred and the secular" (p. 49; ch. 7), thereby revealing precisely that confusion in her own views. Mrs. Tulliver knows that "the linen's so in order that if I was to die tomorrow I shouldn't be ashamed" (p. 86; ch. 9). Most important of all, and most like Weber's predestinarian Protestants, the Dodsons see economic success as indicative of cosmic sanction and financial failure as evidence of providential chastisement. When Mr. Tulliver goes bankrupt they refuse to help the family with money they have already set aside for Tom and Maggie—not only because this would vitiate the important mortuary ritual of proper legacies (and thereby lower the status of the deceased) but also because "there was a general family sense that a judgment had fallen on Mr. Tulliver which it would be an impiety to counteract by too much kindness" (p. 177; ch. 21). In support of the same reasoning Mrs. Pullet observes after Tom succeeds in business that "now Tom's so lucky, it's nothing but right his friends should look on him and help him" (p. 397; ch. 51). In the Dodson view of things you can count the signs of righteousness. Providence has become strictly material, and the providential intention can be found on the bottom line.

This does not mean that the Dodson view of things seems consistent to anybody but themselves. We can easily see that it contains internal contradictions such as those between the rigidities of prescribed behavior and the rational dictates of economic materialism. Mrs. Glegg, for example, feels the pinch of this antithesis when her husband points out that she would be imprudent to call in her loan to Mr. Tulliver even though he has violated family protocol and insulted her. She is getting good interest. More important, in this novel *everybody* has a system that provides a rationale for some particular predisposition or circumstance. The Dodson view is only one of many.

We have seen that in *Adam Bede* the variety of viewpoints corresponds to the differing aims and desires of the individuals who constitute the community. Their diversity can be tolerated because behind most of these perspectives lies a shared sense that the human lot is general and universal. The solidarity of the community is organic, a gemeinschaft perceived by the characters as a common subjection to the mysterious dispensations of life and expressed as variations of a general providentialism. In *The Mill on the Floss* (set thirty to forty years after *Adam Bede*) the community is well on its way to becoming a gesellschaft, a commercial order in which the connections between people are expressed inorganically in terms of money or interest. Under this new order social ties have loosened. The centripetal forces that united Loamshire no longer possess the strength to counteract the diversity of individual aims and viewpoints. Characters tend to think and act in isolation, and what they do and think can separate them more completely from one another.

In fact, the plurality of individual systems for rationalizing experience and justifying action is what gives society in *The Mill on the Floss* its dissociated, fragmented quality. This plurality reflects the erosion of communal habits of mind among the characters. More important, it affects the reader by invalidating any single intellectual frame of reference and by annhilating the possibility that a collective worldview (such as some form of Christian providentialism) could emerge as dominant or structurally central. We have seen that in order to retain their credibility providential explanations for circumstances and events need to be viewed as ultimate explanations, explanations of first causes. But *The Mill on the Floss* effectively denies the priority of *any* single reading of experience. It vitiates the act of interpretation by reducing all interpretations to mere expressions of individual motive. Theories of life are valid only as justifying individual need or desire. The novel thus works toward a harsh and brilliant subversion of assumptions traditional to the providential aesthetic. It achieves this subversion cumulatively, by a subtle process of mutual contradiction among systems and in their refutation by juxtaposed circumstances or events. In order to see how the process works, I want to look carefully at its treatment in relation to three principal characters: Tom, Mr. Tulliver, and Maggie.

Tom Tulliver's system, freighted with values that Matthew Arnold was to term *Hebraic,* is an extension of the Dodson model. The vestigial rituals of the aunts and uncles mean little to him, almost as little as Mr. Stelling's Latin (equally vestigial in a world where the language of commerce is English), but their equation of financial success with personal worth, of wealth with virtue, of capital with honor becomes one of the two major articles of his creed—especially after he loses his repressed hope of winning Lucy. Tom wants to judge by results, by conduct, by what has *"use"* (p. 190; ch. 23). His pervasive utilitarianism leads him to be contemptuous of feelings. He unsettles his father by the too sudden disclosure of his ability to pay off the creditors (p. 283; ch. 34). He says to Maggie that he does not want "to hear anything of your feelings" and that he would "be very sorry to understand your feelings" (pp. 300, 302; ch. 37).

But Tom's system is shown to be a means whereby he justifies the conditions and predispositions of his own inner life. This becomes clear when we realize that the second article of his creed is passionate adherence to archaic patriarchial values—including vengeance upon his father's enemies, promise of which he willingly inscribes in the family Bible at Mr. Tulliver's command. Such an article conflicts with the selection of commercially optimum alternatives characteristic of the rational economic man his Uncle Dean sketches for him as a model of success. When Tom is offered what in St. Ogg's seems a brilliant opportunity, a share in the business of Guest and Company, he asks instead to manage his father's mill: "I'd give up a much greater chance in life for the sake of having the Mill again" (p. 348; ch. 44). It is a regressive step, a Tulliver step. It shows that Tom does go by feelings and that his system consists of conflicting impulses no more consistent with his utilitarian modernity than the family rituals and superstitions of the Dodsons suit their otherwise uniform materialism. Tom's failure to acknowledge this even to himself makes him the most socially and spiritually alienated character in *The Mill on the Floss,* a lost soul full of unshared longing, cut off even from the family rituals of St. Ogg's, a productive social cipher on the periphery of the commercial order unable to commit himself emotionally even to that but unable to do anything else: "I want to have plenty of work. There's nothing else I care about much" (p. 348; ch. 44). Tom inhabits Weber's "iron cage" of alienated care for external goods.

Mr. Tulliver's ethos, of which Tom inherits a cumbersome fragment, hardly deserves the name of system. It is in fact asystematic, a garbled collection of maxims, impressions, and feelings, full of sudden condemnation and affection. As such it is perhaps the most sympathetic and humanly representative in the novel. Like Adam Bede, Mr. Tulliver sees life as mysterious: "This was a puzzling world, as he often said." Wiser in some things than his inlaws, he knows that "one mustn't judge by th' outside" (pp. 14, 17; ch. 3). Associated with trees and the love of trees, he harks back to a pre-Christian, pagan, druidical Britain (pp. 233, 235; ch. 29). It is from him that Maggie inherits her image as a hamadryad (p. 285; ch. 35). He finds it easy to believe in Old Harry and to attribute the legal success of his enemies to that power. He has a fatal and primitive masculine flaw, a belief in the inferiority of women and in the perpetuation of that inferiority; and his choice of Bessy Dodson " 'cause she was a bit weak, like" (p. 18; ch. 3) undoes him when she foolishly gives Wakem the idea of acquiring the mill.

Nevertheless, it is Mr. Tulliver who is truest to the logic of the heart. He cannot bring himself to collect the money his sister's poor husband owes him because "it had come across his mind that if he were hard upon his sister, it might somehow tend to make Tom hard upon Maggie at some distant day" (p. 76; ch. 9). As readers of George Eliot's other novels will recognize, such feelings are the source of wider social sympathies, though they do not have the practical effect of preventing Tom from being hard to Maggie here. And it is the same movement of heart and mind, almost the same logic, which gives rise to the purest religious utterance in *The Mill on the Floss:* "Does God forgive raskills?" asks Mr. Tulliver on his deathbed. "If He does, He won't be hard wi' me" (p. 315; ch. 39). There is little room in St. Ogg's for this degree of anachronism. Mr. Tulliver only "entangles the skein of life" (p. 114; ch. 13).

Maggie, as the Dodsons observe, is her father's child, a child of feeling and passion rather than order and conduct. Nevertheless, more than any other character in the novel, Maggie wants a system. She starts at the age of nine trying to explain to Mr. Riley the pictures in Defoe's *The History of the Devil,* evincing a precocious dissatisfaction with the methods used to identify witches: "If she swims she's a witch, and if she's drowned—and killed, you know—she's innocent. . . . But what good would it do her then, you know, when she's drowned? I suppose, she'd go to heaven, and God would make it up to her" (pp. 16–17; ch. 3).[18] Maggie is too young to know that the reasoning behind the water trial represents a more primitive version of the Dodson providential materialism that holds it an "impiety" to alleviate misfortunes like the Tulliver bankruptcy on the grounds that, as Mrs. Deane puts it, "if trouble's sent . . . it isn't sent without a cause" (p. 183; ch. 23). When Maggie grows older, suffers more, and finds a system that seems to work temporarily for her in the asceticism of Thomas à Kempis, it is a system of unworldliness—antimaterialistic, inner, voiceless—in many respects antithetic to the Dodson paradigm.

Antithetic, that is, except for its providentialism, or the way in which Maggie interprets its providentialism. In *The Imitation of Christ* Maggie believes she has found a theory of life that enjoins passivity: "She saw the possibility of shifting the position from which she looked at the gratification of her own desires—of taking her stand out of herself, and looking at her own life as an insignificant part of a divinely-guided whole" (p. 254; ch. 32). The "divinely-guided whole" may certainly be found in Thomas à Kempis, but the passivity (according, at least, to the narrator of *The Mill on the Floss*) is of a different order. "She had not perceived—how could she until she had

[18]As has often been observed, the trial by water is applied to Maggie herself in various ways throughout the novel.

lived longer?—the inmost truth of the old monk's outpourings, that renunciation remains sorrow, though a sorrow borne willingly." Maggie leaves out the crucial elements of will and responsibility. She "knew nothing of doctrines and systems" but seems conscious of a need for "an emphatic belief" that will somehow justify the passionate anomalies of her condition (pp. 255, 257; ch. 32). When she tries later to explain her system to Philip in the Red Deeps, it sounds like an extreme form of providential determinism: "Our life is determined for us—and it makes the mind very free when we give up wishing, and only think of bearing what is laid upon us, and doing what is given us to do" (p. 264; ch. 33).[19] In such a dissociated state the mind may indeed be free, perhaps unhinged. Certainly it is regressive: "But, dear Philip, I think we are only like children, that some one who is wiser is taking care of. Is it not right to resign ourselves entirely, whatever may be denied us? I have found great peace in that for the last two or three years—even joy in subduing my will." Philip, who has some experience of resignation himself—"the willing endurance of a pain that is not allayed"—tells her, "*You* are not resigned: you are only trying to stupefy yourself" (p. 286; ch. 35).

But Maggie continues to stupefy herself, right up to the end.[20] When she realizes that she cannot sustain the asceticism she finds in Thomas à Kempis she seeks other ethical imperatives. These also are regressive and providential. Just as her asceticism was an expression of her need to be loved and cared for by "some one who is wiser," so her revised system has at its core the idea of past times and past associations: "I desire no future that will break the ties of the past" (p. 389; ch. 49).

---

[19]Stephen Guest uses this logic on Maggie herself: "See, Maggie, how everything has come without our seeking—in spite of all our efforts" (p. 408; ch. 52). It is providential, he implies; but Maggie has her own version.

[20]See Elizabeth Ermarth, "Maggie Tulliver's Long Suicide," *Studies in English Literature,* 14 (1974), 587–601. John P. McGowan observes that "the novel refuses to endorse Maggie's imaginative reveries because they have no referent" ("The Turn of George Eliot's Realism," *Nineteenth-Century Fiction,* 35 [1980], 177).

Unlike Adam Bede, who contemplates the past as a source of knowledge and strength, Maggie (like her brother Tom) codifies it as a rule of conduct. The past becomes her religion, and she denies her own "strongest feeling" because "such feelings continually come across the ties that all our former life has made for us" (p. 394; ch. 50). Her anguished question to Stephen Guest, which she believes to be rhetorical—"If the past is not to bind us, where can duty lie?" (p. 417; ch. 53)—does have other answers than the one she assumes. Stephen, out of his own narrow motive, gives her some of them: in feeling, in truth to the present, in truth to oneself.[21]

To yield to these Maggie would have to free herself from the system she has laboriously constructed to protect her psychological and social liabilities (the function of all systems in this book) and to which she has given an absolute providential sanction. She is not emotionally accessible to persuasion from Stephen because "she had made up her mind to suffer," and we can see that by this time suffering seems safer to Maggie than joy. Beyond this the decision to return to St. Ogg's has the assurance of obedience to a divine command: "I couldn't live in peace if I put the shadow of a willful sin between myself and God." She tells Stephen that Philip "was given to me that I might make his lot less hard." She resumes the puppetry of following the leadings of her providence. Her system is saving her. She is going home: "Home—where her mother and brother were—Philip—Lucy—the scene of her very cares and trials—was the haven towards which her mind tended—the sanctuary where sacred relics lay—where she would be rescued from more falling" (pp. 416, 418, 420; ch. 53). The irony is very bleak. It is also antiprovidential. Maggie has made the "right" decision and she "deserves" to be rescued, but in fact her system has only saved her for one last stupefying cycle.

Maggie's return home does show a certain futile nobility of spirit, and George Eliot powerfully engages our participation

[21]John Holloway points out that Stephen's arguments are "genuine and formidable" (*The Victorian Sage* [New York: Norton, 1965], p. 144). This is not to say that Maggie would have done well to accept Stephen Guest, a question belonging to another order of discussion.

in her conflict. But the events after her return serve primarily to comment on the enslavement her reasoning has revealed. This begins when she turns to Tom as a kind of idol among her "sacred relics": "Her brother was the human being of whom she had been most afraid, from her childhood upwards: afraid with that fear which springs in us when we love one who is inexorable, unbending, unmodifiable—with a mind that we can never mould ourselves upon, and yet that we cannot endure to alienate from us" (p. 422; ch. 54). He had told her earlier, "I shall always take care of you. But you must mind what I say" (p. 207; ch. 25). Now, treated once again like a kind of surrogate providence, he withdraws finally the recognition that she has endowed with such meaning: "I will sanction no such character as yours: the world shall know that *I* feel the difference between right and wrong. If you are in want I shall provide for you. . . . But you shall not come under my roof" (p. 424; ch. 54). With notable individual exceptions (Mrs. Tulliver, Dr. Kenn, Lucy), the inanely mechanical St. Ogg's soon follows his example. Maggie is left to wonder what it was that she came home for, and yet all the while to confirm herself in the rectitude of her return.

Finally a letter comes from Stephen Guest, self-indulgent and insistent, working on her pity—"Whose pain can have been like mine? Whose injury is like mine?"—begging her to come away with him. Again she renounces the temptation and endures a dark night of the soul. When morning comes she finds resource in memories: "the long past came back to her," and with it words from *The Imitation of Christ:* "I have received the cross . . . I will bear it, and bear it till death." She falls on her knees: "Her soul went out to the Unseen Pity that would be with her to the end. Surely there was something taught her by this experience of great need; and she must be learning a secret of human tenderness and long-suffering, that the less erring could hardly know? 'O God, if my life is to be long, let me live to bless and comfort' " (pp. 450–51; ch. 58).

This is the point where, if Maggie's system is to be given support by the narrative of events, if it is to achieve a measure of superiority over the other systems of lesser characters, then traditional application of the providential aesthetic dictates some dramatic and circumstantial response of the kind offered characters in Dickens—Lizzie Hexam, say, on *her* river. And Maggie does seem to get a response, even one that she welcomes: "she was not bewildered for an instant—she knew it was the flood!" This will justify her. She wakes the house, finds the boats, and drifts out into the current: "she had suddenly passed away from that life she had been dreading: it was the transition of death, without its agony—and she was alone in the darkness with God." When she reaches the mill she tells Tom solemnly that "God has taken care of me, to bring me to you" (pp. 451–52, 455; ch. 58).[22]

Maggie's private providential novel, her "romance," is almost over. She has the gratification of watching Tom acknowledge it—"he guessed a story of almost miraculous divinely-protected effort" (p. 455; ch. 58)—just before the end comes. Maggie just has time to feel Tom's embrace, not long enough to undo a system or a theory of life. The reader, however, has more time—enough to realize that Maggie's desperate search for meaning in her suffering has been in vain, that there is no "secret of human tenderness and long-suffering" to justify this event. She does not live "to bless and comfort," or not much. Maggie's system is no more true than the Dodsons' system, or Mr. Tulliver's, or Tom's, or perhaps even Thomas à Kempis's and Bossuet's. We are led to the further conclusion that Maggie's system has betrayed her, and we recognize—as some of the novel's first readers recognized—that her providential premises are invalidated by her catastrophe.[23]

[22]Barbara Hardy argues that "the flood is the Providence of the novel" and that the conclusion provides an example of "the wrong kind of problem solving" that "turns a great psychological novel into a Providence novel." Hardy thus seems to be reading the story that Maggie writes for herself. Hardy objects to "the bad faith that contrasts so strongly with the authenticity of everything that comes before" (*Critical Essays on George Eliot*, pp. 47–50).

[23]"What does it all come to," asked an irritated writer in the *Saturday Review* for April 1860, "except that human life is inexplicable, and that women who feel this find the feeling painful?" (*George Eliot: The Critical Heritage*, p. 117). See pp. 136, 158–61 for contemporary statements on the irreligion of the novel, especially of the ending.

At one period of his gardening activities Mr. Glegg had noticed that "before the burning of York Minster there had been mysterious serpentine marks on the leaves of the rose-trees, together with an unusual prevalence of slugs, which he had been puzzled to know the meaning of, until it flashed upon him with this melancholy conflagration" (p. 108; ch. 12). His reasoning, preposterous as it seems, is no less true than Maggie's. All providential readings of experience and of signs, all theories of life which await justification by consequences, are invalid in *The Mill on the Floss*. There are no conclusive consequences in this text, not even those we rationalize for ourselves. "If we only look far enough off for the consequences of our actions," the narrator observes, "we can always find some point in the combination of results by which those actions can be justified: by adopting the point of view of a Providence who arranges results, or of a philosopher who traces them, we shall find it possible to obtain perfect complacency in choosing to do what is most agreeable to us in the present moment" (p. 289; ch. 35). And since all systems, even Maggie's, subserve this function, their metaphysical status is equally impoverished.

The catastrophe at the end of this novel is indeed arbitrary. It cuts off Maggie and Tom at the instant of their reconciliation, and this troubles readers who desire Maggie's happiness. But this book is about the arbitrary nature of things, including the systems by which characters try to explain events and including those events—like the flood ("that awful visitation of God," [p. 452; ch. 58])—which no character can act upon. The catastrophe is the ultimate arbitrary refutation of the arbitrary causalities that dominate the perspectives of the novel. It is therefore paradoxically consonant, for it has the effect of equalizing all systems, all theories of life, by leveling them.

The nihilistic effect of all this upon what after *Adam Bede* might remain of a providential aesthetic should be clear. In *Adam Bede* the providentialism of the characters, though forced to compete in the reader's attention with naturalistic or anthropological explanations for events, was tolerated, even approved by the narration as a communal effort to bring meaning and value to experience, and in its deeper forms (Adam's or Dinah's) as at least a precious metaphorial expression of human solidarity and love. But in this second novel the cacophony of internally conflicting ethics or systems, all of them infested to varying degrees with egoism and self-indulgence, echoes society's loss of organic unity and prophesies in its evident spiritual deprivation the social alienation to come. And although we as readers may admire one system more than another—as richer, more loving, nobler, more humane—the lessons of this text suggest that our admiration derives not from a true perception of things as they are or from some shared and universal human experience but from an ultimately parochial need to accommodate what we have read to ourselves.

Silas Marner

George Eliot's next novel deals directly with the consolations offered by parochial explanations for events and with the costs of being so consoled. In *Silas Marner* as in *Adam Bede* a tension develops between providential and naturalistic interpretations of the action, and as in *The Mill on the Floss* incongruous and conflicting individual systems of explanation grow out of the peculiarities of personal need and inclination. But in *Silas Marner* an allegorical, fabulous, parabolic quality of the narrative lends itself readily to abstraction. In fact, the story almost seems to demand—as allegories, fables, and parables demand— abstraction by association with literary modes more "primitive" than the more shaded realism of the two earlier novels. This rapidly and insistently abstracting quality permits *Silas Marner* to make what seems to me its special contribution to the uses of the providential aesthetic in George Eliot's fiction: an exploration of the epistemology of providentialism.[24]

[24]Aspects of *Silas Marner*'s providentialism have received serious critical attention. See Thale, *The Novels of George Eliot*, pp. 58–69, and his introduction to the Rinehart edition of *Silas Marner* (New York, 1962), pp. vii– xxii; also, for an investigation of the thematic and structural parallels between the two plots, see David R. Carroll, "*Silas Marner:* Reversing the Oracles of Religion," *Literary Monographs*, I (Madison: Univ. of Wisconsin Press,

In various ways *Silas Marner* raises the broad question of how human beings come to recognize order in events and circumstances and the more specific one of how they come to know what their own lives are about, how they read the text of their experience. Everywhere in the novel characters are in the act of trying to interpret events. In Lantern Yard, Silas's dissenting brethren employ the biblical method of praying and drawing lots, a narrow and evidently fallible technique based on the invocation of a "special providence" and therefore subject to the abuse of hypocrites like William Dane. In Raveloe the methods are more general and various, ranging from the cramped providential logic that prevents Nancy Lammeter Cass from adopting a child to loosely organized discussions at the Rainbow Inn. Mr. Macy, for example, allows that "there's reasons in things as nobody knows on" (pp. 59–60; ch. 6),[25] and this view with its latent hint of unperceived divine purpose receives a gratuitious extension from Mr. Tookey, who doubts "whether it was right to inquire into a robbery at all when the circumstances were so mysterious . . . 'as if there was nothing but what could be made out by justices and constables' " (p. 74; ch. 8). Dolly Winthrop also represents the Raveloe tolerance of mystery and uncertainty, its latitude, by reasoning that human beings can't be better than "Them as are above us" (p. 103; ch. 10). She informs Silas that Eppie was sent to his door by "Them" and that his care of her will bring him luck (pp. 153, 157; ch. 14). She believes that Silas was badly treated at Lantern Yard, but not by "Them" and that he had "no call to lose heart" as he did (pp. 178–79; ch. 16). In Dolly Winthrop's view the fact that Silas will never know the "rights" of the drawing of lots "doesn't hinder there *being* a rights" (p. 224;

1967), 165–200. Carroll treats evidence for the influences of Spinoza and Feuerbach, showing that "love, in each case [Silas's and Godfrey's], determines the meaning of life. And here, as love turns into God, we have the ultimate reversal of the oracles of religion in the novel" (p. 199). I am indebted to these discussions for the underpinning of several of my observations on *Silas Marner*—though my conclusion on the significance of the parabolic elements departs substantially from them.

[25]Page references are to the Rinehart edition.

ch. 21). From this somewhat laborious rationale she and Silas deduce the by no means contemptible conclusion that human beings must "do the right things as fur as we know, and to trusten" (p. 180; ch. 16).

Dolly Winthrop's system of interpretation functions because of the uncertainty it can tolerate. As we saw in *Adam Bede,* this kind of philosophic negative capability, the tolerance for mystery, is an indication of personal strength in the protagonist. It enables him to go on living and working. It is an aspect of Dolly's personal strength that she has no knowledge of the literal meaning of signs. She does not know that the "I.H.S." she pricks into her lard cakes is a graphic symbol for Jesus, though since the same letters may be seen "on the pulpit-cloth at church" she knows "they've a good meaning" (p. 101; ch. 10). Silas and her son Aaron share the cakes in a vague, humane, Feuerbachian version of the sacrament. We feel that the sharing is more important than the letters, or perhaps the meaning of the letters lies not in their literal significance but in the communal sharing.

"I suppose one reason why we are seldom able to comfort our neighbors with our words," says the narrator, "is that our goodwill gets adulterated, in spite of ourselves, before it can pass our lips. We can send black puddings and pettitoes without giving them a flavor of our own egoism; but language is a stream that is almost sure to smack of a mingled soil (p. 95; ch. 10). Like the drawing of lots and other explicit signs, the epistemological status of words is "dark." At the Rainbow, Mr. Macy tells a fine story of the fuddled Reverend Mr. Drumlow's inadvertent transposition of the words *husband* and *wife* during the marriage service of Nancy Lammeter's parents: "I says to myself, 'Is't the meanin' of the words as make folks fast i' wedlock?' For the parson meant right, and the bride and bridegroom meant right. But then, when I come to think on it, meanin' goes but a little way i' most things, for you may mean to stick things together and your glue may be bad, and then where are you?" Mr. Macy is asking a widely debated question: In what does the efficacy and coherence of the ceremony lie, in the signs ("words"), the intention ("meaning"), or somewhere else? After all, the marriage service is a sacrament, and this can give a sacramental importance to the prescribed language. Mr. Drumlow's solution to the problem—" 'Pooh, pooh, Macy, make yourself easy' he says; 'it's neither the meaning nor the words—it's the re*ges*ter that does it—that's the glue' " (p. 61; ch. 6)—offers little in the way of support to language as the expression of a superior reality though it does give us a pleasant insight into the prerogatives of an established church.[26]

But the signs that receive the most interesting and sustained treatment in *Silas Marner* are not primarily verbal (like the words or letters relating to the sacraments of the Church), or explicit (like drawing lots), but unsought eventualities, especially the theft of Silas's gold and the arrival of Eppie. When Silas earns his first guineas in Raveloe, he has no idea what the gold will come to mean to him. When he lived his actively social life in Lantern Yard, he had not loved money for its own sake: "He had seemed to love it little in the years when every penny had its purpose for him; for he loved the *purpose* then" (p. 18; ch. 2). The money, this putative parable tells us, develops for Silas a purpose of its own, the means become ends, the symbol becomes its own significance, the sign becomes substance. Putting it this way, we can see certain parallels to religious orthodoxy, as expressed both in the sacramentalism of the established church ("I.H.S." on the lard cakes), and in the literalism of dissent (drawing lots in Lantern Yard). When the sign begins to be worshipped as the substance, when (as Feuerbach suggested) "love" becomes "God," then humanity becomes spiritually and socially bankrupt.

When Eppie arrives Silas has already lost his money. The man falsely convicted of robbery is himself robbed—to Silas a Job-like infliction of the demon, or "God of lies," whose

---

[26]Not that language is impotent but that it is untrustworthy because it has a life of its own. It tends more to create reality than to describe it: "Of course, every one who had heard the question, not having any distinct image of the peddler as *without* ear-rings, immediately had an image of him *with* ear-rings, larger or smaller, as the case might be; and the image was presently taken for a vivid recollection" (p. 76; ch. 8).

power he felt at Lantern Yard. But, as is not uncommon with George Eliot's protagonists, Silas has set himself up for his own trauma. This trauma makes excellent psychological and aesthetic sense: by feeding his addiction, by permitting himself to become a miser, he begins to approximate the kind of person—morally and psychologically though not legally—the lots declared him to be. He has gone a certain way toward fulfilling their judgment of him as someone to whom money is more important than community of feeling and religious belief. When Eppie arrives he at first takes her golden curls to be his money restored: "Gold!—his own gold—brought back to him as mysteriously as it had been taken away!" (p. 139; ch. 12). In fact, he takes it as an exchange: "The money's gone I don't know where, and this is come from I don't know where." He names her Hephzibah; she is his Jerusalem restored (pp. 153, 157; ch. 14).[27]

There is something wrong with his reasoning. This idea of an exchange of girl for gold can be satisfying only if we condescend in a considerable degree to Silas's capacity for understanding and also are willing to tolerate his egoism in seeing his own needs as central to the event. Or, as a reviewer for the *Dublin University Magazine* unsympathetically observed in April of 1862: "A curious pathological study is the only name we can give to this sketch of a poor daft body whose soul, even to the last, never quite wakes out of the moral catalepsy into which it fell."[28] As Silas himself puts it near the end, when his money has been restored, "It takes no hold of me now. . . . I doubt it might, if I lost you Eppie. I might come to think I was forsaken again, and lost the feeling that God was good to me" (p. 206; ch. 29).

---

[27]"Thou shalt no more be termed Forsaken; neither shall thy land any more be termed Desolate: but thou shalt be called Hephzibah, and thy land Beulah: for the Lord delighteth in thee" (Isaiah 62:4). Silas choses the name also because it was his mother's and sister's, so it combines the providential sign and the naturalistic explanation.

[28]*George Eliot: The Critical Heritage*, pp. 192–93.

It is certainly true that Eppie helps bring Silas into the organic web of his community (a process already begun with the loss of his gold), that in his engagement with his Raveloe neighbors "he recovered a consciousness of unity between his past and present," and that he rediscovers "good i' this world" and the conviction that providence has him in mind—"there's dealings with us—there's dealings" (pp. 177, 181; ch. 16). These developments lead him to "trusten," and to love, to become more fully human. "Since the time the child was sent to me and I've come to love her as myself, I've had light enough to trusten by; and now she says she'll never leave me, I think I shall trusten till I die" (p. 224; ch. 21). Such, as George Eliot formulated it in a letter to John Blackwood, are the "remedial influences of pure, natural human relations."[29] And all this is to the good, leading as it does to a fuller life for the community and to the happiness of Silas and Eppie. It seems to suggest that Silas's providentialism, strongly egocentric like most providentialism in George Eliot's fiction, can be a good thing so long as it does not feed itself at the expense of others, so long as it is taken responsibly, as Silas takes Eppie, so long as the "sign" (evidence of God's care) functions in the service of the "purpose" (social unity or love).

But to see Eppie as a sign from heaven also endows money with a transcendent value. Eppie, in the implicit logic of this view, is *exchanged* for gold. God takes the gold and substitutes the more humanly valuable living child. But God *takes* the gold. What should happen when the gold is returned? In fact, the day Dunsey Cass's body is found and Silas gets his gold back, Godfrey Cass comes to claim his daughter. He offers Eppie a better life, one that his money can buy for her. At that moment Silas's logic leaves him—despite his protests—holding the bag, the money bag. His own theory of exchange has trapped him. Only Eppie's refusal to accept Godfrey's offer can save Silas here—and her refusal bypasses the logic of money

---

[29]Letter of 24 February 1861, *The George Eliot Letters,* ed. Gordon S. Haight (New Haven: Yale Univ. Press, 1954), III, 382.

and providence on the one hand and the claims of biological paternity on the other.

The problem with Silas Marner's reasoning, and its great distinction from Adam Bede's, derives from the fact that his conclusions are formed in complete ignorance of the naturalistic explanations for the events he takes to be the "dealings" of providence. Adam never allows himself or anybody who talks about Hetty Sorel's fate to infer that it was necessary to the good that follows it—his own deepening awareness and eventual union with Dinah. He short-circuits complacent providentialism by insisting that suffering must remain a mystery. In contrast, Silas's logic, and to a lesser extent Dolly Winthrop's, leads to the conclusion that events antecedent to Eppie's arrival either work to achieve Silas's salvation or, more charitably, remain irrelevant to him.[30]

This may be all we should expect from "a poor daft body" subject to involuntary mental and physical lapses, but the reader knows the whole sordid story, Godfrey Cass's story and the story of Eppie's alcoholic, opium-addicted mother. It is a story of abandonment, deceit, self-indulgence, reliance upon chance, abdication of marital and parental responsibility. The fact that Godfrey, as has often been pointed out, reforms under the influence of his wife's loving rectitude and comes to see a "retribution" in his own life (p. 198; ch. 17) does not alter the case. As Godfrey himself puts it (they are his last words in the novel), "It *is* too late to mend some things, say what they will" (p. 219; ch. 20). The reader who rests content with

[30]"But it is not altogether impossible," wrote Richard Simpson in October 1863, "to discover the irony of making Marner's conversion depend altogether on human sympathies and love, while he, simple fellow, fails to see the action of the general law of humanity, and attributes everything to the 'dealings' which regulate the accidents. *Silas Marner* contains an apology for Providence arbitrary and petitionary as the silliest of religious novels, and an apology for the special doctrines of Feuerbach's humanitarianism worked up with the utmost dialectic and psychological ability. There is great ingenuity in this method of planting opinions which one wishes to eradicate, and of hiding a subtle argument for error under a specious defence of the truth" (from the *Home and Foreign Review*, quoted in *George Eliot: The Critical Heritage*, p. 229).

the simple providential explanation must possess a determining preconception about the appropriate moral line in English fiction.[31] The reader who condescends to Silas's view of things and assumes the point to be that it is good for poor daft bodies to feel themselves loved and watched over because this makes them happy and society stable (an "opiate of the masses" approach) must posit a kind of moral superciliousness in this novel inconsistent with George Eliot's other work. And even elaborate recent analyses which view the parallel plots of Godfrey and Silas as mutually illuminating because they reveal similar truths about human nature, its egoism or its growth through love, or because they make similar comments about society, its inhibition or its liberation of the self—even such analyses seem to me to miss the extreme but central point of this "legendary tale."[32]

This point is that what Godfrey "knows" about Eppie's arrival at Raveloe and what Silas "knows" about her advent in his life are forever contradictory and incompatible. What Godfrey knows is of course closer to what most readers would recognize as realistic, as a naturalistic explanation. But that explanation does not appear to have meaning for Silas. He does not challenge it or even ask about it. What Silas knows about Eppie is that she was "dealt" to him to save him. Only the parabolic explanation is *real* to him; he *knows* it to be true because his money was taken. In the meeting between Silas and Godfrey there is no communication, except the communication from Eppie that she chooses to stay with Silas—a choice that has nothing to do with signs, with ordering the universe around oneself, with providence, but exclusively with her feelings. These are self-validating and what most readers want her to have: "I wasn't brought up to be a lady, and I can't turn my mind to it. I like the working folks, and their

---

[31]That so many did so for so long testifies to the continuing strength of simple providential expectations among readers of English fiction for generations after *Silas Marner* was published. A school edition of the novel in 1903 referred to its "tender religious charm" (ibid., p. 18).

[32]George Eliot's term for it (*Letters*, III, 382).

victuals, and their ways. . . . I'm promised to marry a working-man, as 'll live with father, and help me to take care of him" (p. 216; ch. 19). But her choice entails the rejection of a wider sphere of knowing; it is a conservative choice—confined, ignorant, loving.

"O father," says Eppie on her wedding day, "what a pretty home ours is! I think nobody could be happier than we are" (p. 227; Conclusion). The novel lets us believe that she may be right, but a serious reading of the novel also requires that we take in the series of rejections that led to this happiness: Godfrey Cass's rejection of Eppie's mother and his consignment of Eppie to Silas; her rejection of Godfrey and Nancy and the wider life they can offer her; Silas's rejection of claims and explanations that might impinge upon his centrality in Eppie's life and the providentialism reawakened by it. What Silas, Eppie, Dolly Winthrop, Mr. Macy, the landlord at the Rainbow, even Nancy Cass all agree on seems to be that once you have found the system that works for you, that makes you happy or secure, you hold onto it and lock the door. The consensus at the Rainbow Inn is that only a fool would stand in the dark looking for ghosts he did not want to see (pp. 63–66; ch. 6). Once you find what you are looking for, your own Eppie, your Jerusalem restored, you stop if you want to be happy. In this circumscribed vision of happiness, the signs—words, events, other people, money—have epistemological validity only in that confined arena of personal need and desire where they can be arranged in patterns of reassurance and safety, where they become the counters, the currency of our individual "special providence." Most of us admit no evidence of any other. We can't afford to. We hoard what we have.

Thus the story does say that Silas's providentialism, his treatment of the exchange of girl for gold, has made him happy. But the story also prevents us from resting content with the logic that makes him so. On the other hand, if we take the elitist view that such logic is good for little people like Silas and Eppie and that money in this story is best seen as a symbol for social interaction, then we find ourselves in the uncomfortable position of supporting various forms of mental stasis.

And we find ourselves opposing the complex social causalities and the doctrine of personal responsibility for action that George Eliot elaborated so tellingly in her other novels.

"No," says Godfrey Cass at the end, "there's debts we can't pay like money debts, by paying extra for the years that have slipped by" (p. 217; ch. 20). I want to agree with him. I think his story—and Silas's—both argue the limitations, the fundamental weakness of clinging to signs and symbols. Money is not a sign; it is not a symbol. It is money—worth so much and no more and no less. Eppie is Eppie and gold is gold. And the novel *Silas Marner,* which seems so much like a parable or an allegory, contains an indictment of these ways of reading the world.

At the conclusion of *Silas Marner* only Godfrey Cass has left the door open. He is the only character still growing. He is still critically reading the text of experience. And the novel leaves him proportionately less satisfied and less at rest than the others. *His* money has not been exchanged for a daughter. Eppie rejected it. His wife Nancy attributes his restlessness, his unconsoled melancholy over the hiatus in his life, to their childlessness. No doubt she is right. Godfrey does not have his Eppie, and not having her, he, unlike the others, can still learn. And this austere alliance between longing and knowledge is the other, bleaker, more abstract moral of the book, its criticism of a parabolic or allegorical view of things that it at once exploits and subverts.

Romola and *Felix Holt*

George Eliot's manipulation of important aspects of traditional providentialism continues in *Romola* and *Felix Holt,* but in neither of these does she employ the possibilities of a providential aesthetic as a central structuring principle. Here the primary focus turns on politics and political life, its dialectic and consequence. *Romola* and *Felix Holt* are more candidly *worldly* than the three early novels, and although important

characters are deeply involved with religious thought and practice, their involvement is treated as a function of politics: in
relation, that is, to the life of the state or to the wider social
forces at work in their specific temporal contexts. The providentialism of Dinah Morris or Maggie Tulliver or Silas Marner
is (as we have seen) central to the thematic conflicts and tensions that dominate their novels. That of Romola or Savonarola or the Reverend Mr. Lyons is not, and neither Tito
Melema nor Felix Holt can be said to have a recognizably
providential worldview—perhaps the first major characters in
George Eliot's fiction who do not. In *Romola* and *Felix Holt*
characters function in what has become an essentially historical
context, less metaphysical, less abstract and philosophical, less
congenial to George Eliot's previous exploitation of a providential intention even in its limited application as a metaphor
for human solidarity.

This in itself constitutes a most important development.
Among the characters, political rationalizations tend to absorb
or supplant providential habits of mind. The thematic direction
of the novels becomes more secular. This process involves a
movement away from the metaphorical or generalizing power
of those symbolic devices dependent upon traditional providentialism as expressed in fiction, the traditional structuring
power of the providential aesthetic. The narrative voice itself
seems to become more explicit and didactic as if to compensate
for this loss. George Eliot's convictions have not changed, but
the machinery of her art has. It moves away from the vaguely
nostalgic past of the bucolic setting to the turmoil of 1492–
98 in cosmopolitan Florence or to the election of 1832 in
"Treby Magna," away from generally representative types to
ostensibly specified historical characters, away (or so it seemed
to most of her contemporaries) from universal human themes
to particular historical problems.

Most general critical studies of George Eliot deal with this
change in her art after *Silas Marner,* a change immediately
noticed in the contemporary reviews of *Romola* and *Felix Holt.*
Clearly it has importance not only in the development of her

own fiction but for the development of English fiction generally. My present concern, however, is limited to tracing those innovations that bear directly on her exploitation of a providential aesthetic. For this purpose *Romola* and *Felix Holt* serve primarily to elaborate certain lines of thought begun in the three preceding novels and to introduce important new elements that receive fuller treatment in *Middlemarch* and *Daniel Deronda*.

In *Romola* Tito Melema seems at first a kind of advanced version of the male characters like Arthur Donnithorne and Stephen Guest, who assume that the universe is in place to serve their own desires. Like them, he at first feels himself to be a favorite of fortune (p. 81; ch. 7), and he assumes that the "end of all life" is "to extract the utmost sum of pleasure."[33] But closer attention to Tito's thoughts and casual remarks shows him to be something new in George Eliot's fiction, a cynical believer in the vicissitudes of fortune and the meaninglessness of the universe. He ridicules Tessa's simple providentialism with mild but revealing irony ("Perhaps the *Aves* fetched me only it took them a long while," p. 139; ch. 14). When Nello the barber asks him about Bardo's "great work" of scholarship in which he is supposed to be a dedicated assistant and "which is to astonish posterity," Tito replies, "Posterity in good truth, whom it will probably astonish as the universe does, by the impossibility of seeing the plan of it" (p. 126; ch. 13). In a planless universe everything is permitted, and Tito trusts only in the strength of his own policy and practice. Like certain advanced villains in Dickens, his nihilism serves his selfishness; his cynicism permits moral license. In Tito we have a character—the first in George Eliot's fiction—where egoism is sustained not by a self-serving providentialism but by nihilism. His ethic is that of Raffles in *Middlemarch,* and he reappears typically in *Daniel Deronda* as Grandcourt.

[33]*Romola* (New York: Harper and Brothers, 1869), p. 81, ch. 7; p. 111, ch. 11.

Tito's opportunistic nihilism appears at first to be the opposite of Savonarola's special providentialism. What could be more different from holding that the universe is without perceptible order than holding that Florence is its divinely specified center? Morally and socially, however, their actions have similarly disastrous results, to Florence and to themselves. When Savonarola tells Romola that "the cause of my party *is* the cause of God's kingdom" (p. 439; ch. 59), the immediate political implications and the historical consequences show him to be effectively a moral ally of the Tito who betrays him. Both men, indeed, betray their friends and the wider social life around them. Savonarola's evasion of the trial by fire and Tito's planned escape from Florence have similar motives, and both ultimately fail as the result of a train of consequences they have set off themselves. The crowd that assembles to capture Savonarola chases Tito into the river. The special providentialism of Savonarola has its reversed image in the special nihilism of Tito. It is a fresh point in George Eliot's work, one aimed at an intellectually aggressive audience whose ambitions (like those implicated in the programs of Comte and Spencer) involve political consequences.

In fact, one of the major themes of *Romola* is the pervasiveness and superiority of a wisdom greater than learning and more powerful than political manipulation. When Tito is still young in Florence with some traces of innocence about him, he feels "that loving awe in the presence of noble womanhood which is, perhaps, something like the worship paid of old to a great nature-goddess, who was not all-knowing, but whose life and power were something deeper and more primordial than knowledge" (p. 94; ch. 9). He senses the power of what Romola ultimately comes to embody. But Tito loses the guidance of this primordial wisdom because he lacks the elemental moral sense that lies beneath and behind pagan and Christian religious life, "the initial recognition of a moral law restraining desire" that "checks the hard, bold scrutiny of imperfect thought into obligations which can never be proved to have any sanctity in the absence of feeling" (p. 112; ch. 11). Like Romola's brother Dino and like Savonarola as well, he cuts himself off

from "the human sympathies which are the very life and substance of our wisdom" (p. 152; ch. 15), the sympathies that
Romola discovers in her service to the poor of Florence and
confirms as part of herself in the plague-stricken land she lights
on after "drifting away."

The two most important coincidences of the novel act in
aid of this primordial and (as represented here) female wisdom.
Romola's landing in the pestilential village, herself an image
of the Madonna complete with a "Hebrew baby" in her arms,
strikes the afflicted community like a providential advent. Legends grow out of it. And such humane service, we are made
to feel, is not only what the villagers require but what Romola
needs as well. She had set off in her boat feeling "orphaned
in those wide spaces of sea and sky. She read no messages of
love for her in that far-off symbolic writing of the heavens,
and with a great sob she wished that she might be gliding into
death" (p. 450; ch. 61). She wakens to the benign warmth of
the sun and to the exercise of those duties of human sympathy
which will help to renew her and which still bring her to
mysterious primeval wisdom that her father, her husband, and
her priest—the masculine representative constituents of Florence itself—so distinctly lack. Her landing at the village seems
providential—too providential, many readers have thought,
for a novel treating chiefly of historical realpolitik. It is in fact
an application of a device traditional to providential fiction,
the merited but uncontrived fulfillment of desire that I have
called inconsequent actualization.

Romola's waking at the village immediately follows the murder of Tito by Baldassare, also an event that strains probability
in what at first looks like another awkward attempt to reveal
a providential intention or at least to serve poetic justice. Just
as the Mediterranean floats Romola to the village where she
is needed, so the Arno flings Tito onto the bank where Baldassare lies waiting. It seems too good to be true, not to
Baldassare, whose design of revenge leads him to expect it,
but to readers who for sixty chapters have been learning to
live realistically with Tito. Is this the novel in which to look
for a providential intention, and is George Eliot the author

likely to supply it? She seems to have anticipated these questions, for the chapter ends: "Who shall put his finger on the work of justice and say, 'It is there?' Justice is like the kingdom of God—it is not without us as a fact, it is within us as a great yearning" (p. 489; ch. 67).[34] So we are warned against the traditional interpretation, and the next chapter begins with Romola's waking. The warning is significant, the juxtaposition of improbabilities is doubtless significant—but of what?

The novel really is unclear on these points, and Romola's fortunate voyage and Tito's well-earned murder do violate the tone and atmosphere of historical realism so laboriously achieved in the preceding sixty-six chapters. Unlike, say, the fortunate arrival of Eppie in *Silas Marner,* which can be traced to the willful indulgences of her parents, human agents whose actions have human consequences, these events in *Romola* are brought about by the currents of sea and river, natural agents not governed by human will. Romola goes to sleep at sea and wakes up at the village. Tito loses control of his course in the river before it casts him up violently two yards from a man he betrayed. This tells us that the narrative interrupts the concatenation of willed human events in order to place the fate of the principals at the disposal of nonhuman natural elements, a movement not typical of George Eliot's fictional causalities.

But here, perhaps, lies the necessary clue to the meaning of the voyage and the murder. They have nothing to do with politics, or at least not with the manipulations, evasions, and brutalities that go by that name in Savonarola's Florence. They have nothing to do with scholarship either, that excessive faith in rational aggrandisement which leaves the possessor blind and acrimonious, the solitary guardian of a library. By giving the Arno and the Mediterranean the enigmatic last word in the destinies of Tito and Romola, the novel suggests (though

---

[34]George Levine offers a valuable speculation as to why these events are in the novel (though not a complete analysis of what they mean there): "George Eliot herself has put justice in the world. Her own great yearning for it sought a method by which to embody it: the method was romance" ("*Romola* as Fable," *Critical Essays on George Eliot,* p. 96).

it certainly fails to explain) the influence of that "great nature-goddess" whose "life and power were something deeper and more primordial than knowledge"—or than the practice of politics. These problematic events dramatize an important critical point that comments retrospectively on the machinations that precede them. And although here they lead to lapses in the realistic decorum, the apparent violation of naturalistic explanation and probability reappear in triumphant complexity and richness in *Daniel Deronda,* a novel where willed but unimplemented occurrences are mysteriously but less arbitrarily actualized.

In *Felix Holt* the causes of almost all the important events, including those in the distant past that result in Esther's right of inheritance to Transome Court, may be traced to the willed actions of human agents. This fact, however, does not prevent a good deal of mouthing of the word *providence* and the hypothetical enlistment of the providential intention in English politics, a diffused Podsnappery with echoes of Savonarola's Florentine chauvinism. Mrs. Transome learned in her youth that "the providential government of the world, though a little confused and entangled in foreign countries, in our favored land was clearly seen to be carried forward on Tory and Church of England principles."[35] The Reverend Mr. Lingon rationalizes his support of his radical nephew Harold Transome with the assurance that family ties are part of the scheme of things, "as if Providence couldn't take care of the country without my quarreling with my own sister's son!" (p. 122; ch. 3). Sir Maximus Debarry justifies toleration of Harold Transome's candidacy with the observation that "we may surely wink at a few things for the sake of the public interest, if God Almighty does; and if He didn't, I don't know what would have become of the country" (p. 180; ch. 7). Mr. Johnson, the corrupt election agent from London, asserts that "it was a most providential thing in the Mugham election last year that Putty was

[35]*Felix Holt,* ed. Peter Coveney (Harmondsworth: Penguin, 1979), p. 105; ch. 1.

not on the Tory side" (p. 282; ch. 17). Mr. Wace the brewer thinks that "providence and the good sense of the country" will protect the institutions of church, king, and rational free enterprise (pp. 301–2; ch. 20). But these views prevent no one from engaging in the politics of faction and self-interest, and all the political figures act as if providence can use all the help it can get.

There is nothing fundamentally contradictory in this: providence—if it works at all—employs human agents to reveal the true order of things in society. Just how sincerely a belief in this process can be held is revealed by its embodiment in the dissenting minister Rufus Lyon. Mr. Lyon loves debate and has enviable confidence in his powers of persuasion. Knowledge for him really is power, and he leaps at his imagined opportunity to serve God and country by debating the representative of the Establishment in the person of the Reverend Augustus Debarry. When Felix Holt tries to moderate these expectations, the minister (sounding like a lovable Casaubon) assures him: "My young friend, it is a case wherein the prearranged conditions tend by such a beautiful fitness to the issue I have sought, that I should have forever held myself a traitor to my charge had I neglected the indication" (p. 328; ch. 22). But the rector, Mr. Debarry, is horrified by this literal application of a commonplace courtesy (his nephew's offer of service to Mr. Lyon). He sees Lyon as a quixotic but formidable agent of the leveling forces at work ("losing all the results of civilization, all the lessons of Providence" [p. 330; ch. 23]) and decides to send a curate in his stead. The curate defects and Mr. Lyon stands alone before his disgruntled audience. His opportunity to speak is thwarted. Perhaps it was not a providential leading.

He does not learn his lesson. When Esther gains a legal right to Transome Court he sees the event as a providential "command," not because she merits high station in herself, but because it means that wealth and power might pass from members of the Church of England to the "body of congregational Dissent." Or as he puts it to her, "your education and peculiar history would thus be seen to have coincided with a long train of events in making this family property a means of honoring and illustrating a purer form of Christianity than that which hath unhappily obtained the pre-eminence in this land" (pp. 505, 506; ch. 41). His logic as a dissenting radical is no better than that of the Establishment. Both sides see providential justification for their own interests and providential patterns in their own actions.

But Esther gives up her claim to the estate and Mr. Lyon loses again. Providence does not give him much external encouragement. What makes him lovable is that he loses and yet he keeps the faith. He is constantly denied—denied the longed-for debate, denied his daughter's conversion to Dissent, denied predestinarian signs of approval such as wealth and honor. But he goes on loving and believing despite the losses. His love for Esther's mother had been "irreconcilable with that conception of the world which made his faith" (p. 166; ch. 6), and his affections have been wayward ever since. He loves the radical in Felix Holt. He respects Esther's freedom of thought. He can above all tolerate uncertainty— that sine qua non of moral health in George Eliot's fiction— and even be witty about it. When Esther remarks that "everything is uncertain" he responds: "Truly . . . the uncertainty of things is a text rather too wide and obvious for fruitful application; and to discourse of it is, as one might say, to bottle up the air, and make a present of it to those who are already standing out of doors" (p. 508; ch. 41).

Esther has to learn what it means to live in the moral open air. Her father's cumbersome providentialism does not help her ("There was no illumination for her in this theory of providential arrangement" [p. 505; ch. 41]). When she goes to live with Harold and his mother at Transome Court, the temptation for her is to imagine "what it would be to abandon her own past" in some painless way, to achieve a transition into proffered new life (apparently suited to her predispositions almost as dangerously as Pip's great expectations are to his) without irreparable loss. "It was difficult by any theory of providence, or consideration of results, to see a course which she could call duty" (p. 524; ch. 43). If Esther rejects her

father's idea of a providential "command," what "consideration of results," what legitimate causality should guide her?
The question is a serious one, asked as it is at what could be
called the historical moment of deprivation, the loss of the
securities inherent in the providential intention as popularly
represented in English fiction. There is a chill here like that
felt in the great spaces of *Middlemarch*. And Esther's method,
her solution, is one that is not consistently employed by any
major character in the earlier novels.[36] She begins to look very
carefully at other people, first at Felix Holt and then at Harold
Transome and his mother.

In Mrs. Transome, Esther finds a study in self-defeat, a
women condemned by her own values and convicted by her
own system. Mrs. Transome is a providentialist who hopes
that the return of her son will set her right with the order of
things, "to feel that the doubtful deeds of her life were justified
by the result, since a kind Providence had sanctioned them"
(p. 89; ch. 1). If her son proves loving and submissive it will
mean that she is forgiven for her adultery and for her tyranny
over her husband. Harold Transome is instead sexist and self-
confident. This and the events that follow, including the potential loss of the estate, she sees "through the medium of certain
dominant emotions that made them seem like a long-ripening
retribution" (p. 456; ch. 36). Her son's male chauvinism
("Women. . . . It doesn't signify what they think" [pp. 115–
17; ch. 2]) has its reflection in her despairing sense of imprisonment in her own sex. Her protest has a certain validity when
it is directed against Harold or Jermyn and their complacen-
cies, but this should not blind us to the pathological elements,
the self-hatred and fatalism of her deeper revelations: "A woman's love is always freezing into fear. . . . God was cruel when
he made women" (p. 488; ch. 39). "Always the edge of calam-
ity had fallen on *her*. Who had felt for her? She was desolate.
God had no pity" (p. 595; ch. 50).

This is what Esther penetrates; this is the deadness of Transome Court; and this is the ghastly possibility for herself that

---

[36]With the exception of Philip Wakem, who nevertheless lacks Esther's
balance and hence her freedom.

she rejects. When she decides to return to her father and to ally herself with Felix, she is not following a "consideration of results" based on a determining providentialism—her father's or Mrs. Transome's—but on her own keen insight into wider possibilities based on her comprehension of a person who seeks them. In prison Felix tells her that "the only failure a man ought to fear is failure in cleaving to the purpose he sees to be best. As to just the amount of result he may see from his particular work—that's a tremendous uncertainty: the universe has not been arranged for the gratification of his feelings." He shows her, though, that he accepts her choice for herself, even assuming that choice to be mistress of Transome Court. He does not tell her that her opportunity is an arrangement of providence or a determining condition of her womanhood. Instead, he calls it "a case of fitness that seems to give a chance sanction to that musty law" (p. 557; ch. 45). She may well feel that there is more open air in Felix Holt's cell than in all the rooms at Transome Court.

This openness to the wider possibilities of life with its attendant uncertainties, this refusal to accept the limitations of preconceived patterns or anticipated results, is what it means to be truly radical in *Felix Holt*. As Denner vainly tries to persuade Mrs. Transome, "Things don't happen because they're bad or good. . . . There's good chances and bad, and nobody's luck is pulled only by one string." Mrs. Transome tells her that she talks "like a French infidel," but Denner is not afraid and her mistress is full of fears (p. 103; ch. 1). Or, as Tommy Trounsem, the last of his line, puts it: "I were deep enough, but its no use being deep, 'cause you can never know the law. And there's times when the deepest fellow's worst frightened" (p. 379; ch. 28).[37] Esther's choice nullifies the preposterous labyrinthine concatenations of the law of entail, that bulwark of nationalized providentialism. In fact, she rejects all systems that explain experience by prescribing conduct. In deciding

[37]G. S. Venables, in an 1866 review of *Felix Holt,* observed that "the law supplies to modern novels the place of that supernatural machinery which was once thought indispensable in epic composition" (*George Eliot: The Critical Heritage,* p. 280).

not to accept Harold Transome and Transome Court, Esther really choses the unknown over the known.[38] She thus becomes someone who cannot be bribed. She achieves this by means of an "inward revolution" which—given the degeneracy of the allied political and providential systems in *Felix Holt*—seems to be the only form of personal action free from the absurdities of self-contradiction. Finally, Esther's private inward revolution, her radical rejection of prescriptive systems and the enslavement of mind they represent, points us toward its wider social application in the great work that follows.

Middlemarch

Middlemarch is the most worldly of George Eliot's novels. Her contemporaries felt this at once and found themselves depressed by what David Carroll terms "the absence, the wilful denial of any spiritual dimension to Middlemarch society." In a review in the *Spectator* R. H. Hutton complained that this author was "always harping" on the "discordant string" of atheism. George Eliot, he said, "is a melancholy teacher,—melancholy because skeptical. . . . The whole tone of the story is so thoroughly noble, both morally and intellectually, that the care with which George Eliot excludes all real faith in God from the religious side of her religious characters, conveys the same sort of shock with which, during the early days of eclipses, men must have seen the rays of light converging towards a centre of darkness." A less acute writer for the *Saturday Review* suggested that Dorothea would have done better to abjure social reform and to "comfort herself in the belief that the eye of Providence never sleeps." Edith Simcox characterized the author's "large theory of the universe" as "at once so charitable and so melancholy that it would be fairly intolerable (although true) without the sauce of an unsparing humour."[39] These writers and

---

[38]For a valuable discussion of the "virtual rather than real" implications of Esther's choice, see Caserio, *Plot, Story, and the Novel*, pp. 108–12.

[39]*George Eliot: The Critical Heritage*, pp. 29–30, 293, 302, 313, 316, 325.

others, even those prepared to admit some truth in the narrator's view of things, felt the cosmic loneliness of *Middlemarch*, the "coldness" and "darkness," as they called it, of its spaces.

Their responses were based on accurate readings of the text, despite the fact that from a metaphysical perspective *Middlemarch* contains nothing new. No new position on the cosmic order of things is advanced, no theory of the universe not at least implicit in George Eliot's previous fiction. What has changed, what is new, is the treatment of the providentialism of the principal characters.[40] In earlier novels the religious convictions of Dinah Morris and Silas Marner, to take the most prominent examples, are indulged, even petted as being morally valuable if not theoretically sound. And even as late as *Felix Holt* the strained providential logic of the Reverend Mr. Lyon seems to be tolerated as the excess of a generous nature. *Middlemarch,* however, lacks this indulgence and this tolerance. Here the providential habit of mind as embodied in the chief characters, particularly in the chief male characters, becomes a moral and spiritual disorder.

Bulstrode, Casaubon, Lydgate, and Fred Vincy each believes that he possesses a key whereby the secret of the order of things, the pattern that gives significance to the cosmos, can be unlocked and disclosed. With varying degrees of awareness each places himself at the center of that order. Each commits an irrevocable act based on this illusion of centrality. Each finds himself forced to abandon his illusion in the searing light of a new knowledge, an awareness that involves the painful illumination of the otherness of the world and of other people. And although certain of the female principals—Dorothea most evidently but also Rosamond, Celia, and Mrs. Bulstrode—may be seen to participate in different stages of this pattern, only these four male characters are forced to dance the whole figure. In this novel the involvement of *man's* egoism with a providential habit of mind has become inescapable, has become in

[40]Peter Jones gives a brief account of the providentialism of *Middlemarch*'s chief characters in *Philosophy and the Novel* (Oxford: Clarendon, 1975), pp. 36–40.

fact a complex single identity, so that masculine complacency and the providentialism of these chief male characters (Garth, Farebrother, and Ladislaw escape) can serve by the end as troubling intimate representations of one another.

Fred Vincy is the simplest of the four. He can be seen as the typological offspring of Arthur Donnithorne, Stephen Guest, young Godfrey Cass, and Harold Transome. Fred's key to the order of things lies in the assumption that that order is fitted to himself. When he needs money he counts on a "providential occurrence" to supply it. "It would have been sheer absurdity to think that the supply would be short of the need: as absurd as a faith that believed in half a miracle for want of strength to believe in a whole one." And the absurd in something close to its modern existential meaning is what confronts him. Featherstone's present of five twenty-pound notes "actually presented the absurdity of being less than his hopefulness had decided that they must be. What can the fitness of things mean, if not their fitness to a man's expectations? Failing this, absurdity and atheism gape behind him" (pp. 99, 100; ch. 14).

This sounds like an appropriate sardonic tone to take with a young gentleman very much too full of himself. But the problem is in fact a serious one. If the young man's sense of order has been founded on an illusion of the fitness of things to himself, then the classic response to this kind of disappointment *is* atheism and the confrontation with absurdity. What he took to be solid and ordered becomes (to use Nietzsche's telling word) "weightless."[41] Fred's redeeming sense of inferiority to Mary and to Mr. Farebrother saves him from this weightlessness, and his rescue is aided by their affection and— equally important—by his intellectual inability to achieve the range of abstract consciousness necessary to a full appreciation of absurdity. He seizes the beneficent opportunity to work off his egoism in apprenticeship to Caleb Garth, frightened along by Mr. Farebrother's noble disclosure of his love for Mary

[41]See Karl Jaspers, *Nietzsche and Christianity* (Chicago: Henry Regnery, Gateway ed., 1961), p. 14.

with its threat of rivalry. Fred Vincy runs the course through providential egoism, the unpardonable (and unpardoned) act of contracting a debt that the Garths must pay, to a new awareness attained through a recognition of the competing needs and hence the otherness of others.

Mr. Casaubon's limitations provide no such protection. His massive good fortune in marrying Dorothea, instead of stimulating him to growth and a saving awareness, becomes transformed in the tragic alchemy of his secret insecurity into the presiding circumstance of his destruction. This alchemy is founded upon the principles and elements of his own pervasive providentialism, a providentialism that dominates his view of other people, of himself, and of his life's work. When Dorothea makes her mistimed suggestion that their wealth be redistributed in Ladislaw's behalf, he tells her that "these . . . are providential arrangements" (p. 274; ch. 37), a commonplace justification of the economic status quo. When he writes his grotesque proposal of marriage, his letter identifies Dorothea as a gift from providence to him: "Some deeper correspondence than that of date in the fact that a consciousness of need in my own life had arisen contemporaneously with the possibility of my being acquainted with you." His own "foreshadowing needs" for her are therefore "providentially related thereto as stages towards the completion of a life's plan"— God's plan, that is, for Mr. Casaubon's life. To be her husband "I should regard as the highest of providential gifts" (pp. 31–32; ch. 5)—though as the narrator later observes, "Whether Providence had taken equal care of Miss Brooke in presenting her with Mr. Casaubon was an idea which could hardly occur to him. . . . As if a man could choose not only his wife but his wife's husband!" (p. 206; ch. 29).

Dorothea initially thinks of Mr. Casaubon as, among other models, "a living Bossuet . . . a modern Augustine," two of the greatest expounders of providence, of God's will acting through human time and human history. And Casaubon's ambition seems to be on a scale with their achievements. In his projected "Key to All Mythologies" he proposes nothing less than the reconciliation of all known systems of cosmic order to "a tradition originally revealed" (pp. 17–18; ch. 3)—that is, to historical facts as recorded in the Bible.[42] To this grandiose and desperate intellectual venture Casaubon binds himself irretrievably. His work can be seen as the public reflection of an inner logic—Fred Vincy's logic—that places him and his personal fulfillment as a pivot in the supreme order of the divine plan. The same providence that provided a Dorothea to meet Mr. Casaubon's "foreshadowing needs" revealed itself originally in biblical history, probably in the initial order of human society before the Tower of Babel and before the Flood. All mythologies must be corruptions of that original tradition. But if Dorothea (associated with the pagan Ariadne in the Vatican Museum scene)[43] proves not to be the passive adjunct to Mr. Casaubon's needs, if the various splinter mythologies (the religions of the world) resist accommodation to his vision of the original tradition, then indeed "absurdity and atheism gape behind him." The phrase that seems satirical banter as applied to Fred Vincy describes the actual terror of the loss that threatens Casaubon: "Even his religious faith wavered with his wavering trust in his own authorship, and the consolation of the Christian hope in immortality seemed to lean on the immortality of the still unwritten Key to All Mythologies. For my part I am very sorry for him" (p. 206; ch. 29).

It is not easy to be sorry for Mr. Casaubon. He has taken a good deal upon himself—all mythologies and Dorothea Brooke. And it is not easy to admire him, especially as young Ladislaw could set him right about both errors in a twinkling. And yet Casaubon does have something admirable about him. The same egoism that permits him to take Dorothea as his due gives rise to his monstrous, preposterous, grotesque intellectual enterprise—an operatic example of Faustian scholarly

---

[42]See W. J. Harvey, "The Intellectual Background of the Novel," in *Middlemarch: Critical Approaches to the Novel,* ed. Barbara Hardy (New York: Oxford Univ. Press, 1967), pp. 33–34.

[43]For the full significance of this association see Gerhard Joseph, "The *Antigone* as Cultural Touchstone: Matthew Arnold, Hegel, George Eliot, Virginia Woolf, and Margaret Drabble," *PMLA,* 96 (1981), 26–28.

heroism in the medieval manner, a *Summa* in fact. We are told that "it was as free from interpretation as a plan for threading the stars together" (p. 351; ch. 48). Baseless, insubstantial, indefensible as ego itself, it nevertheless represents the search for a key. There may be no such key. Mythologies may arise as spontaneously and independently as Dorothea's opinions. There may be—*Middlemarch* seems to say so—no key at all. But Casaubon's search, his failure, his pathetic terror as he apprehends Dorothea's otherness from himself, his despairing resignation as his marriage becomes an invasion, an "outward requirement," all reflect, however distortingly, the universal human need to find sweet reason somewhere, what Camus lyrically identified as "the wild longing for clarity whose call echoes in the human heart."[44]

Even Casaubon's final bizarre act of presumption, his dying request that Dorothea avail herself of the deadly "Synoptical Tabulation for the use of Mrs. Casaubon" to devote her life to the "Key," has a frantic truth of purpose in it. After all, *if* the key exists, *because* the key exists, it must be revealed to the world. Not to make the humiliating request of the only human instrument available to him would be cowardly—provided always that one accepts the providential first principles of the endeavor. Of course most readers feel that it would be wrong of Dorothea to rear this brainchild, that she is right to reject it. But that is because we apply principles of discreteness that a thoroughgoing providentialist would not admit. We hold with *Middlemarch*'s narrator that certain liberating distinctions must be made between private and professional life and that marriage must be actuated by different motives and forms from those that govern scholarship. We believe that the dead cannot and ought not to dictate to the living. We are more sympathetic to Dorothea's course than she is herself (as her message of retraction to her dead husband suggests), because we have accepted more fully the loss of that vision of unity that Casaubon refuses to relinquish. Like the narrator, we are uninhibited

[44]Albert Camus, *The Myth of Sisyphus*, trans. Justin O'Brian (New York: Vintage, 1955), p. 16.

by the remorseless integrity of a complete providential worldview.

It is often said that although Lydgate's professional ambition and his marriage contain many parallels to Casaubon's, he receives more sympathetic treatment from the narrative. It has also been repeatedly observed that Lydgate's chief fault lies in attending with scientific accuracy to his research while ignoring the subtle but numerous signs that Middlemarch society contains dangerous traps and that his is baited with Rosamond. Correct as such observations are, they overlook the most basic parallel between Casaubon and Lydgate, the most damaging one. This is that Lydgate, like Casaubon, applies the same fundamental premise to his private life as to his scientific research and that this premise is a secular manifestation of a providential habit of mind. Lydgate assumes that what he wants to be there *is* there. He wants to become a great researcher, to "make a link in the chain of discovery." To achieve this, he attempts to discover the nature of the "primitive tissue," the key to organic life (pp. 108, 110; ch. 15). He does not ask whether such tissue exists: he assumes it.[45] Its existence suits his sense of order and of his place in that order. His science relies on a faith as arbitrary as Casaubon's. And so does his choice of Rosamond. Though he has had a striking lesson to suggest a different approach, he judges Rosamond not according to her representation of herself—and she represents herself with unconscious accuracy—but according to threadbare masculine assumptions about what women are like, assumptions that place him at the center of things.

Despite these parallels Lydgate does stand higher than Casaubon in the values that *Middlemarch* supports. He cares about the sufferings of others; he shows ready sympathy and compassion; his personal and intellectual life is passionate. And Lydgate seems more sympathetic than Casaubon not only because he sustains these qualities but also because we are more privileged witnesses of his disillusionment and because this

[45]George Eliot's most current evidence suggested that it did not. See Harvey, "The Intellectual Background," pp. 35–37.

disillusionment seems closer to our own. His ambition does not derive from an arcane and anachronistic mythography but belongs instead to the heroic saga of modern scientific advance. His sense that his wife and household furniture should be tributary to this enterprise may be painfully recognizable to many of us.

In addition to these sources of sympathy the narrator offers us more intimate knowledge of Lydgate's melancholy pilgrimage than we have of Casaubon's. Lydgate's decline is better lighted. At the end his knowledge of Rosamond's implacable otherness and of the irremediable disaster of their marriage seems more complete, more fully acknowledged. His spiritual "murder" at her hands has a peculiar modernity about it—psychological collapse in confrontation with absurdity, admission of the inevitability of continuing defeat. "We are on a perilous margin," says the narrator, "when we begin to look passively at our future selves, and see our own figures led with dull consent into insipid misdoing and shabby achievement" (p. 574; ch. 79). It is a passivity that Casaubon never quite reaches, that the ancient bulwarks of his orthodox providentialism save him from. Lydgate's more tenuous initial sense of order buckles irreparably with the undermining of his masculine egoism—"I am no longer sure enough of myself," he tells Dorothea (p. 562; ch. 76)—as he too is forced through the pattern of disillusionment and isolation.

To Nicholas Bulstrode, Lydgate is only one entry in the all-absorbing account of his stewardship to providence. When Lydgate arrives in Middlemarch, Bulstrode hails his "advent" as a "gracious indication that a more manifest blessing is now to be awarded to my efforts" (p. 92; ch. 13). When Lydgate's financial difficulties become public, Bulstrode abandons him and the hospital: "The original plan, I confess, was one which I had much at heart, under submission to the Divine Will. But since providential indications demand a renunciation from me, I renounce" (p. 500; ch. 67). The reasoning is remorseless, reminiscent on a much higher level of awareness of that Dodson instinct in *The Mill on the Floss* to regard adequate financial assistance for the Tullivers as an "impiety" and then to rally round Tom when he gets lucky. Like theirs, but much richer and more delusive, Bulstrode's providentialism is of an evangelical, distinctively Calvinist kind, predestinarian in implication, in which all events, circumstances, and individuals become signs and tokens of God's will. Even the believer's own thoughts, feelings, and actions have only a secondary meaning in themselves but serve primarily as the crucial indices of salvation or damnation in a lifelong symbolic drama of unveiling from which the strained attention seeks evidence of election.

To this drama Bulstrode has brought a characteristic and subtle twist, well beyond the reach of the secularized Dodsons. He has severed in his own consciousness the essential connection between personal desire and moral action, thus permitting himself a radical latitude of behavior for which he is accountable in no human context. The severance derives from a corruption of evangelical providentialism. Bulstrode has made a deal with God: if he treats his own inclinations as irrelevant, as of no more account than the impulses of a being infinitely unworthy, if he becomes nothing more nor less than an "instrument" and has ontological value only as his "instrumentality" proves servicable to divine purpose, then his election may be assumed as a matter of course and personal accountability can be waived in advance of action.[46] Bulstrode thus sees himself as no more and no less than a medium for the providential intention to make itself known. As he continuously refines out the corruptions of his human nature (his own desires), consciousness itself becomes for him a seamless record of the *momenta* of God's will. And all action, even or especially such action as leads to the death of an enemy, is ultimately referable to providence (p. 526; ch. 71).

Bulstrode's false "key" resides in his belief that he can thus rise above his own humanity and that his centrality in the order of things follows from his discipline of spiritual refinement. The practical weakness of his conception lies in the fact that it requires complete isolation and can be realized only in

---

[46]For Bulstrode's belief in his instrumentality see p. 385, ch. 53; pp. 450–52, ch. 61; and pp. 516, 519, ch. 70.

total privacy: "Sin seemed to be a question of doctrine and inward penitence, humiliation an exercise of the closet, the bearings of his deeds a matter of private vision adjusted solely by spiritual relations and conceptions of the divine purpose" (p. 384; ch. 53). In contrast to Casaubon's proofs, Bulstrode's lie totally inward, and his converse nemesis arrives not as a failure of domestic intimacy but as public exposure. His perverted egoism, repeatedly pointed to by the narrator and other characters, is the egoism that denies its own action and thereby permits itself a licentious autonomy. When his inequity—his betrayal of a mother and daughter—becomes public, Bulstrode must see it with other eyes and must account for it to other people. This public accounting the intrinsic isolation of his system precludes.

But Bulstrode has never cared much to conciliate public opinion at large, and it is not public opinion itself that destroys him. What destroys him lies in what public exposure implies according to the logic of his cosmic paradigm. Public exposure wipes out his temporal influence and power. It annhilates his validity as God's agent. But once an instrument always an instrument. The remorseless logic of Bulstrode's own system— he has had plenty of practice in applying it to others—shows him to be supremely discarded, with the eternal consequences of such rejection: "If he turned to God there seemed to be no answer but the pressure of retribution" (p. 550; ch. 74). As with Casaubon and Lydgate, a providential system inextricably involved with personal egoism traps its subject in an unforeseen consequence of its own application.

In antithesis to these fatal egocentric providential paradigms *Middlemarch* celebrates a charitable, responsible, asystematic pragmatism represented among the male personae by Caleb Garth, Camden Farebrother, and Will Ladislaw. Although Garth regards his appointment to the management of the Freshitt and Tipton estates as "a great gift of God" and although he has a vaguely providential notion that "things hang together" (pp. 295, 297; ch. 40), he never places himself at the center of the universal order or draws conclusions about it from the province of his own experience. Mr. Farebrother retains too acute an awareness of his own personal liabilities, particularly evident in his shifts to supplement his income, ever to apply his idea of the proper order of things (whatever that idea may be) to his own humanity. And Ladislaw lets in light and fresh air by his simple refusal to systematize experience. He demands latitude for himself and he gives it to others. "It ought to lie with a man's self that he is a gentleman," he tells Bulstrode (p. 457; ch. 61). He recognizes instinctively the otherness of other people and he values it—particularly in Dorothea.

Ladislaw's lack of system is misinterpreted by Casaubon, Hawley, and Mrs. Cadwallader as an absence of moral purpose, and by some past and present-day writers as a distressing and somehow revealing failure of masculinity. It has in fact proved difficult to say anything about him, especially in relation to his fitness for Dorothea, which is more revealing of the character in question than of the prejudices of the critic—a fact that comments in part at least on the enduring association between the assertion of prescriptive values (the possession of a moral paradigm) and qualification as a masculine romantic principal. And Ladislaw's credo—"To love what is good and beautiful when I see it" (p. 287; ch. 39)—is almost totally nonprescriptive. It depends upon a ranging sensibility made up of such qualities as spontaneity, ready sympathy, and the capacity to be "ardent." These are the qualities of George Eliot's great heroines—Maggie Tulliver, Romola, Esther Lyon, Dorothea Brooke—and in giving them to Ladislaw she was not only taking an aesthetic risk but making a moral comment. *Middlemarch* suggests that such an affinity of sensibility is not only desirable in itself but only becomes possible when the baggage of prescriptive systems, including and especially all forms of providentialism, has been thrown away—when men, like the women in Ladislaw's description, are free to "change from moment to moment" (p. 142; ch. 20).

Survival in the world of *Middlemarch,* English provincial society at the time of the First Reform Bill, depends upon the capacity to change. Prescriptive providential paradigms of universal order have fragmented from their hypothetical status of a "coherent social faith," that "medium" for "ardent deeds" that the narrator with a kind of ostensible nostalgia posits as the context for St. Theresa's heroic achievement (p. 3, Prelude; p. 612, Finale).[47] This fragmentation places the greatest value upon the asystematic and flexible qualities, the pragmatic qualities, such as spontaneity and ready sympathy. Here one survives not by codes and systems, plans and paradigms, but by a kind of fellow feeling and compassion. Dorothca, who finishes as a richly credible composite of these diffuse characteristics, develops not by holding on but by giving up—giving up her early evangelical religiosity, her plans for cottages and other reforms, her hope of learned partnership in great religious enterprises.[48] She had thought to be a kind of surrogate providence in herself, dispensing goodness without the encumbrance of personal desires, and all her early schemes were tainted with elements of prescriptive value reminiscent in various ways of the masculine paradigms I have examined. "I have no longings," she told Ladislaw when she was still trying to help Casaubon (p. 287; ch. 39). When she yields at last to her passion and breaks down the social barriers of her wealth (that "providential arrangement" of Mr. Casaubon's), she is reduced at last to the liberating contemplation of practical arrangements: "We could live quite well on my fortune— it is too much—seven hundred a-year—I want so little—no new clothes—and I will learn what everything costs" (p. 594; ch. 83). It is not hieratic, it is not hitting high C, but it will work. Dorothea enters the world by taking the best option that world offers in the form of the man whose personal qualities now most closely resemble her own—the qualities best suited to survival in the emerging context.

---

[47]For a discussion of George Eliot's narrators in their hortatory capacity and as characters *in* the fiction (rather than as thinly disguised authorial mouthpieces) see Elizabeth Ermarth, "Method and Moral in George Eliot's Narrative," *Victorian Newsletter,* No. 47 (1975), 4–8.

[48]Garrett shows that Dorothea's early illusions about Casaubon "are sustained through the period of their engagement by her tendency to interpret him as she would a sacred text or providential design" (*The Victorian Multiplot Novel,* pp. 150–51).

One final observation seems necessary to conclude this examination of the providential elements in *Middlemarch*. Although the novel relentlessly attacks and condemns providential paradigms at every level—religious, social, psychological—there lies behind the condemnation what looks from our present-day perspective like a kind of faith or optimism that arrests the tendency toward nihilism or anarchy. The book asserts that the best way to live in a society devoid of "coherent social faith and order" is to become not less but more fully socialized. The moments of greatest potential and meaning are moments of social encounter and contact: Farebrother's warning to Fred Vincy, Dorothea's consolation of Lydgate, her two visits to Rosamond, Ladislaw's "farewell" visit to Dorothea all have diffuse and complex consequences that tend toward unity and happiness. This is not always the case—Lydgate ignores Farebrother's admonitions to avoid financial entanglement, Ladislaw spurns Bulstrode's cagey offer of restitution—but the weight of the evidence suggests that the social web can transmit the effects of individual sympathy and compassion, that "souls live on in perpetual echoes" (p. 119; ch. 16), that a "fine act . . . produces a kind of regenerating shudder through the frame" (p. 495; ch. 66), that the effect of Dorothea on others "was incalculably diffusive" (p. 613; Finale). Such assertions, substantially borne out by the resolutions of the various subplots, strongly suggest that an organic solidarity subsists—an elemental social mythos for which no key exists, a tissue too basic for analysis—and that despite its subtlety and resistance to systematization it remains subject to representation in narrative.

Daniel Deronda

George Eliot's last novel takes up the immense challenge of asserting this elemental social mythos, this fundamental tissue of human solidarity left largely implicit in *Middlemarch*. *Middlemarch* is the last word, the ultimate statement about consequence, in the representation of a rational causality in English fiction. At the end the reader of *Middlemarch* knows how everything happens—or if not quite everything then at least how it is that causes may become known.[49] This knowledge is great, greater than in any other English novel, but it is a cold knowledge, a terminal knowledge. Amid such knowledge the social web survives by a kind of faith quite independent of the kinds of knowing that the intellectual face of the novel seems to approve, survives beneath even that ready sympathy and ardent advocacy characteristic of Will and Dorothea.

Daniel Deronda really is about the heart of the social matter—what it is that holds human beings together, what unites a family, a nation, a people, the human species, and what the true value of these identities can be for the individual constituents. In its treatment of this elemental coherence, which is here neither destiny nor providence, the novel employs structural devices reminiscent of the traditional providential aesthetic: coincidence, a sense of fatality, the inconsequent actualization of individual desires, the interpretation of individual and social history to show plan or pattern. These devices led George Eliot's contemporaries to speak of *Daniel Deronda* as a romance rather than a novel, of her movement from realism toward idealism. In a review of September 1876 R. H. Hutton saw in it the signs of an ancient and profound providentialism: "It would be as idle to say that there is no conception of Providence or of supernatural guidance involved in the story, as to say the same of the Oedipean trilogy of Sophocles. The art of this story is essentially religious."[50]

In our day U. C. Knoepflmacher has recast this view with a narrowed focus:

> Miss Evans, the one-time "infidel *esprit*" of the *Westminister Review*, has been partially displaced by her predecessor, the ardent Evangelical. . . . Deronda's messiahship

---

[49]Raymond Williams observes that "what is found in *Middlemarch* is a knowable community, but knowable in a new sense," and he develops the point (*The English Novel from Dickens to Lawrence* [New York: Oxford Univ. Press, 1970], pp. 89–94).

[50]*George Eliot: The Critical Heritage*, pp. 382–98, 415, 366.

and his redemption from a negative skepticism are purely "providential," based as they are on his coincidental rescue of the drowning Mirah and of his discovery of her lost brother Ezra. . . . But his schooling is not that of experience. It is providence that prepares him as the new Daniel by furnishing him with a ready-made tradition already tested by the experiences of history and heredity. . . . It is thus that the reader is left only with Deronda's "calm benignant force," oscillating uneasily between the ideal and the real.[51]

However we appraise the accuracy of such commentary, Hutton's as well as Knoepflmacher's, we must agree that it could not have been written by weak readers, by readers who do not have some vigorous idea of what the traditional aspirations of the novel have been. That their assertions, as I believe and will argue, fall so far off the mark—so much farther off the mark than the analyses they both offer of *Middlemarch*—indicates the immensity of the challenge, then and now, that *Daniel Deronda* poses.

In order to apprehend the newness of this work, its novelty as contrasted with what has been taken to be its regression or retreat, I propose to examine those of its structural devices which recall the elements of the traditional providential aesthetic, elements central to the fiction of Brontë and Dickens for example, and which George Eliot exploited in her novels from *Adam Bede* through *Romola*. It is the radical transmutation of these devices, their application to the theme of a distinctly human solidarity, a social coherence exclusively temporal, that advances *Daniel Deronda* beyond not only traditional providential fiction—that advance George Eliot accomplished long before—but beyond the rational, empirical causalities of *Middlemarch* as well.

Coincidence in traditional providential novels almost always points in the end to a divine intention at work in the lives of

---

[51]Knoepflmacher, *Religious Humanism and the Victorian Novel*, pp. 138, 140, 144–45, 148.

the characters. The initially unperceived causality behind the coinciding events is referred in the growth of awareness gradually achieved by characters, narrators, and readers to a pattern of opportunities, actions, and consequences offered by providence. In *Daniel Deronda,* however, George Eliot takes some pains to attribute the surprise or wonder of coincidence, that unperceived or unimagined causality, to human ignorance and egoism. When (to take a simple example) Hans Meyrick discovers that Anna Gascoigne is Gwendolen's cousin, he is at first struck by the coincidence. But "on reflection I discovered that there was not the least ground for surprise, unless I had beforehand believed that nobody could be anybody's cousin without my knowing it. This sort of surprise, I take it, depends on a liveliness of the spine, with a more or less constant nullity of brain."[52] Hans has the intelligence and imagination to posit a world of causes beyond his own apprehension. In contrast, when Grandcourt makes an unscheduled stop at Genoa for repairs to his yacht and meets Deronda at the Albergo dell'Italia, he dismisses the fact that the encounter cannot be prearranged, denies his own ability to reason from the evidence—denies, that is, evidence for a causality beyond his knowledge—and takes the event as further indication of a conspiracy against him" (pp. 740–41; ch. 54).[53] His consequent irritation in part at least leads him to the fatal insistence that Gwendolen accompany him sailing. Neither Meyrick nor Grandcourt regards these coincidences as providential. The point is that in both cases the unexpectedness of the convergence of events may be traced back to individual ignorance, blithely admitted by one and disastrously denied by the other.

But what about the more impressive coincidences, the determining coincidences that have led some readers to see the plot

---

[52]*Daniel Deronda,* ed. Barbara Hardy (Baltimore: Penguin, 1967), p. 707; ch. 52.

[53]Grandcourt's stale witticism to Lady Mallinger—"I heard somebody say how providential it was that there always happened to be springs at gambling places" (p. 322; ch. 25)—delivered so dryly as to bewilder his auditor, is perfectly in character, satirizing the foolishness of those unable to order causes shrewdly.

of *Daniel Deronda* as essentially providential? As readers we are more privileged than Hans Meyrick in our knowledge of Gwendolen's family tie to the Gascoignes, and we know, more than Grandcourt, how Deronda happens to be in Genoa. But how is it that shortly after saving Mirah, Deronda comes so immediately upon Mordecai, not only once in the bookshop but the same evening again at the Cohens'? That Joseph Kalonymos picks him out at that synagogue in Frankfurt? That desiring to be a Jew he is a Jew? "Blood! How things come about!" exclaims the dismayed Monks in *Oliver Twist,* suddenly aware of the cosmic implications of his ignorance. But Monks lives in the straightforward providential world of early Dickens where coincidences are explicitly referred to divine planning. No such references are made by the narrator of *Daniel Deronda*. The epigraph from Aristotle that heads chapter 41—"It is a part of probability that many improbable things will happen"—refers us ultimately to the limitation of individual experience and knowledge, as our sense of the probable depends upon the range of our awareness. Thus one thing the coincidences in the novel suggest is that our awareness has its limits and that what lies beyond these will strike us as improbable, that we must beware of making Grandcourt's revealing error, of failing to imagine, to posit to ourselves, a vastness of cause and effect well beyond the circle of our own light.

But Deronda's discovery of Mordecai and the other real coincidences (those whose causality is never sequentially laid out for the reader), mean more than this. They are the ultimate evidence for the elemental social coherence the novel celebrates. At the end of my discussion of *Middlemarch* I suggested that the web of social life is represented there as a tissue too basic or "primitive" for analysis, an organic solidarity subsisting beneath analytic penetration, but that it nevertheless lends itself to representation in narrative. In *Daniel Deronda* the intellectual perspective has shifted and the representation of this solidarity has become the thematic foreground where the stylistic and structural devices subserve it. Thus the meaning of the coincidences in *Daniel Deronda* is central, but this meaning is not delivered hortatively (as the discursive propensities of the narrator might lead us to expect) but dramatically (the method perfected in *Middlemarch*), in particular by means of the development and action of the chief characters. It is in relation to them that the coincidences and other devices traditional in the providential aesthetic make sense, a sense that is not providential.

Gwendolen's relatives often refer her to providential design as an explanation for circumstances that distress her, and she quite as often rejects their reasoning. Her mother tells her that "we must resign ourselves to the will of Providence." Gwendolen answers, "But I don't resign myself. I shall do what I can against it. What is the good of calling people's wickedness Providence?" (p. 274; ch. 21). Despite what Mr. Gascoigne knows about Grandcourt he can say to Gwendolen, "If Providence offers you power and position—especially when unclogged by any conditions that are repugnant to you—your course is one of responsibility, into which caprice must not enter" (p. 179; ch. 13). But we are told that Gwendolen takes to gambling abroad in the general view "that in this confused world it signified nothing what anyone did, so that they amused themselves" and that "no religious view of trouble helped her" (pp. 194, 317; chs. 15, 24). What Gwendolen relies on is her regressive infantile sense that somehow the universe will, like her mother, love her best and treat her like the princess she feels herself to be. This "spoiled child" element is usually presented by George Eliot as a correlative of naive providentialism (Arthur Donnithorne, Hetty Sorel, Tessa, Rosamond and Fred Vincy), but not here. Although Gwendolen wants to believe herself the center of the cosmos, she possesses no cosmology to support her inclination. This makes her a peculiarly modern, peculiarly vulnerable character. She has no way of justifying her caprice; her egoism is unsustained by any justifying system.

What Gwendolen is left with is a desire for personal power—power dissociated from responsibility. This the novel terms *mastery:* "Gwendolen's confidence lay chiefly in herself. She felt well equipped for the mastery of life" (p. 69; ch. 4). Her idea of the proper order of things is grossly primitive, correlative in fact of unmodified, unsocialized ego. It means being on top. She marries, in what is actually the greatest coincidence of the novel, precisely the man most calculated to teach her the full value of this single motive. Like her own, Grandcourt's bearing and appearance recommend him as the ultimate human refinement of his culture while his inner being is a terrifying pathological extension of infantile will.[54] He is a typological descendant of Tito Melema, a morbid forerunner of Meredith's Sir Willoughby Patterne. Unlike Grandcourt, however, Gwendolen possesses the rudiments of a social self, an instinctive "dread of wrong-doing" (p. 342; ch. 27). Whereas Grandcourt is actuated by the single motive of asserting his mastery, Gwendolen unwillingly but inescapably harbors a social element, a psychological constituent of human solidarity. It is this that finally makes the "gamble" of her marriage "a terrible *plus*" to her (p. 659; ch. 48). Intimacy with a man entirely free from that element which she has tried to deny in herself is made unendurable by the knowledge that she has violated her promise to Mrs. Glasher and thus made her own "gain out of another's loss" (p. 500; ch. 36). Her remorse and shame, the stirrings of the social element in her consciousness, is what gives the single-minded Grandcourt the coveted mastery in their marriage.

"Always she was the princess in exile" (p. 71; ch. 4). The image suggests the childishness of fairy tale and the fairy-tale emphasis on superiority and power. It also suggests the dissociation of the highest qualities of the self from its social context, and the existential panic to which Gwendolen is subject serves as the emotional corollary to this isolation:

> Solitude in any wide scene impressed her with an undefined feeling of immeasurable existence aloof from her, in the midst of which she was helplessly incapable of asserting herself. The little astronomy taught her at school used sometimes to set her imagination at work in a way

[54]For a discussion of Grandcourt's arbitrary willfulness, see Felicia Bonaparte, *Will and Destiny: Morality and Tragedy in George Eliot's Novels* (New York: New York Univ. Press, 1975), pp. 100–102; and Neil Roberts, *George Eliot: Her Beliefs and Her Art*, pp. 213–14.

that made her tremble: but always when some one joined
her she recovered her indifference to the vastness in which
she seemed an exile; she found again her usual world in
which her will was of some avail, and the religious
nomenclature belonging to this world was no more identified for her with those uneasy impressions of awe than
her uncle's surplices seen out of use at the rectory. With
human ears and eyes about her, she had always hitherto
recovered her confidence, and felt the possibility of winning empire. (pp. 94–95, ch. 6).

Without orthodox religion or any other system of cosmic or
moral order, Gwendolen has only "empire." This does not
help her when the moment of choice comes and she accepts
Grandcourt. Then, when she has violated her primitive "dread
of wrong-doing," the liability to "fits of spiritual dread" that
had seemed in her maidenhood only "brief remembered madness, and unexplained exception from her normal life" (p. 94;
ch. 6) become the quotidian, the normative reality for Gwendolen. She can no longer use others as celebrants in the service
of her sense of mastery. She can no longer use "the possibility
of winning empire" to feed the baseless imperialism of her
ego. She finds herself alone with Grandcourt. It is as if she
were condemned to survive alienated forever from the part of
herself which could have made that adult contact with others
requisite for sanity and were forced to embrace instead her
own static, infantile will.[55]

Gwendolen's fear of her own condition saves her, and this
fear she ties not to God but to Deronda. In this capacity, as
a contemporary notice in the *Saturday Review* pointed out, "he
suggests the idea of a Providence,"[56] and in Gwendolen's

[55]Garrett, among others, notices Gwendolen's similarity to her spouse, "a
distorted reflection of herself" (*The Victorian Multiplot Novel*, p. 171).

[56]*George Eliot: The Critical Heritage*, p. 381. Albert R. Cirillo describes
Deronda's relation to Gwendolen "as an ideal which overcomes her narrow
egoism. In these terms he is an objectification of moral life, the moral life
Gwendolen finally achieves; he is the object that Feuerbach spoke of when
he said that 'man is nothing without an object'" ("Salvation in *Daniel
Deronda*," *Literary Monographs*, I [1967], 203).

primitive state of social development this is exactly what she needs. Her anger after he returns her necklace "had changed into a superstitious dread" in which he becomes a "priest" or spiritual monitor, an "outer conscience." He brings to Gwendolen "that judgment of the Invisible and Universal which self-flattery and the world's tolerance would easily melt and disperse. In this way our brother may be in the stead of God to us, and his opinion which has pierced even to the joints and marrow, may be our virtue in the making. That mission of Deronda to Gwendolen had begun with what she had felt to be his judgment of her at the gaming table" (pp. 374, 485, 833; chs. 29, 35, 64). For Gwendolen such a presence is necessary to transform her rudimentary fear of wrongdoing into a moral sense; her spiritual development demands it; it is an intermediate step in her pilgrimage toward social being.

Gwendolen's last step in the novel is the recognition of Deronda's humanity, of the fact that he does not exist exclusively for her and that his human limitations must separate him from her. In her absolute, childlike dependence "she did not imagine him otherwise than always within her reach, her supreme need of him blinding her to the separateness of his life . . . we are all apt to fall into this passionate egoism of imagination, not only towards our fellow-men, but towards God." In giving up Deronda to his own mission, Gwendolen surrenders at last the childhood assumption "that whatever surrounded her was somehow specially for her." She has the sense of "something spiritual and vaguely tremendous that thrust her away, and yet quelled all anger into self-humiliation." Gwendolen is losing the only God, the only providence, she has ever had, and one that she had had only very briefly. Her acceptance of the cosmic loneliness that this implies—"I shall be better"—clothes her with heroism at the end (pp. 867, 876, 879; ch. 69).[57] That this heroism has a hysterical edge to it may be attributed to the shock of the light in which she discovers her nakedness.

[57]Darrel Mansell comments on the "tragedy" of Gwendolen's isolation in "A Note on Hegel and George Eliot," *Victorian Newsletter*, No. 27 (1965), 15.

We can see that Gwendolen's development has its large analogue in what George Eliot saw as the social development of
humanity—from primitive fear of wrongdoing (symbolized by
the figure fleeing the drowned face in the picture), through
fear and love of an absolute external monitor (elementary providentialism), toward a more generalized awareness of diffuse
social responsibilities. In modification of the now weary cliché,
it may be said that Gwendolen's spiritual ontogeny recapitu-
lates humankind's social phylogeny. No doubt this derivation
of what at first looks like a loosely positivist allegory from the
most celebrated of George Eliot's psychological studies will
arouse some resistance.[58] But what may strike us as a conflicting double agenda was a single movement for readers steeped
in the providential aesthetic. Jane Eyre and Lucy Snowe, Mr.
Dombey and Pip are no less psychologically credible because
they live in providential fictions. Their providences are part of
their realities. So Gwendolen's development is part of the
developing human context, the context of emerging solidarity
in which her creator believed.

This emerging solidarity reaches its fullest representation in
Mirah and Mordecai and in Deronda's relation to them. As
most critics have observed, there are serious aesthetic problems
with the "Jewish half" of the novel. The problems, however,
are neither incidental nor arbitrary, but integral to the thematic
emphasis of the whole narrative. For example, the apparently
complete suspension of George Eliot's characteristic irony in
the delineation of Mirah makes her rather hard to take. Like
that of Dickens's first virtuous heroines, her credibility as a
character is perpetually threatened by her representative thematic function. She seems to have only good thoughts and
generous impulses, rather simple thoughts and impulses for a
woman whose art (according to Herr Klesmer) has reached a
high level of sophistication. She is a naive providentialist,
interpreting Deronda's appearance in her hour of despair as

---

[58]W. J. Harvey points out that George Eliot declined Frederick Harrison's
1866 invitation to retail a positivist program in her fiction (*The Art of George
Eliot*, pp. 177–78). See also *Letters*, IV, 300.

"God's command" to her to live (pp. 231, 234; ch. 17). She instinctively rejects the "hell" of her childhood surroundings among which there seemed to be "no great meanings" (p. 257; ch. 20). She approaches the faith of her brother Mordecai in asserting that "if people have thought what is the most beautiful and the best thing, it must be true"—which is to say, as Deronda interprets it for her, that "it is a truth in thought. . . . It lives in the idea" (p. 523; ch. 37). But her primary thematic function is to pose an alternative to Gwendolen, not just in her rather wearing virtue but in her self-containment and in the legitimate mastery she has achieved through her art. Her singing represents the opposite of gambling, something learned, achieved, developed. Mirah is always represented as calm and strong when she has to perform. Like Klesmer, she knows that "it is safer to do anything—singing or anything else—before those who know and understand all about it" (p. 544; ch. 39). No action could contrast more vividly with Gwendolen's secretive, deceptive gambling—the attempt to gain from another's loss. The true mastery of art is generous, revealed, profoundly social. Mirah serves the chief thematic concern of the novel in representing it that way; and her intellectual simplicity perhaps allows this representation to emerge more clearly than it does with a somewhat more shaded figure like Klesmer.[59]

Mordecai's expectations of Deronda also appear at first to be naively providential. The narrator tells us that the "thoughts of his heart . . . seemed to him too precious, too closely inwoven with the growth of things not to have a further destiny," that he imagines a "more executive self" to realize his ideas, that he in fact comes to expect a "being answering to his need" (p. 530; ch. 38). Deronda arrives just as Mordecai had imagined, right down to details of landscape and lighting. He will use Deronda to give substance, body, to his vision. Deronda will be his surrogate: "that my vision and passion should enter into yours—yea, into yours; for he whom I longed for afar,

---

[59]Mirah's art is also a moral and psychological stay to her, a development of Caterina's singing in "Mr. Gilfil's Love-Story," *Scenes of Clerical Life*, p. 195.

was he not you whom I discerned as mine when you came near?" (p. 821; ch. 63). From a conventional or worldly stand-point Deronda can see the strain in all this: "To take such a demand in the light of an obligation in any direct sense would have been preposterous." Indeed, Mordecai's assumption of Deronda as a surrogate has some of the repellent quality of Miss Havisham's appropriation of Estella in *Great Expectations.* But Deronda does not feel that, and what really needs explain-ing, what really strains our credulity, is not Mordecai's appar-ent fanaticism—which is, as the narrator says, "abundant enough" in the world—but Deronda's accessibility to it (pp. 570, 568; ch. 41). That Mordecai after developing his ideas and expecting an "executive self" to implement them for, as he tells us, "these five years" should fix on some younger man is not improbable (p. 550; ch. 40). What seems improb-able is that the man he fixes on should feel a need to be precisely the agent of such a vision, the executor of such an idea. The problem the novel raises with their discovery of each other is that of widening the range of our apprehension of causality so that the precise complement of their antecedent needs does *not* have to be referred to providence.

"You would remind me that I may be under an illusion," says Mordecai to Deronda early in their relationship. "*So it might be with my trust, if you would make it an illusion. But you will not*" (p. 560; ch. 40; George Eliot's emphasis). The two italicized remarks do a great deal of work. First they show us that Mordecai has a fund of self-awareness suggestive of sanity. Secondly, they show that he acknowledges the possibility that Deronda has power and freedom of his own, the power and freedom to turn Mordecai's "trust" into an "illusion." Finally, they suggest his confidence that Deronda will *choose* to advance Mordecai's aims. Unlike Casaubon with Dorothea or Bul-strode with Lydgate, Mordecai does not regard Deronda as a cipher in the divine account or a celestial sign or gift to himself. Mordecai counts on Deronda's will, on his exercise of his own freedom—his freedom, that is, as a Jew.

Deronda's Jewishness places him in the same *context* with Mordecai, in the same historical and social moment. This is what Mordecai counts on—not providence but history and the social consciousness as expressed in a collective identity. He counts on time and the felt necessities of his people to send him a Jew who will work to provide a national habitation for Jews. Both Mordecai and Deronda have what the novel terms, in a phrase evocative of much of George Eliot's scholarly background, a "world-historic position" (p. 815; ch. 63). Mordecai tells Deronda that he is "not listening to one who raves aloof from the lives of his fellows" (p. 555; ch. 40). His "vision," that is, is intensely social, the image of a vast force for which he provides the prophetic human voice. "Let the torch of visible community be lit," he says (p. 596; ch. 42). This torch lights Deronda's way to him. The force of this collective desire for a "visible community" acts in numberless unanalyzable ways; it is the historical extension into nationhood of the elemental social impulse. It is what forces Deronda's mother to obey her dead father, what he finally calls "that stronger Something" that has "determined that I shall be all the more the grandson whom also you willed to annihilate" (p. 727; ch. 53). It is what produces the major coincidences in the novel.

The "Jewish half" of *Daniel Deronda* does not result solely from a large-minded impulse of the author to reduce the barriers of social prejudice.[60] The Jews in the novel and the Jewish nationalism they invoke locate a particular expression of a concern evident throughout George Eliot's fiction. This is the movement of the social impulse in individuals to achieve identity in a "visible community." The vagueness of Mordecai's vision and Deronda's plans for realizing it have irritated critics for a century, but their very lack of specificity permits generalization. In this way the Jewish aspirations are not parochial but representative. The "Jewish half" of the novel really tells

---

[60]Though this of course is important. See for example Graham Martin, "*Daniel Deronda:* George Eliot and Political Change," *Critical Essays on George Eliot,* pp. 148–50; and especially Avrom Fleishman's decisive essay "Daniel Charisi," in *Fiction and the Ways of Knowing* (Austin: Univ. of Texas Press, 1978), pp. 86–109.

the collective half of the human story—that families, peoples, nations move toward the fulfillment of all social aspiration, the higher expression of human solidarity, and that individuals have the opportunity of a willed participation in this enlargement, an opportunity not sent by providence but developed by the human struggle through time. "I like to mark the time," says the narrator early in the novel, "and connect the course of lives with the historic stream, for all classes of thinkers" (pp. 121–22; ch. 8).

The relationship between Mordecai and Deronda, with Mordecai as the visionary and Deronda as the "executive self," thus participates in the novel's general concern with social development, particularly in its emphasis on the importance of ideas and the way in which ideas become actualized, realized. Deronda tells Gwendolen that to care about ideas "is a sort of affection" (p. 470; ch. 35). Mordecai tells Deronda that "beloved ideas" came to him and that these ideas "were a trust to fulfil." Their realization he takes to be his responsibility and Deronda's as they participate willingly in the emerging zeitgeist. Or, as Mordecai puts it: "The world grows, and its frame is knit together by the growing soul; dim, dim at first, then clearer and more clear, the consciousness discerns remote stirrings. As thoughts move within us darkly, and shake us before they are fully discerned—so events—so beings: they are knit with us in the growth of the world. You have risen within me like a thought not fully spelled: my soul is shaken before the words are all there. The rest will come—it will come" (pp. 554, 559; ch. 40). And, indeed, for them it does come. Deronda turns out to be a Jew. He can carry Mordecai's "torch of visible community." Ideas, aspirations, do achieve realization; human beings do enjoy "rare moments when our yearnings and our acts can be completely one, and the real we behold is our ideal good" (p. 817; ch. 63). Through their participation in the same generous social idea, by ardently desiring what is good, people do sometimes get what they deserve. Mordecai gets Deronda, Mirah gets Mordecai, Deronda gets Mirah and Judaism. It looks like providence but it is not. It is a kind of coincidence whose causality lies in the complex and nebulous movement of ideology and history, what might be called the social time of the novel, and this force (we are urged to believe) can achieve striking effects of realization in individual lives.

It is this process of realization that links the "Gwendolen half" of *Daniel Deronda* with the "Jewish half" in what finally constitutes a powerful thematic unity. For Gwendolen too ideas are realized.[61] When Grandcourt is knocked overboard, her "vision" of "some possible accident," her "dream" of "a white dead face" becomes actual, real (pp. 737, 738; ch. 54). "I only know," she says, "that I saw my wish outside me." What practical consequence Gwendolen's desire for Grand-court's death—her pronounced desire to kill, "strong as thirst"—may have had in the event, what actually followed from her momentary pause as he cried for help, can never be known in the sense that the purely physical effects of a purely physical act can be known (pp. 761, 756; ch. 56). But however charitably we choose to interpret the moment of hesitation (Deronda interprets it most charitably), the link between the idea and its realization is a link of moral responsibility. It constitutes a betrayal of her social being, and Gwendolen's horror at her failure is appropriate.

Because Gwendolen's vision (Grandcourt's dead face) does not derive from or lend itself to a larger social context, its realization provides a moment of extreme isolation, the isolation toward which Gwendolen's selfishness has been tending throughout the novel and which precedes the tentative heroic first steps of her recovery. In contrast, Mordecai's vision (and Mirah's and Deronda's) leads toward unity and contact. In *Daniel Deronda* ideas can kill, but they also give life and growth. Everything depends upon the generosity, the social element, of the impulse. Gwendolen's infantile egoism separates her

---

[61]Garrett notes this among other "analogies between the novel's 'higher' and 'lower' worlds" in *The Victorian Multiplot Novel*, pp. 174–78. See Elizabeth Ermarth, "Incarnations: George Eliot's Conception of 'Undeviating Law,' " *Nineteenth-Century Fiction*, 29 (1974), especially pp. 278–81, for a treatment of the "objects of culture" as "embodied ideas" which shows how central such linkages are in George Eliot's thought.

from others in something of the same way that the "Gwendolen half" of the novel seems to be separated from the "Jewish half." But what links both halves powerfully together is the process of realization: the realization of Gwendolen's idea proves that the process in which Mordecai places his trust works throughout the social web. The realization of her secret, private, isolated vision of horror generalizes and validates his public, philosophic, social aspiration. The causality behind their respective coincidences is the same in kind, however diverse the moral and historical consequences.

In this way the exquisite narrative of Gwendolen's development illuminates and strengthens Mordecai's assertion that "all things are bound together in that Omnipresence which is the place and habitation of the world" (p. 818; ch. 63). Such an identity precludes the action of a providential intention. God in this novel does not act upon the world. The world acts, the world in its largest historical and social bearings, "for the divine Unity embraced as its consequence the ultimate unity of mankind" (p. 802; ch. 61). God can become love. It is the thematic achievement of the novel to show how this happens. And George Eliot's artistic triumph in *Daniel Deronda* is the corresponding transmutation of the major traditional elements of the providential aesthetic—the sense of fatality or destiny, the inconsequent actualization of individual desire, the reading of plan and pattern in individual and social history, and above all the discovery of coincidence—in the imagination of an entirely human world.

INDEX

INDEX